Understanding and Teaching
American Slavery

The Harvey Goldberg Series
for Understanding and Teaching History

The Harvey Goldberg Series for Understanding and Teaching History gives college and secondary history instructors a deeper understanding of the past as well as the tools to help them teach it creatively and effectively. Each volume focuses on a specific historical topic and offers a wealth of content and resources, providing concrete examples of how teachers can approach the subject in the classroom. Named for Harvey Goldberg, a professor renowned for his history teaching at Oberlin College, Ohio State University, and the University of Wisconsin from the 1960s to the 1980s, the series reflects Goldberg's commitment to helping students think critically about the past with the goal of creating a better future. For more information, please visit www.GoldbergSeries.org.

Series Editors

John Day Tully is an associate professor of history at Central Connecticut State University and was the founding director of the Harvey Goldberg Center for Excellence in Teaching at Ohio State University.

Matthew Masur is an associate professor of history at Saint Anselm College, where he is codirector of the Father Guerin Center for Teaching Excellence. He is a member of the Teaching Committee of the Society for Historians of American Foreign Relations and writes on American-Vietnamese relations.

Brad Austin is a professor of history at Salem State University. He has served as chair of the American Historical Association's Teaching Prize Committee and has worked with hundreds of secondary school teachers as the academic coordinator of many Teaching American History grants.

Advisory Board

Kevin Boyle   Northwestern University
Ross Dunn   Professor Emeritus, San Diego State University
Leon Fink   UIC Distinguished Professor of History, University of Illinois at Chicago
Kimberly Ibach   Meeker High School, Meeker, Colorado
Alfred W. McCoy   J.R.W. Smail Professor of History, Director, Harvey Goldberg Center for the Study of Contemporary History, University of Wisconsin–Madison
David J. Staley   Director, Harvey Goldberg Center for Excellence in Teaching, Ohio State University
Maggie Tran   McLean High School, McLean, Virginia
Sam Wineburg   Margaret Jacks Professor of Education and (by courtesy) of History, Director, Stanford History Education Group, Stanford University

Understanding and Teaching American Slavery

Edited by
BETHANY JAY
CYNTHIA LYNN LYERLY

The University of Wisconsin Press

The University of Wisconsin Press
1930 Monroe Street, 3rd Floor
Madison, Wisconsin 53711-2059
uwpress.wisc.edu

3 Henrietta Street, Covent Garden
London WC2E 8LU, United Kingdom
eurospanbookstore.com

Printed in the United States of America

Library of Congress Cataloging-in-Publication Data

Understanding and teaching American slavery / edited by
Bethany Jay and Cynthia Lynn Lyerly.
pages   cm. — (The Harvey Goldberg series for understanding and teaching history)
Includes bibliographical references and index.
ISBN 978-0-299-30664-9 (pbk.: alk. paper)
1. Slavery—History—Study and teaching—United States.
I. Jay, Bethany, editor.   II. Lyerly, Cynthia Lynn, 1960-, editor.
III. Series: Harvey Goldberg series for understanding and teaching history.
E441.U45 2016
306.3'62071073—dc23
2015010259

Contents

Contents

Part Three: Sources and Strategies
for Teaching Slavery

Contents

Acknowledgments

Together, we would like to acknowledge the wonderful work of the many scholars who have contributed to this book. When we first proposed the manuscript, we created a "wish list" of potential contributors, and we feel privileged that so many of those on our list have agreed to work with us on this project. In particular, we would like to acknowledge Ira Berlin's early and consistent support of this project. Dr. Berlin's faith in the value of this resource has pushed us to create a product that lives up to his lofty example of scholarship and pedagogy. Similarly, several of our contributors, namely Ira Berlin, Joanne Pope Melish, Eric Kimball, Steven Oliver, and Lindsay Randall, gave their time and expertise by discussing their contributions to the book at several conferences. Those experiences were formative in helping us to structure a book that educators need, and we appreciate the generosity of the scholars who participated in them.

Of course, this book is just one volume in the Harvey Goldberg Series for Understanding and Teaching History. We are thankful that the series editors, Brad Austin, Matthew Masur, and John Day Tully, asked us to edit this volume, and we are indebted to them for the support they have provided along the way.

Last, we would like to acknowledge our students, who inspire us and teach us every day. It is a privilege to share this volume with them.

Each of us also has accumulated our share of individual debts.

I would like to thank my Salem State University colleagues, particularly Brad Austin, Andrew Darien, Michele Louro, Donna Seger, and Jessica Ziparo, who have offered advice and support when they all had other work that they needed to do. I look forward to returning the favor for many years to come. I would also like to thank my coeditor, Cynthia Lynn Lyerly. It was Lynn's class at Boston College that inspired my passion for this topic, and it has been an honor to work with her on this project. I would like to acknowledge the support of my family, in particular my wonderful and giving parents, Ruth and Rich, and my sister, Amy Waywell. Without you, none of this would be possible. Last, I would like to thank my husband, Hunter, and my children, Harper, Kathleen, and Madelyn. You make life complicated and wonderful, and you have all been endlessly patient with my "book stuff." Nothing is complete until you are a part of it. I share this book with you.

BETHANY JAY

I thank my patient, supportive, and wonderful husband, Michael Pollens; Beth Jay, who had the idea for this volume and whose commitment to pedagogy (and family) is inspiring; and John Boles, Mark Lyerly, and Anne Lyerly, the three most amazing teachers in my life.

CYNTHIA LYNN LYERLY

Foreword

The Short Course for Bringing Slavery into the Classroom in Ten Not-So-Easy Pieces

IRA BERLIN

African American slavery is a difficult subject for any public forum and even more so for the classroom. This is especially true in the United States, where the painful legacy of slavery remains tangled with the vexed matter of race. In the classroom, students squirm uncomfortably and look at their shoelaces as they wait hopefully for someone, someone else—anyone but themselves—to speak up. When that voice is at last heard, it may not always be welcome, as discussions of slavery can explode in angry, often uninformed rants. These are just the kind of nightmarish classroom scenarios that every teacher dreads and, as a result, most avoid. But discussions about slavery and race can awaken students to a deeper appreciation of both, precisely because of their explosive nature. Despite the stony silence, students care. They may be uninformed or willfully ignorant. They may claim the case is closed—as if the book on any historical subject can be shut—or assert that discussion will only open old wounds. But they have opinions that demand a hearing. Open conversation clears the air and flushes out errant notions. It also provides students with an opportunity to wrestle with complex ideas that are wrapped in moral judgments and vice versa, a far cry from the mindless memorization they often equate with historical study. Occasionally, such discussions can even carry students to new levels of understanding, which presumably is the very essence of education. For myself, if discussions of slavery have generated some of my worst classroom experiences, they have also produced some of my best. I treasure those priceless moments when I have witnessed my students' world change, and I presume they do as well.

But, alas, classroom discussions of slavery are not a matter of choice—a gamble made at will—but a necessity. Teaching slavery is essential to any understanding of American society, along with an appreciation of America's place in the world. Even more important, it is a necessary step in coming to terms with the legacy of race that the American past has bequeathed our students. Like it or not, slavery must be in our classrooms just as it is in our literature, cinema, TV docudramas, museums, and politics. The question is not whether to teach slavery and the associated matter of race but how to do it in a way that allows students to incorporate slavery into their understanding of society and self, whether they are black, white, or, increasingly, neither black nor white. As with any subject, no single curriculum is best for all circumstances, but all should incorporate ten essential elements.

1. Slavery holds a special place in the history of the United States. Slavery shaped the American economy, politics, law, culture, and the fundamental beliefs of the American people. For most of American history—the two hundred and fifty years between the founding of Jamestown, the Confederate surrender at Appomattox, and the ratification of the Thirteenth Amendment—the mainland colonies and then the American Republic were a society of slaveholders and slaves.

The American economy was founded upon the production of slave-grown crops, the great staples of tobacco, rice, sugar, and finally cotton, which slave owners sold on the international market and which brought capital into the colonies and then the young Republic. That capital eventually funded the creation of an infrastructure upon which rests three centuries of American economic success. In 1860, the four million slaves in the American South were conservatively valued at three billion dollars. That was almost three times the value of the entire American manufacturing establishment including all the railroads, steamship lines, and carriages in the entire United States, about seven times the net worth of all the banks in the United States, and nearly fifty times the expenditures of the federal government.

The great wealth slavery produced allowed slave owners to play a central role in the establishment of the new federal government in 1789, as they quickly transformed their economic power into political power. Between the founding of the Republic and the Civil War, the majority of the presidents—everyone from Washington, Jefferson, Madison, Monroe, and Jackson through Tyler, Polk, and Taylor—were slaveholders, and generally substantial ones. The same was true for the Supreme Court, where, for most of the period between the ratification of the Constitution and the Civil War, a slaveholding majority was ruled over by two successive slaveholding chief justices, John Marshall and Roger Taney. A similar pattern can be found in Congress, and it was the struggle for control of Congress between the slaveholding and non-slaveholding states around which antebellum politics revolved.

The men who controlled politics also made the laws, which were essential to slavery's existence. The Founding Fathers designed the nation's preeminent charter, the Constitution of the United States, to protect property and slave property in particular. From the passage of the first fugitive slave law in 1793 to the second in 1850, slaveholders had a friend in court, as did white people generally. Not only did slave codes of the Southern states incorporate white supremacy, but so too did the laws of the Northern ones. The law elevated white over black, in the North as well as the South.

The power of the slave-owning class, represented by the predominance of slaveholders in the nation's leadership, gave it a large hand in shaping American culture and the values central to American life. It was no accident that a slaveholder penned the founding statement of American nationality and that freedom became central to the ideology of the American Republic. Men and women who drove slaves understood the meaning of chattel bondage, as most surely did the men and women who were, in fact, chattel. And if it is no accident that Thomas Jefferson wrote that "all men are created equal," then it was most certainly no accident that some of the greatest spokesmen for that ideal, from Richard Allen and Frederick Douglass through W.E.B. Du Bois and Martin Luther King Jr., were slaves, former slaves, and the descendants of slaves. The centrality of slavery in the American past is manifest.

2. As important as slavery is to the American past, chattel bondage was not the sole concern of the United States. Slavery existed from the earliest history of human society. As the center of the plantation complex, it flourished throughout the Atlantic world between the fifteenth and nineteenth centuries. Even after its formal abolition by every nation state, it continues to exist. Sadly, the number of people held in bondage today is increasing.

Although modern slavery (since the fifteenth century) was identified with people of African descent, probably the majority of human beings who ever trod the earth lived and labored in some kind of coerced relationship. Africans and people of African descent are only some of the many peoples who suffered enslavement. No peoples, however defined—by lineage, nationality, religion, and color—escaped enslavement at one time or another. In world history, slavery is the rule, freedom the exception.

3. The relationship of slavery and race is neither obvious nor direct, but problematic and debatable. Over the course of human history, men and women were enslaved for a variety of reasons. But the origin of modern plantation slavery was singular: the planter's near insatiable appetite for labor. Native Americans and Africans from across the Atlantic were taken from their communities not to debase, humiliate, or degrade them in the eyes of white people, although slavery would do all of those things. The purpose of plantation slavery was not to elevate white people over black ones, although slavery served that function as well. Rather, slavery's purpose was to make some white people rich. For that reason, slavery—whatever its various effects and however it became tangled with the matter of race—was first an institution of class exploitation.

4. Whenever and wherever slavery existed, it rested on a contradiction, for slaves were both human beings and property. Denying men and women the essence of their humanity—their volition—made slavery logically impossible, a relationship that one Spanish legal code called "against natural reason." Throughout history, that contradiction remained at the heart of the slave relation. It manifested itself in every aspect of slave life, from the most public prosecutions of slave criminals (men and women allegedly without volition charged and punished for willfully violating the law) to the most intimate relationship between slave owners and slaves (for surely there was no pleasure to be gained in having sex with a slave if the slave was just furniture). What made slaves valuable to their owners was that they had wills of their own; they could make choices, could learn, and could improve themselves. Slave owners appreciated this and often encouraged their slaves to become better artisans, servants, and laborers. At various times, they found it useful and beneficial for slaves to travel independently, gain

knowledge of the geography, carry a gun or knife, and educate themselves. Yet, the more valuable the slave became and the greater the slave's worth, the more adamantly slave owners pressed their claims of ownership and insisted that their right to property in human beings was sacrosanct. Moreover, if educating slaves by training them in a trade, allowing them to gain knowledge of the landscape, or securing a modicum of literacy increased the value of the slave, it also made the slave more dangerous, increasing both the slave's desire for freedom and his or her means to secure it. Slavery, by definition, was a problematic relationship.

The same contradiction between the slave as person and property that defined slavery also defined opposition to slavery. This was especially true in the United States. American nationality rested on the principle that all human beings were self-evidently free and entitled to "life, liberty, and the pursuit of happiness." Opponents of slavery drew strength from the Republic's founding statement. But if the Declaration of Independence staked a claim for the universality of freedom and made equality normative, the Constitution—the bedrock of the American government—protected property, and slave owners insisted that the state (both the national and local governments) honor their right to property in man. From the beginning, the struggle between the slaves and slave masters, freedom and slavery, was embedded in the struggle over the essence of the American Republic and the meaning of the American experience.

5. Slavery was both death and life. Slavery was a killing machine. It necessarily rested on violence and the willingness of slave owners to use every means necessary to bend slaves to their will. Slaveholders and their allies murdered, mutilated, traumatized, and demeaned millions of men and women. Mean, nasty, heinous violence that denied human beings the essence of their humanity, that excluded them from a full participation in society, and that left them in a perpetual state of fear was an essential element in the institution of chattel bondage. When slaveholders were denied a monopoly of violence—backed by the power of the state—slavery collapsed.

But while slavery killed, mutilated, traumatized, and demeaned millions of people, enslaved people never gave in to the process of dehumanization. While slavery was death, slavery was also life. Slaves did not surrender to the imposition, physical and psychological. They refused to be dehumanized by dehumanizing treatment. The history of slavery was not only the story of victimization, brutalization, and exclusion. On the narrowest of grounds and in the most difficult of circumstances, enslaved peoples created and sustained life in the form of families, churches, and associations of all kinds. These organizations, often clandestine and fugitive, fragile and unrecognized by the larger society, became the site of new languages, aesthetics, and philosophies as expressed in story, music, dance, and cuisine. They produced leaders, institutions, and ideas that countered the culture and ideologies of the slave-owning class. The slaves' oppositional culture continues to inform American life, so much so that it is impossible to imagine American culture without slavery's creative legacy.

What makes slavery so difficult for our students, and for ourselves, to comprehend is that it embraces two conflicting ideas—slavery as death and slavery as life—that are equally compelling. One states that slavery is one of the great crimes in human history; the other that men and women transcended slavery's inhumanity, grew strong because of it, and made enslavement one of the great sites of human creativity. One speaks to the deep nightmare of chattel bondage; the other to its hard-earned, life-affirming legacy. Both elements of slavery's history are essential to tell slavery's story. On the one hand, if the soul-wrenching violence is excised, the history of slavery becomes an empty vessel without weight or meaning. It is a gigantic fraud that denies the suffering of millions and the struggle to create life under the most difficult of circumstances. On the other hand, if slavery is only the story of murders, mutilations, and the denials of humanity, and if it fails to recognize what slaves created in the most difficult of circumstances, the story of slavery is an equally hollow charade. It ignores the great struggle of enslaved people and what they created at such great cost.

The true history of slavery must tell both stories and tell them simultaneously. Doing so presses against a Manichean urge to make slavery's history one thing or the other. It is always a difficult task.

6. The extremes in which slavery manifest itself—death and life—were reflected most concretely in the daily interchanges between slaves and slave owners, affirming that slaves could not exist without the master and vice versa. The master-slave relation took multiple forms that defied the most vivid imagination. Only the most talented artist can imagine the fullness of the tragedy of human bondage.

The master-slave relation has provided novelists with fertile ground for exploring the entire realm of human behavior. Some of the best fiction from Stowe to Twain, Faulkner to Wright, and Ellison to Morrison pivots around slavery and its aftermath. But if only great imagination can capture the fullest of those relations, slavery's history defines their essence.

Slave masters believed that ownership licensed them to abuse the slave in the most vicious and appalling manner, while at the very same time they asserted that they loved their slaves and, in turn, were loved by them. In countless ways—but most especially when the arrival of freedom allowed them to abandon their owners—slaves exposed the fantasy of the world their masters had made. At those moments, no one felt the pain of betrayal more sharply than the owning class. But slave-holders were not the only ones who felt the pain of self-deception. While they encouraged the master's belief in their mutual affection, perhaps in hopes of moderating the slaveholder's cruelty, self-interest led to imaginative projections for slaves as well as their owners, compounding the complexity of an already complex relationship.

The convolutions that characterized the relationship between master and slave played out in fields and workshops, the Big House and the quarter, but perhaps was nowhere more visible than in the bedroom. Slave masters abused slave women sexually (the sexual abuse of slave men was also routine although not nearly as well documented), forcing themselves upon their subordinates in the vilest manner. While rape was the commonplace of master-slave sexuality, some of those relationships, even ones begun in ugly force, turned into life-long loving unions that can only be fairly described as marriages. And, like all marriages, the presumably loving ties between master and slave took different forms. Thomas Jefferson (president, 1801–9) lived with Sally Hemings and their children but refused to recognize publicly either their relationship or their children; Richard Mentor Johnson (vice president, 1837–41) not only openly embraced his black wife but also brought his entire family to Washington, introduced his daughters to Washington society, and married them to white men of his own class. These, of course, were only two of the many configurations of relationships between white masters and black slaves, since most of the sexual relations between slaveholders and the enslaved neither led to cohabitation nor recognition. Yet, they confirm that the study of slavery, at base, is the study of social relations.

7. Slavery was an institution of power. Slave owners labored to break the slaves' will and make enslaved peoples an extension of their own person. Slaves refused to bend, asserted their autonomy, and ultimately maintained their humanity. In this struggle, the slave owner—who claimed the title of "master"—enjoyed enormous advantages, so much so that slavery is often characterized as an institution of total domination. But slaves were never without power themselves. Because slaves had some power—if only the smallest of mites—slavery was not only an institution of domination, but also an institution of negotiation. Those negotiations were not those of the level playing field that Americans prized, but negotiations among profound unequals. Understanding how men and women with little power and no independent standing were able to work their wills is to understand the essence of slavery.

For most of slavery's history, the unequal struggle between slave and owner was such that no one could win, at least in the short run (which, for most, lasted a lifetime). Despite their monopoly of violence, slave masters failed miserably in transforming human beings to their ideal of a commodity without will or volition—mere extensions of their will. Slaves maintained a hold on their own humanity. But if they succeeded in countering their owner's claim that they were mere commodities, slaves could deny the day-to-day reality of the slave master's power. Save for the great revolt in Saint Domingue, slave rebels failed to break the slave master's grasp. With neither side able to claim victory, slaves and slave owners fought an endless guerrilla war.

The deadlock necessitated compromise, in which each temporarily surrendered its claim—the master to total domination and the slave to existential freedom. Under this grudging truce, slave owners granted slaves privileges—to establish families, travel freely, market the product of their labor, and even hold property—which slaves immediately claimed as rights. The exact nature of these privileges or rights were subject to constant negotiation and endless renegotiation, in which slaves tried to expand their rights, while their owners labored to shrink them. Such negotiations were freighted with danger, as either party—if pushed too hard—might peremptorily repudiate the entire agreement, reopening overt warfare. Indeed, for slaves, most acts of resistance—flight, arson, and even open rebellion—were not rooted in the outrage of slavery itself, but in the violations of generally understood accords. The contingencies upon which such bargains rested revealed the fragility of slavery, so that—in a moment—so-called "good" owners could turn vicious and so-called "good" slaves could turn rebel.

8. Because the circumstances of the negotiations between slave owners and slaves were always different, slavery itself was always different. Slavery changed over time and through space. It depended upon the terrain of enslavement (geography); the nature of enslaved populations and the balance of numbers between master and slave, white and black, men and women, and adults and children (demography); and the nationalities of the slave and slave owner (Igbo, Kongo, Mande; English, French, Spanish) and their standing (African or creole), among other things. These endless permutations meant that slavery took different forms and, moreover, that those forms were constantly changing. Such differences affirm that slave societies, whatever their essential commonalities, only can be understood as historical creations.

Much the same is true for the slaves themselves. Slaves, no more than their owners or white and black nonslaveholders, never thought and acted the same way. Their aspirations, ideologies, and actions manifested themselves in endless variety. If, given the realities of slavery, some were content to learn a skill, gain a place in the Big House, earn money, and cut the best deal they could to mitigate the horrors of bondage, others refused to bide their time and await the Jubilee. Instead, they searched for ways to speed—with varying degrees of success—the arrival of freedom for themselves, their families, and their people. Homogenizing the slave experience of necessity distorts it.

9. Ownership did not define the lives of enslaved peoples. Like every other human being who ever lived, the slave was a product of his or her circumstances, only one part—a significant part, to be sure—of which was that he or she was owned. Among their other attributes, slaves were husbands and wives (even in the absence of legal standing) and parents and children; they were skilled and unskilled, field hands and house servants; and they were Christians and Muslims, Methodists and Baptists. Knowing that a person was a slave does not tell everything about him or her. Put another way, slaveholders severely circumscribed the lives of enslaved people, but they never fully defined them. The slaves' history—like all human history—was made not only by what was done to them, but also by what they did for themselves.

What were the circumstances that shaped the lives of slaves in the United States? Americans generally point to three: cotton, black belt residence, and the Afro-Christian religion, although for most of slavery's history on mainland North American few slaves grew cotton, lived in the deep South, or embraced Christianity. Freezing the history of slavery at its zenith, Americans have read it backwards. This perhaps is a tribute to the abolitionist movement and its ability to shape popular understanding of the history of slavery or the enormous place of the Civil War in the American imagination, but it is a disservice to the experience of the slaves and us—their descendants—who are left to wrestle with slavery and its legacy of racial injustice with partial knowledge.

10. Finally, slavery insinuated itself into every relationship, institution, and action in a slave society. While the slave master and the slave stood at the center of slave societies, no one was untouched. The relationship between master and slaves deeply affected the standing of white and black nonslaveholders (who, in the antebellum American South, composed the vast majority of the population), as it did between the slave master and his wife and his children. It defined manhood and womanhood. The slave society's politics, its economy, its social structure, and its culture all rested upon the existence of chattel bondage. One way or another, slavery shaped everything from what people ate to how they loved. In the words of Frank Tannenbaum, "Nothing escaped, nothing, and no one."

Appreciating these ten elements in the history of slavery opens the door to a conversation that may transform not only our students but also the society in which they live. But, like all of history's lessons, they will not be the end of the discussion, but a fuller beginning.

Understanding and Teaching
American Slavery

Introduction

BETHANY JAY and CYNTHIA LYNN LYERLY

The scenes are unforgettable. A pregnant slave lies in a hole dug to accommodate her swollen belly so that she can be beaten without endangering her master's investment in her unborn child.[1] Though a buyer is willing to purchase them together, the slave trader, deaf to the pleas of the slave mother, Eliza, separates her from her daughter, Emily, preferring instead to auction the girl to white men looking for concubines.[2] James Henry Hammond, a prominent southern politician, instructs his son to take care of several slave children who were fathered either by Hammond or by his son because "slavery in the family will be their happiest earthly condition."[3]

Other scenes inspire. A cook's husband on Burleigh plantation convincingly feigns blindness and is assigned to the light work of helping his wife in the kitchen. After the Civil War, this now free man makes eighteen good crops and is "one of the best farmers in the country." For seven years, a young mother hides in an attic crawl space to avoid the lecherous designs of her master, leaving only to escape to freedom in the North. On plantations across the South, slaves compose hymns like "Go Down Moses" and "Wade in the Water," giving credence to Paul Robeson's celebration of the "healing comfort to be found in the illimitable sorrow of the spirituals."[4]

In slavery, we and our students see the best and the worst of humanity. American slavery is one of the most challenging and emotionally fraught subjects we teach. No other field in American history has changed so dramatically in modern times.[5] Slavery is also such a difficult topic that it is tempting to give into a progressive narrative that centers on runaways and abolitionists and excludes the everyday complex realities of slavery.

3

There are many challenges for teachers of slavery. How do we get our students to understand the racist underpinnings of American slavery, while still acknowledging its traces in contemporary America and critiquing its assumptions? How do we recognize slaves' agency while acknowledging the brutality and inhumanity of human bondage? How do we work with sources that have obsolete and racist terms, images, and ideas in them? How do we overcome students' shame, guilt, and denial about American slavery? Additionally, the mythology of slavery has been enshrined in so much of our popular culture. We are taught that the nation was founded on the principle that "all men are created equal." In this view, slavery was the aberration to the grand narrative of American freedom until the abolitionist North fought a war to end it, destroying an idyllic and genteel southern culture in the process. Because of all of these difficulties, it may be tempting to omit or minimize discussions of American slavery rather than wade into these treacherous waters.

Scholars teaching about slavery must face these challenges and explode the myths before we can start. The essays in this book address these problems. Beginning with Ira Berlin's brilliant foreword on the essential but "not-so-easy" elements of teaching slavery, several essays discuss the broad context of slavery in the classroom. James Loewen's essay discusses strategies for introducing this content into the classroom by exploring its contemporary relevance with students. Steven Oliver offers instructors a step-by-step guide to creating a comfortable classroom environment for these difficult discussions.

As Berlin has noted, slavery was an integral part of the American economy and political system. Slavery was the economic engine for much of western capitalist development, and northern industry depended on slavery. Several essays expand on these themes and provide resources for the classroom. Laird Bergad's essay picks up on the importance of slavery outside the North American continent by charting the development of modern slave societies in Central and South America and in the Caribbean alongside the one in the United States. Using the examples of Rhode Island and New York, Christy Clark-Pujara demonstrates the ways that the northern economy was built on slavery, as northern merchants and industries tirelessly dealt in products made by or intended for the slaves in the slaveholding centers of the Deep South and the West Indies. Joanne Pope Melish reminds us that slavery existed in the North, that it was important to the northern economy, and that it

4

produced a legacy of racism in the region that far outlived the institution itself. Deirdre Cooper Owens shifts the focus to southern slavery in her essay, which shows the importance of slave-produced cash crops to the economy and the ways in which work routines affected the lives and culture of the enslaved. James Brewer Stewart rounds out this discussion by exploring a method to teach students about contemporary slavery.

Slavery was so important to the economy that protections for slavery were built into the American Constitution, and several generations later southern men went to war to protect it. Legal historian Paul Finkelman's essay demonstrates the power that slaveholders wielded in the debates surrounding the Constitution and the long-term impact of Constitutional protections for the institution. Bethany Jay examines slavery and the Civil War, exploring the institution as a cause of the war and highlighting the ways that free and enslaved African Americans affected the prosecution of the war and the policy of emancipation.

Berlin's foreword also reminds us of the many contradictions of slavery—as Berlin puts it, "human beings and property," "death and life." Sowande' Mustakeem's essay demonstrates the transformation of human beings into property in her discussion of the violence and degradation of the slave trade. Kenneth Greenberg and Antonio Bly further explore these contradictions in their chapters on slave resistance and runaway slave ads, respectively. Though slave resistance encompassed violent uprisings, attempts at permanent freedom, and smaller everyday decisions, each of these acts was an expression of slaves' humanity. Through his discussion of slave culture, particularly slave spirituals, Bernard Powers demonstrates Berlin's statement: "On the narrowest of grounds and in the most difficult of circumstances, enslaved peoples created and sustained life." By offering a responsible method of role-playing in the classroom, Lindsay Anne Randall's essay demonstrates a strategy to allow students to consider the ways that these contradictions affected individual slave lives.

As Berlin notes, if slavery presents problems for the educator, it also presents opportunities. Teachers of slavery have a tremendous array of resources to use in the classroom. Slave narratives, runaway ads, spirituals, contemporary films, and material culture all help students to develop a deeper understanding of American slavery and a keener appreciation for the historian's craft. All sources have biases, but the sources our book discusses are often particularly one-sided, forcing students to confront how the source was produced, the prejudices of the creator, and its purposes. Many teachers are afraid of these sources because of their biases, but Cynthia Lyerly, Antonio Bly, Ray Williams, Ron Briley, and Sarah Miller and her coauthors provide strategies to incorporate them into the curriculum in sophisticated ways. The stories these sources tell engage students on a visceral level, and teachers can use that engagement to make them think in more complicated and profound ways about slavery and about history.

As Edmund Morgan so eloquently reminded us, slavery is an American "paradox," and "it behooves Americans to understand it if they would understand themselves."[6] This book is our effort to move beyond myth and forgetting and to grapple with the ugly truths of America's past. Our authors bring together the most recent scholarship on this subject to demonstrate how to integrate slavery into the broad chronological and geographical sweep of American history. Beginning with Ira Berlin's powerful foreword, these essays illustrate the stubborn humanity of the powerless, the creativity that can persevere in the midst of unimaginable degradation and brutality, and the unexpected influence that the enslaved had on domestic and international policy.

NOTES

1. Moses Grandy, *Narrative of the Life of Moses Grandy; Late a Slave in the United States of America* (London: C. Gilpin, 1843), 28.

2. Solomon Northup, *Twelve Years a Slave* (Auburn, NY: Derby and Miller, 1853; Mineola, NY: Dover, 2000), 83–88. Citations refer to 2000 edition.

3. James Henry Hammond to Harry Hammond, February 19, 1856, in James Henry Hammond Papers, SCL, in Drew Gilpin Faust, *James Henry Hammond and the Old South: A Design for Mastery* (Baton Rouge: Louisiana State University Press, 1982), 87.

4. Paul Robeson, *Here I Stand* (New York: Beacon Press, 1958; New York: Beacon Press, 1998), 15.

5. See, for example, Peter J. Parish, *Slavery: History and Historians* (Boulder, CO: Westview Press, 1990), and Edward E. Baptist and Stephanie M. H. Camp, eds., *New Studies in the History of American Slavery* (Athens: University of Georgia Press, 2006).

6. Edmund Morgan, *American Slavery, American Freedom* (New York: W. W. Norton, 1975; New York: W. W. Norton, 2003), 5.

PART ONE

Slavery and the Classroom

Methods for Teaching Slavery to High School Students and College Undergraduates in the United States

JAMES W. LOEWEN

> The black-white rift stands at the very center of American history. It is the great challenge to which all our deepest aspirations to freedom must rise. If we forget that—if we forget the great stain of slavery that stands at the heart of our country, our history, our experiment—we forget who we are, and we make the great rift deeper and wider.
>
> KEN BURNS, "Mystic Chords of Memory"
> (University of Vermont speech, September 12, 1991)

When I give workshops for high school history teachers, I point out that their task is not to teach US history textbooks. Rather, they are supposed to teach US history. I suggest that they develop a list of thirty to fifty topics they *want* to teach—topics that they deem so important that no eighteen-year-old should leave high school without having considered them deeply. Each topic should connect importantly with students' lives today.

This list cannot be completely arbitrary. A list without the making and use of the Constitution is not acceptable. Neither is a list without slavery.

The Importance of Slavery

Although there are problems in teaching slavery, there are bigger problems in *not* teaching slavery. Some teachers let their worries about teaching the subject deter them from giving slavery the attention it deserves. When they do, as the filmmaker Ken Burns notes, they participate in making "the great rift" between blacks and whites deeper and wider. Moreover, it's bad history. Surely slavery, which caused and underlies this rift, was the most pervasive single issue in our past. Consider: contention about slavery forced the Whig Party to collapse; caused the main Protestant churches to separate, North and South; and prompted the Republican Party to form. Until the end of the nineteenth century, cotton—planted, cultivated, harvested, and ginned by slaves and then by ex-slaves—was by far our most important export. Our graceful antebellum homes, northern as well as southern, were mostly built by slaves or from profits derived from the slave and cotton trades. Slavery prompted secession; the resulting Civil War killed about as many Americans as died in all our other wars combined. Black-white relations were the main theme of Reconstruction after the Civil War; America's failure to let African Americans have equal rights then led inexorably to the struggle for civil rights a century later.

Slavery also deeply influenced our popular culture. From the 1850s through the 1930s (except, perhaps, during the Civil War and Reconstruction), the dominant form of popular entertainment in America was minstrel shows, which derived in a perverse way from plantation slavery. Two novels have been by far our most popular—both by white women, both about slavery. *Uncle Tom's Cabin* dominated the nineteenth century, *Gone with the Wind* the twentieth. During the nineteenth century, *Uncle Tom's Cabin* was also by far our most popular play, with thousands of productions; during the twentieth, *Gone with the Wind* was by far our most popular movie (in constant dollars). The most popular television miniseries ever was *Roots*, the saga of an enslaved family; it changed our culture by setting off an explosion of interest in genealogy, ethnic backgrounds, and slavery. In music, slavery gave rise to spirituals and work songs, which in turn led to gospel music and the blues. Other essays in this book show how slavery influenced the adoption and some of the language of our Constitution. It affected our foreign policy, sometimes in ways that were contrary to our national interests.

Most important of all, slavery caused racism. In the United States, as a legal and social system, slavery ended between 1863 and 1865, depending upon where one lived. Unfortunately, racism, slavery's handmaiden, did not. In turn, white supremacy, the ideology that slavery begot, caused the Democratic Party to label itself the "white man's party" for almost a century, into the 1920s. Also during the 1920s, white supremacy led to the "science" of eugenics (human breeding), IQ and SAT testing, and restrictions on the immigration of "inferior races" from southern and eastern Europe as well as Asia and Africa.

Obviously, then, because of its impact throughout our past and in our present, we must teach about slavery. The question is how.

Relevance to the Present

The first step in introducing a unit on slavery is to help students see slavery's relevance to the present. One way to begin is with the *Skymall* catalog, until recently the most widely distributed catalog in the United States.[1] For twenty-five years, it awaited travelers in the seat pocket in front of them on every major airline. Amtrak also distributed it, retitled *TravelMall*. Over the years, *Skymall* offered thousands of different items for the consumer. It was a catalog of catalogs. It had items from Brookstone, Frontgate, and Hammacher Schlemmer. It sold trampolines, doggie beds, and live lobsters. It even had a doorbell that rings all over the house.

About the only thing it *didn't* have was people of color.

To be sure, occasionally the catalog listed a product that itself was an exception. For example, *Skymall* used to sell a photo of Mookie Wilson's ground ball dribbling past Boston first-baseman Bill Buckner to give the New York Mets victory in game six of the 1986 World Series—considered the most famous at-bat in Mets history. Both Wilson and Buckner signed the photo, and Wilson is African American. In a different example, *Skymall* offered a garden sculpture modeled on the Moai statues found on Easter Island; the statues too depict nonwhite people. I'm not talking about such cases, where the *product itself* is interracial. I'm talking about the models hired by the catalog and by the companies that make the products sold in it. Here the merchants had discretion as to the races of the models they chose. They exercised it. The absence of people of color among the hundreds of models shown using products in *Skymall* was overwhelming. From 2006 to 2014, typical issues included about two hundred photos that showed models using products. Usually one or two photos included an African American. As well, two or three showed whites who might have been Latino, and one or two showed images, often tiny, that were in between and hard to classify.

The population of the United States was about 64 percent non-Hispanic white in 2010 and is less white today. Issue after issue, *Skymall* came out nearly 97 percent white, less than 1.7 percent black, less than .9 percent Hispanic, and about .8 percent Asian. Could this have been by accident? I teach sociological statistics, so I did the math to find out. Having so many white images, drawn from a population "only" 64 percent white, in just one catalog could happen by chance far less often than once in a billion.[2] The possibility that two consecutive catalogs could wind up this way by chance is actually much less than one billionth times one billionth.[3] We can conclude that the almost total exclusion of people of color from *Skymall* was no accident.

Most readers of *Skymall*, even many African American readers, never noticed its whiteness. It just seemed "natural." But by "natural" in quotation marks a sociologist means not natural at all but something so deep in our culture that we neither notice nor question it. Since the whiteness of *Skymall* could not happen by chance, it most certainly was *not* natural. It was racial. Absent slavery, race would not influence model choice, just as eye color does not.[4] Then African Americans would be about 12 percent of the models in *Skymall*; Hispanics, Asians, and Native Americans would be represented roughly proportionately, as well. Moreover, if not for slavery, Americans would have noticed the astonishing absence of African Americans (and others) rather than taking it for granted. Finally, if not for slavery, Americans would surely have protested this absence, at least by refusing to buy from such a catalog.

Of course, *Skymall* is the tip of an iceberg—an iceberg students might explore further. In the 2010 census, African American families made about two-thirds the median income of white families. In tiny part, the reason was that African Americans—except for a handful of light-skinned persons—could not be models for *Skymall* or the companies that advertised in it. Of course, *Skymall* is only a synecdoche—a figure of speech in which a part stands for the whole.[5] Research shows that companies in many fields are still reluctant to hire African Americans. To cite just one study: in about 2005, economists sent five thousand résumés to some 1,250 companies in Chicago and Boston that had posted help-wanted ads. Ahead of time, they talked with human resources managers at some of the companies and came away thinking that black applicants would be *more* likely to get called for job interviews. "Employers said they were hungry for qualified minorities and were aggressively seeking diversity." The résumés varied. Some had stereotypically "white" names such as Greg; others had "black" names such as Tyrone. Every employer got four résumés: an average white applicant, an average black applicant, a highly skilled white applicant, and a highly skilled black applicant. The researchers measured only one outcome: callbacks. Résumés with "white" names triggered 50 percent more requests for interviews than those with "black" names. Indeed, even lower-skilled white applicants got more callbacks than highly skilled blacks.[6]

Studies finding similar results appear every few months, sometimes dramatically on television. Even when affirmative action was at its height, in the mid-1990s, white people knew that blacks still faced discrimination. For example, white parents in Riverside, California, objected to a proposal to name a local high school after Martin Luther King Jr., saying such a name might cause their children to be perceived as coming from a "black" school, which would hurt their chances of getting into good colleges. If they really believed that affirmative action was widespread while discrimination was a thing of the past, they would have relished having their kids graduate from a high school named for King.[7]

Since that time, having an African American president may have helped, but more recent judicial attacks on affirmative action have hurt. Now few programs exist to counter racial discrimination such as that shown in *Skymall* or in the résumé study. No wonder median black household income as a proportion of non-Hispanic white income fell from about 65 percent in 2000 to 59 percent by 2010.[8]

Even more important than the income differential is the black/white wealth ratio, which shows a far greater disparity. While the income ratio in 2010 was 3:5, the wealth ratio was about 1:11. That is, the median white family has eleven times as much wealth as the median black family. To some degree, this enormous wealth gap derives from the income gap. A family making $32,000 (the median black household income in 2010) can find it hard to save a dime. Meanwhile, a family making $54,600 (the median white income in 2010) can save $20,000 and still live better than the black family. Income differences alone, however, do not explain the wealth gap. Within each income category, white families own much more than black families. That's due to history: white families have been much more likely to receive gifts from parents and other relatives in the form of down payments on first homes, money for college educations, and bequests in wills. In turn, the money for these gifts came mostly from the equity that white parents and grandparents built up in their homes over time.[9]

Why didn't black families build up the same net worth in their homes? This home ownership gap stems from specific historical causes during the suburbanization of the United States after World War II. Between 1947 and 1968, millions of middle-class and working-class families bought their first homes. They were helped by the Veterans Administration (VA) and the Federal Housing Administration (FHA). These programs almost completely excluded African Americans (and some other nonwhites).[10] So for decades black families paid rent in the city while white families paid off mortgages in the suburbs. If not for slavery and the assumptions about black inferiority that it engendered, whites would never have thought to keep blacks from benefiting from the VA and FHA programs—and then we would not see such a wealth gap by race today.

Moreover, when suburbs formed, about 80 percent of them flatly barred African Americans, formally or informally, from living in them. Only in the 1990s did many suburbs, such as Hemet, near Los Angeles; Cicero, bordering Chicago; and Livonia, near Detroit, begin to allow black residents.[11] Even today, many whites think it "natural" for African Americans to live in the inner city and for European Americans to populate the outer suburbs. Again, absent slavery, whites would never have excluded blacks from suburbs across the United States.

For that matter, if not for slavery, people from Africa would not have been identified as a race in the first place, let alone stigmatized as an inferior race. Race as a social concept, along with the claim that the white race is superior to other groups, came about as a rationale for slavery. As Supreme Court Justice William O. Douglas famously put it in 1968, racism is a vestige of "slavery unwilling to die."[12] This is terribly important for students to grasp, because otherwise many of them (and

14

not just black students) imagine that racism is innate, at least among white folks.

Many Americans imagine today that humans "naturally" come divided into three races—black, yellow (!), and white—not realizing that this classification system is also a product of history. Three is no magic number. Sometimes Europeans (and European Americans) came up with three races, sometimes five, sometimes seven, sometimes more. The Library of Congress was built in 1897. Carved in stone, above its windows, are thirty-three male heads, representing the *thirty-three* "races" of mankind extant in 1897. Each is intended to "exemplify all the average physical characteristics of his race," according to an explanation put out by the library at the time:

1, Slav; 2, Blonde European; 3, Brunette European; 4, Greek; 5, Persian; 6, Circassian; 7, Hindoo; 8, Hungarian (Magyar); 9, Semite or Jew; 10, Arab (Bedouin); 11, Turk; 12, Modern Egyptian; 13, Ethiopian; 14, Malay; 15, Polynesian; 16, Australian; 17, Negrito (Andaman Islands, etc.); 18, Bantu; 19, New Guinean; 20 Sudanese; 21, Pygmy; 22, Fuegian; 23, Botocudo (South America); 24, Pueblo Indian; 25, Eskimo; 26, Plains Indian; 27, Saami (Lapp); 28, Korean; 29, Japanese; 30, Ainu; 31, Burmese; 32, Tibetan; 33, Chinese.[13]

The basic point remains: as racism grew, owing to slavery, Europeans began to think of themselves as a group—"whites"—and classified others as "nonwhites."

In sum, slavery still influences how people think, where they live, how much money they have, and even who gets chosen to model in a catalog. Students should leave this discussion able to form useful ideas about slavery's impact on our past and present in response to the question "Why must we learn about slavery?"

How Not to Teach about Slavery

Here's an example of how *not* to teach about slavery, from a student teacher who was observing a social studies teacher in New York City. The teacher was white; most of his students were black. He began the unit on slavery by burying "his nose in his notes" and lecturing, with no introduction. "The students were visibly upset by what they were hearing," according to the student teacher, "but the

15

teacher just kept going until the end of the period, at which point he finished the lecture, put down his papers, and sent them on to math class."[14]

Perhaps the teacher worried about how his students *would* have reacted, so he taught in such a way as to allow no reactions. It is not a "feel-good" topic, after all. Teachers of majority-black classes may worry that all they will accomplish is making their students mad. Teachers of classes with only a handful of African Americans do not want those students to feel singled out. Teachers of all-white classes don't want parental complaints from students who infer they are supposed to feel guilty. These issues are less salient on the college level, but white college students all too often respond to units on slavery and race by shutting down, afraid to say anything substantive lest they might be thought racist.

Begin with Meta-Discussions

Showing slavery's impact on the present is the first step in introducing a unit on slavery. The second might be to hold a meta-conversation—a conversation about the unit we're about to start. A way to begin is by the teacher confessing (if true) that in previous years she did not always give enough time and attention to slavery. The teacher can ask, "Do you have any idea why I didn't?" Students may come up with some of the answers:

- It's contentious.
- The teacher was afraid white students would clam up.
- The teacher was afraid black students would get angry.
- The textbook doesn't cover slavery very well.
- The teacher didn't think she knew enough to do a good job.
- The teacher was worried about falling behind the schedule.

The the teacher can ask, "Was I *right* to worry?" She can also tailor a question to the demography of her class: "People warned me that college freshmen—especially in a racially mixed [or almost all-white, or whatever] class—would not be mature enough to handle a discussion about slavery. Were they right?" In my experience, students *never* agree that they're immature; in the process, they sign on to be mature. Follow with a second challenge: "We will have to go beyond the textbook and learn more about slavery—and the racism that derived from it—on our own. It's important. It might be interesting. Can you do that?"

Students also need a second meta-discussion, on what I call "racial nationalism." One way to begin is to ask students to jot down the names of several heroes of theirs. In classes that have reasonable numbers of African Americans, one can then ask the black students to volunteer a few names. If they name black folks—and some surely will—then the teacher can explore this: "Do you think you might have thought of these people because you're black?" Probably they will agree. That's okay.

Teachers might then explore the white students' choices; especially in a context of race relations, some are likely to name Mahatma Gandhi, Martin Luther King Jr., Nelson Mandela, Serena Williams, or other nonwhites. That too is okay, of course. An approach I use is to volunteer a hero of my own: the architect Frank Lloyd Wright. He invented the carport, I point out. Until then, we kept cars in free-standing enclosed garages distant from our houses—mainly because in earlier times we wanted to keep our houses free from the odor of horse manure! He also designed some beautiful houses and other structures, complete with new styles of furniture and leaded glass windows, I go on. Then I admit that I take an "in-group" kind of pride in his excellence, as if it somehow implies something good about *me*. We're both from Illinois, for example. I have been very interested in architecture and even designed (and built) a house. And, I admit, Wright and I are both white (and male, too). There's a kind of "we" there.

I call that sort of pride "racial nationalism." Of *course* I realize that I had nothing to do with Wright's genius and that his accomplishments do not really reflect positively on me. Nevertheless, I still kind of think that way. So do most of us, I suspect, including our students. So I point out my racial nationalism to my students, label it irrational but understandable, forgive myself for it, and ask them to examine their own versions.

Then I ask, "Okay, if it's irrational for me to take pride in Frank Lloyd Wright, as *a white person*, is it rational for me to feel bad as *a white person* because white people enslaved people of color?" The answer, which we want students of all races to see, is no. Review "anachronism," and ask for examples. Students need to understand that to hold anyone alive today responsible for someone's having been a slave or a slave owner or for slavery in general is anachronistic.[15] A unit on slavery isn't about proving a group bad. No white person should feel guilty because some other whites, many decades ago, enslaved people. No black person should feel ashamed because some other blacks, many decades ago, were enslaved. Indeed, if a white student teases a black student today— "Your people used to serve my people . . ."—or if a black student rages at a white student today—"You people have always been racist . . ."— they themselves are displaying vestiges of slavery unwilling to die. At the end of this meta-conversation, students should know to chorus "no" when asked, "Is anyone in this classroom responsible for enslaving?" "Is anyone in this classroom responsible for being enslaved?" That does not mean we are off the "moral hook," though. We are responsible for treating people fairly, without racism, and for treating slavery honestly, without sugar-coating, from here on, for the rest of our lives.[16]

Every student also needs to learn about antislavery activists like Edward Coles, the Grimké sisters, and Elizabeth Van Lew. Then none can graduate thinking all whites were racist. All need to know about antislavery activists like Frederick Douglass and the people who rebelled at Destrehan Plantation in Louisiana. Then none can graduate thinking blacks accepted slavery and did little about it.

Slavery Led to Racism

The next step is to hold a conversation about racism. Many students of all races—in both high school and college—are unsophisticated as to what racism is and where it comes from. In the past few years, racism has come to be considered socially unacceptable, at least in interracial settings. That's a welcome development, because it is both unfair to individuals and bad for our nation to treat people unfairly on the basis of their racial group membership. On the other hand, since it's unacceptable to be racist, white people in particular have begun to define "racism" so narrowly as to exclude most human behavior!

A simple and useful definition of "racism" is this: treating people differently and worse owing to their racial group membership. Consider *Skymall*. How did it treat a handsome model who happened to be African American? Differently and worse, according to the statistics, as we saw. Because he is black, such a person had almost no chance to be hired by *Skymall* or one of its advertisers. We cannot reserve the word "racist" for those few people who shout, "Go home, nigger!" *Skymall* was definitely racist, even if no one who worked there used the "n-word," did anything to keep African Americans out of her neighborhood, or worked consciously to maintain the astounding wealth gap that whites enjoy over blacks.

Skymall was also culturally racist. That is, as part of American culture (like *Gone with the Wind*), it implied that African Americans don't jump on trampolines, eat live lobsters, or even use doorbells. This is part of a process sociologists call "otherizing." It makes racial minorities appear different from "us." Surely no one at *Skymall* meant to do this, but the exclusion of African Americans (and, to a degree, other minorities) inevitably had this effect.

Many Americans think people are "naturally" racist or that at least *white* people are. I have heard college professors, social scientists, and lawyers say that whites are racist by nature—that is, genetically. Nonsense. No one is born with the notion that the human race is subdivided by skin color, let alone that one group should be dominant over others. Racism is a product of history, particularly of the history of slavery. We've already discussed "naturally," and teachers can let students in on what sociologists do with that term. Racism was an *historical* invention.

Racism is thus neither innate nor inevitable. Students must never be allowed to say that it is without being contradicted—preferably by other students. Of course, showing how racism developed to rationalize slavery does not mean that whites adopted the idea consciously and hypocritically to defend the otherwise indefensible unfairness of slavery. Whites sincerely believed in racial differences. Indeed, between 1855 and 1865, white supremacy in turn prompted the white South to mount a fierce defense of slavery. During the Nadir of race relations—that terrible period from 1890 to about 1940, when the United States was more racist in its thinking than at any other point—whites used racism to justify the otherwise indefensible unfairness of removing blacks from citizenship.[17]

Slavery was not always caught up with race. Europeans have enslaved each other for centuries. The word itself derives from "Slav," the people most often enslaved by their neighbors before 1400 because they had not organized into nation-states and could not defend themselves adequately.[18] Native Americans and Africans likewise enslaved their neighbors long before Europeans arrived. Ethnocentrism—the notion that our culture is better than theirs—has long existed among human groups. Perhaps all societies have been ethnocentric. Saying "we're better than they" can rationalize enslaving "them." But then the enslaved grow more like us, intermarry with us, have children, and speak our language. Now ethnocentrism can no longer rationalize enslaving them.[19]

One way to show the development of racism is through Shakespeare's play *Othello*. Shakespeare wrote the play in 1604, but it derives from a story written down in 1565 by Giovanni Battista Giraldi but that probably dates back still further. Giraldi and Shakespeare considered Othello's blackness exotic but not bad. European nations, beginning with Portugal in the middle of the 1400s, had already begun to enslave Africans. Eric Kimball explains in his essay in this volume that Europeans at this time stopped enslaving Slavs and instead picked on African villages, avoiding those Africans who had organized into nation-states or enlisting them as allies. Black slaves came to be seen as better than white slaves, who could more easily run away. By 1600 most slaves in Europe were black and most blacks in Europe were enslaved, so slavery began to be seen as racial. Since their color still identified them as slaves even after they had acculturated to "white" society, it seemed appropriate to keep Africans' children enslaved.[20]

Racism increased as this "new" slavery intensified. By 1700, white slave traders were carrying thousands of Africans every year to Brazil, the Caribbean, and the southern United States, where they and their children would work, unrecompensed, forever. This bothered many white people. Bartolomé de las Casas, for example, a Spanish conquistador who became a priest, recanted his suggestion that the Spanish replace enslaved American Indians, who were dying in slavery, with Africans. Referring to himself in the third person, he later wrote that he "was unaware of the injustice with which the Portuguese take them and make slaves of them, and would not have given that advice for all the world." He prayed to God to have mercy upon his soul, Las Casas went on, "but he does not know if God will do so."[21]

Other white people used racism to ease their guilt. Montesquieu, the French social philosopher, ironically observed in 1748: "It is impossible for us to suppose these creatures [Africans] to be men, because, allowing them to be men, a suspicion would follow that we ourselves are not Christian." Here Montesquieu is presaging the social psychologist Leon Festinger's idea of cognitive dissonance—that people mold their ideas to rationalize their actions. Rather than conclude, like Las Casas, that they were wrong to enslave Africans, most whites chose to believe that Africans' inferiority was demonstrated by their having *been* enslaved and that slavery—even perpetual bondage—was appropriate for such inferior persons. This notion of innate black inferiority grew until, by 1850, black actors could not play Othello! White actors in black-face had to take the role, because Othello kisses his wife, Desdemona, and it seemed improper to force a white actress to kiss an inferior black person, even if only on stage.[22]

Historiography and Slavery

After clearing the air about race and racism, professors and teachers might continue their discussion of slavery in America by asking students to evaluate their textbook. What are the main things we need to know about slavery? Students can work in pairs to draw up the important questions. The teacher might seed some questions:

- How many slaves came to the British colonies and later the United States?
- From where?
- Where within the United States did they wind up? Why did slavery die out in the North but intensify in the South? (Be careful; other chapters in this book show it's not as simple as "climate," "crops," or "topography.")
- How did slavery affect US foreign policy?
- What were slaves' lives like? How did people respond to enslavement?
- Why were there fewer slave revolts in the United States than in Haiti, Jamaica, Brazil, and elsewhere in the Americas?
- Was slavery ending by 1860?
- How did the monetary value of slaves compare to other investments in the United States?

Other chapters in this book should give rise to additional points that students might reasonably expect textbooks to treat. For example, Eric Kimball emphasizes that European colonists *chose* to use slaves, but some textbooks imply it was "natural."[23]

After generating an overall question list, students can examine their textbook to see how it measures up. If they feel it answers their questions, wonderful! Let them work together to uncover the answers. I suspect they will find that it doesn't. In that case, teachers must help them to go beyond the textbook and learn more about slavery and its impact on their own. (That's where this book comes in, of course.)

One reason many textbooks treat slavery (and related issues) poorly is that publishers want to sell to states in the South, all of which are controlled by southern whites. Every southern state adopts textbooks statewide, so publishers study their adoption requirements carefully. After about 1890, as the Nadir of race relations set in, white southerners began to demand that history textbooks call the Civil War the "War between the States." This was an anachronism: no one called it that while it was going on. Nevertheless, publishers caved in to the pressure. They still do. Students can examine, for example, what their textbook says about secession and states' rights. One fairly recent example, *The American Journey*, writes: "Southerners justified secession with the theory of states' rights. . . . Now because the national government had violated that contract—by refusing to enforce the Fugitive Slave Act and by denying the Southern states equal rights in the territories—the states were justified in leaving the Union."[24] This is nonsense. All of the key statements Confederates made as they left the Union, beginning with South Carolina's "Declaration of the Immediate Causes Which Induce and Justify the Secession of South Carolina from the Federal Union," blame northern states, *not* the "national government," for "refusing to enforce the Fugitive Slave Act."[25] Southern leaders were clear that they were *against* states' rights when northern states exercised those rights against slavery. Southerners seceded *for* slavery. James McPherson is listed as one of *Journey*'s three authors. Students can compare *Journey* with what McPherson himself wrote in *Battle Cry of Freedom*.

We have mentioned how two novels about slavery—*Uncle Tom's Cabin* and *Gone with the Wind*—have dominated US popular culture. Students can compare the very different views of slavery these books portray. *Uncle Tom's Cabin* shows the pain slavery caused and how slaves yearned for and sought independence. *Gone with the Wind* gives a rose-tinged view of slavery and laments its passing. These books exemplify the sea change in thinking about slavery that took place during the Nadir. In that era, white supremacists reimposed the rigid racial hierarchy set up during slavery. They stopped black southerners from voting, serving on juries, using libraries, and enjoying other basic civil liberties. Northern whites did nothing, even though the new state constitutions that accomplished this reactionary revolution violated the Fourteenth and Fifteenth Amendments to the US Constitution.[26]

During the Nadir, nostalgia for slavery swept the nation. Blackface minstrel shows grew wildly popular. Antebellum plantations became major tourist sites. *Gone with the Wind* was appropriate for this new worldview.

Examining historical sources such as textbooks and novels by locating their authors in time and social space exemplifies historiography. Professors need to teach students the concept—most simply put, the "history of history"—and get them to buy into the term.[27]

Key Points about Slavery as a Lived Experience

Now that we are slowly getting past the Nadir, teachers are freer to teach and students are freer to learn more accurate information about slavery. Historians have identified four key problems of slave life. Most important was slaves' lack of independence. They could not decide whether to work, or where, or how; what to eat or when to eat it; or even what to do from moment to moment, during much of the twenty-four-hour day. Archaeologists have been surprised to find almost no remains of tableware or even tables in slave quarters. That's because many owners did not allow slaves to have or even make tables, plates, knives, or forks.[28]

A related problem was slaves' inability to control their own careers, to decide whom to marry, or to maintain relations with their families. In the slave narratives taken down in the 1930s, old African Americans tell of having their parents sold away from them while the narrators were still children and of being unable to plan for the future. On many plantations, this anxiety peaked every year around Christmas, when some slaves were rented out for the next year to another employer. That meant it might be a year or even more before husband saw wife or child saw parent again. Most slaves also had no way out of slavery, even for their children, no matter how hard they worked.

The third key problem slaves faced was violence. Paul Escott studied more than two thousand slave narratives taken down during the 1930s. He found that when interviewers asked ex-slaves to assess their owners, the attribute they mentioned most often was whipping. Whippings could be life-shattering experiences. In the 1930s an ex-slave still remembered a whipping he received as a young boy, seventy years earlier: "I just about half died. I lay in the bunk two days, getting over that whipping—getting over it in the body, but not the heart. No, sir, I have

Slavery was a penal system. This photograph shows the cells attached to the Franklin and Armfield slave trading firm in Alexandria, Virginia. On their home plantations, few people had to be kept under lock and key. There the enslaved had family ties, friendships, and routines that were hard to break. Moreover, rural life afforded few options for escape. White patrollers challenged any African American traveling without a pass as a potential runaway. In cities, keeping African Americans in bondage was more of a problem. The anonymity of urban life made it harder for whites to know whether a black person was free, rented out, or absent from their owner without leave. To cope with this problem, many Southern hotels had basement rooms with barred windows and doors that locked from the outside, to draw the trade of owners traveling with valets, cooks, coachmen, or people to sell. Owners could lock their slaves in for the night, then retire to their own quarters secure in the knowledge that none could run away. Franklin and Armfield also provided this service for slave owners visiting Alexandria, advertising "safe keeping at 25¢ per day." Image courtesy of James Loewen.

that in the heart till this day." Some overseers then rubbed salt in the wounds. Escott found that about 70 percent of the slave narratives included stories of being whipped as slaves—and these narratives came from people who were on average only about ten years old when slavery ended.[29]

The final problem was the sense of black racial inferiority that slavery created and that most whites believed and many blacks half-believed. The mansions that planters had slaves build for them played a role in getting people to believe that whites were superior people—impressive, elegant, worthy of our respect. On the other end of the social spectrum, on some plantations, planters had slave children eat from troughs, with or without wooden paddles or spoons. As one old woman remembered seventy years later: "There was a trough out in the yard where they poured in mush and milk, and us children and the dogs would all crowd 'round it and eat together. We children had homemade wooden paddles to eat with, and we sure had to be in a hurry about it, because the dogs would get it all if we didn't." Even without dogs, children often competed with one another for basic sustenance. Meanwhile, the children of the plantation owners were learning which fork to use with which course. The contrast suggested that slavery was right: white children eat like gods, while black children eat like animals.[30]

For most slaves, these issues were insurmountable. Enslaved people could persevere, but they could not overcome. Music can help students perceive bondage as experienced by African Americans. Let them sing or read aloud together spirituals: "*Nobody* knows the trouble I've seen." "Got hard trials in my way; Heaven shall be my home."

The Influence of Slavery on US Government Policies

Slavery cannot readily survive without secure borders. This is one reason that slavery had such influence over US foreign policy. Even before the creation of the United States, colonials attacked Native American settlements because they provided havens for escaping slaves. Similar concerns fueled our conflicts with Spanish Florida, the Seminole Wars, the secession of Texas from Mexico, and the Mexican War.

Worried about encouraging slave revolts, Thomas Jefferson swung our foreign policy away from supporting Haiti against France and toward encouraging France to retake Haiti. Yet it was in our national interest to deter French colonialism, and when Haiti defeated France anyway, Napoleon was prompted to sell us the European rights to the Louisiana Territory. Similarly, Mexico's opposition to slavery helped cause the Confederacy to favor France's attempt to conquer Mexico in 1861.

The influence of plantation owners caused the US government mostly to ignore the illegal international slave trade. Supposedly the government stopped the US trade in 1808, but in fact it continued until it was finally stopped by the Civil War. It's very hard to estimate the extent of this necessarily underground activity, but probably it was the most widespread illegal activity in US history until Prohibition. Another aspect of the illegal slave trade might be called the "reverse underground railroad": kidnapping free blacks into slavery. Both parts of this trade were hard to stop, owing to jury nullification in the slave South.

Other Issues

The remainder of this chapter cannot outline all the themes and topics students need to understand about slavery. (The rest of the book helps!) All three segments of the international slave trade deserve attention. Students need to understand the extraordinary profits slavery made possible and the political clout that resulted from this wealth. How enslaved people reacted must be part of the story. Students should not conclude that slaves were only victims. While blacks did sometimes buy into the notion that whites were superior, at other times they knew better. Some escaped and hung out in the woods for weeks as a way to repay an owner for unfair treatment and to negotiate better terms for the future. Some even escaped to Mexico, the North, or Canada or stayed with Indian tribes. Most enslaved people never had a good opportunity to escape, but they helped one another in everything from giving birth to performing funeral ceremonies. They developed sly stories and jokes in which African Americans got the best of their "masters." They resisted slavery in subtle ways (like doing bad work that had to be repeated), stole extra food (but not enough to be noticed), or became indispensable (to win better treatment). Some learned to read and informed themselves of political affairs. They built a religious faith that promised a better life to come. Simply staying alive, remaining sane, building whatever community they could, and retaining the hope of eventual freedom were forms of resistance to enslavement.

As slavery continued, it did *not* get more humane; on the contrary, it grew more rigid. After 1820, several states passed laws interfering with the rights of owners to free their workers. Some made it impossible to free slaves without getting them out of state. In 1859, Arkansas passed a law requiring all "free Negroes" to leave the state within the year or be enslaved. In Maryland, Virginia, and Kentucky, owners were increasingly finding that their biggest source of profit was people. So they split up families and sent children and young adults hundreds of miles away, to slave markets in Natchez, New Orleans, or Mobile. In the Deep South, these children and young adults would clear land and grow cotton or cane sugar, destined never to see their parents or friends again. Racism as an ideology intensified in the period 1830 to 1860, as slave owners labored to justify slavery's injustice.

Nothing in the development of American slavery suggested it was on its last legs or would soon come to an end. Cotton had become so profitable that Natchez, Mississippi, claimed to have more millionaires per capita in 1860 than anywhere else in America. Egypt and India could not compete with "King Cotton," as it was called—planted, cultivated, and picked by unpaid labor.

Courses in US history cover many topics and cannot spend excessive time on just one. Middle and high school teachers can use the new requirements of the "Common Core Standards," however, to justify giving adequate attention to slavery. These mandate learning fewer topics in greater depth and encouraging students to read, critique, and use original sources such as the secession documents. College professors, too, can use slavery to teach important concepts like historiography and *verstehende*. Skills and understandings gained while studying slavery transfer to other topics, just as slavery itself remains relevant to other issues.

NOTES

1. "Teaching Slavery," chapter 8 in James W. Loewen, *Teaching What Really Happened* (New York: Teachers College Press, 2010), suggests a different way to link slavery to the present. *Skymall* went bankrupt in 2015, stopped publication, was purchased, and may be relaunched.

2. Here is one way to grasp how unlikely such a white outcome is: consider that the likelihood that the very first photo would include only whites if models were drawn at random. It would be .64. (Actually, it would be less if the photo showed more than one person, but I did not count number of people, only number of photos with only white people.) The probability that a second photo would also include only whites would be .64 times .64, or .41. The likelihood that a third photo would be all-white would be .64 times .41, or .26, and on it goes, rapidly becoming a very small number.

Since some photos *did* include nonwhites, we cannot simply do the calculation as I have shown it. Instead, I used the t-test for the difference of a sample proportion versus a population, comparing 96.6 percent (percent non-Hispanic white in *Skymall*) and 64 percent (percent non-Hispanic white in the United States). The t value for the difference of two percentages for the first catalog, which had 292 photos with models, = 31. T-tables usually provide probabilities only for values of t that range from 2 to 5, which correspond to a probability of less than .05 (t = 2) to less than .0001 (t = 5). A value of t = 31 is dramatically less likely. In fact, it corresponds to a likelihood by chance of less than .00000000000 000000000000000000000000000000000000000000000000000000000000000000000 000000000001.

3. Simply doing this multiplication requires that we assume statistical independence. Because some advertisers used the same photos in issue after issue, we should not. We can avoid this violation by counting only *new* photos in the second catalog. Doing so decreases the number of cases in that catalog, but the resulting t value is still so high that the probability that the new photos alone could be so white if drawn randomly from the US population is again far less than one in a billion.

4. Eye color *could* be a way to discriminate, as Jane Elliott showed. See the first half of William Peters, "A Class Divided" (PBS Frontline Video, 1986).

5. Teachers of history can also simultaneously teach English, so why not introduce students to "synecdoche"? My favorite way is with this example: many analysts claim that the United States cannot reduce its armed forces significantly, even though the Cold War has ended, owing to the clout of the military-industrial complex. The largest single member of that complex is General Electric, which makes everything from Gatling guns to jet aircraft engines. A commentator might dismiss any new proposal to cut our spending on war with the phrase "It won't play in Schenectady." Since Schenectady is the headquarters of General Electric, the phrase is a synecdoche for GE and indeed for the entire military-industrial complex. It is, in short, the Schenectady synecdoche!

6. Research summarized by Courtland Milloy, "Out from under the Thumb of White Bias," *Washington Post*, January 26, 2005. Interestingly, highly qualified black applicants drew no more calls than did average black applicants.

7. Owen J. Dwyer and Derek H. Alderman, *Civil Rights Memorials and the Geography of Memory* (Chicago: Center for American Places at Columbia College, 1996), 10.

8. Brad Plumer, "These Ten Charts Show the Black-White Economic Gap Hasn't Budged in 50 Years," *Washington Post*, August 28, 2013, http://www.washingtonpost.com/news/wonkblog/wp/2013/08/28/these-seven-charts-show-the-black-white-economic-gap-hasnt-budged-in-50-years/. To be sure, there were other causes of the income gap, including less stable black families and more arrests among young black men, but these variables did not change much from 2000 to 2010.

9. See Dalton Conley, "Forty Acres and a Mule Isn't Enough," *Le Monde Diplomatique* (Paris), September 2001, en.monde-diplomatique.fr/2001/09/08 richconley.

10. John Palen, *The Suburbs* (New York: McGraw-Hill, 1995), 58.

11. James W. Loewen, *Sundown Towns* (New York: New Press, 2005), 81, 119, 144-45.

12. Douglas opinion, *Jones v. Alfred H. Mayer Co*, 392 US 409, 445-47 (1968).

13. Herbert Small, *Handbook of the New Library of Congress* (Boston: Curtis & Cameron, 1897), 13-15. I changed some spelling to match modern usage.

14. Angus Johnston reports this incident in "Why I'll Add a Trigger Warning," *Inside Higher Ed*, May 29, 2014, insidehighered.com/views/2014/05/29/essay-why-professor-adding-trigger-warning-his-syllabus#ixzz36QjoCja2.

15. I don't intend this discussion as a comment on the issue of reparations. My stand on reparations depends upon what kind of reparations are sought, for what actions, and to whom they will be paid and by what governments or corporations.

16. That might even involve doing something about the *Skymall* catalog and similar instances of racism in our present world.

17. Loewen, *Teaching What Really Happened*, 189-208, describes the Nadir of race relations, justifies dating it from 1890 to 1940, and explains in what ways it was "more racist" than other eras, such as having the highest incidence of lynching.

18. Mongols and North African Muslims also enslaved Slavs; Western Europeans mostly stopped after Slavs became Christians.

19. As well, the enslaved came from nearby tribes. Even if "we" consider "them" inferior, our cultures share many similarities, from what we eat to how we live. Even if we Venetians usually subjugate the Slavs, we Iroquois usually defeat the Hurons, or we Tutsis usually dominate the Hutus, on occasion "they" win. Then we have to trade captives back and forth. So conquerors had to consider the conquered as people, even if somewhat inferior. The power imbalance that European nation-states increasingly enjoyed, however, allowed Venice and Crimea to enslave huge numbers of Slavs, the British to run roughshod

over the Irish, and the Spanish to conquer the Canary Islanders. To rationalize such conquests, the victors depicted the victims as savage, pagan, and inferior by nature. Such activities and thinking helped make Europeans ready to be racist.

20. On *Othello*, see William Harris and Judith Levey, eds., *The New Columbia Encyclopedia* (New York: Columbia University Press, 1975), 1088. On the rise of black slavery, see Hugh Thomas, *The Slave Trade* (New York: Simon & Schuster, 1997), 64. Ironically, Portuguese leaders at first resisted racism and tried to teach their subjects and other Europeans about African empires, which had been impressive but were now slipping into disarray. See Felipe Fernández-Armesto, *Millennium* (New York: Scribner, 1995), 196–97.

21. Las Casas quoted in Marcel Bataillon, "The Clerigo Casas," in Juan Friede and Benjamin Keen, *Bartolomé de las Casas in History* (DeKalb: Northern Illinois University Press, 1971), 415–16.

22. Montesquieu quoted in Felix Okoye, *The American Image of Africa: Myth and Reality* (Buffalo, NY: Black Academy Press, 1971), 37. Cf. Leon Festinger, *A Theory of Cognitive Dissonance* (Evanston, IL: Row, Peterson, 1957).

23. In *A History of the United States*, for example, Daniel Boorstin and Brooks Kelley write, "Empty land creates slavery" (Needham, MA: Pearson/Prentice-Hall, 2005), 52.

24. *The American Journey* (New York: Glencoe McGraw-Hill, 2000), 455.

25. These documents are collected in James W. Loewen and Edward Sebesta, eds., *The Confederate and Neo-Confederate Reader* (Jackson: University Press of Mississippi, 2010).

26. See Loewen, *Teaching What Really Happened*, chapter 8, for a discussion on how to teach the Nadir.

27. Kenneth Greenberg's essay treats the historiography of slave resistance without using the term.

28. Archaeologist Teresa Singleton, private communication, 1992.

29. Paul Escott, *Slavery Remembered* (Chapel Hill: University of North Carolina Press, 1979); George P. Rawick, ed., *The American Slave* (Westport, CT: Greenwood, 1972 [1941]), 18: 43–44.

30. Mia Bay, *The White Image in the Black Mind: African American Ideas about White People*, 1830–1925 (New York: Oxford University Press, 2000), 127–28.

Dealing with Things as They Are

Creating a Classroom Environment for
Teaching Slavery and Its Lingering Impact

STEVEN THURSTON OLIVER

History teachers working with middle and high school students often ask me how they should go about introducing the most challenging aspects of US history to their students. Many teachers feel ill equipped to handle such discussions and unwittingly engage in what could only be described as an act of avoidance. The visceral discomfort so many feel in being forthright and honest about the ways in which the United States has at times fallen far short of its ideals is rooted in fear.

As a sociologist of education interested in the ways in which race, class, gender, and sexual orientation affect access to educational opportunity, I find it useful to explore the sources of this fear in order to fully understand it. Schools, whether elementary, secondary, or postsecondary, function as microcosms of the larger society. Whatever issues we find in society, we will find those issues reflected in our schools and, by extension, in ourselves. The fear and uncertainty that teachers express result from the present conditions in our society, typified by a heightened sensitivity around issues of race. Many examples demonstrate that one mistake can end a career, so it is understandable that many teachers want to be careful. In some ways it is the downside of the push for political correctness. While in general terms I would argue that this has been a good thing, it has had the unintended consequence of creating a situation where people, even well-intentioned people, are not willing to engage in conversations at all. Many teachers also are immobilized by the fear that bringing up issues of race in the United States and the subtexts of slavery, Jim Crow, the civil rights era, and present-day disparities will create extreme discomfort for themselves and their students. In multicultural classrooms teachers may fear that such discussions will stir up racial and ethnic tensions and give students new reasons to dislike and distrust one another. Rather than having the desired effect of raising awareness and engendering empathy and compassion, they fear discussions of race may give students access to new language to be used as insults and taunts and provide a motivation for bullying on the basis of differences. Additionally, teachers—especially white teachers— can be fearful that in attempting to cover these issues they may make mistakes that could somehow implicate them as being racist or, at the very least, totally unprepared to facilitate difficult dialogues.

After nearly two decades of doing work around diversity and inclusion in various contexts, I fully understand and appreciate that engaging in difficult conversations about slavery, racism, and other forms of discrimination remains challenging. An essential goal for all educators is to cultivate our—and our students'—capacity simply to stay in the difficult conversation and avoid the temptation to water down, avoid, or run away altogether. Teachers should be aware that these conversations can provoke frustration and anger and be mentally and spiritually exhausting. I often find myself offering up my knowledge, insight, and personal narrative, including some of my most painful experiences, to people who, because of their privilege, may not care and who will never change. At times I have been tempted to give up the work altogether as a simple act of self-preservation. What has kept me invested in doing this work has been the people who are willing to engage in a lifelong process of engaging across differences and who are inevitably transformed by the exchange of ideas. These people in turn have the potential to change others. I also believe that it is important work and that my own continued growth is dependent upon my willingness to sit with discomfort and the messiness of life. It is perhaps this realization that has informed my teaching and made me okay with the idea of making students uncomfortable. The very discomfort that we seek to avoid and at times shield our students from can, in fact, be a powerful catalyst for growth and transformation. Dealing with things as they are and inviting students to be part of imagining a better reality is a real gift educators can offer. This essay shares important insights, perspectives, and strategies that teachers can incorporate into their own pedagogy. In short, my advice to those whose primary job is the teaching of history is to tell your students the truth, create a safe space for students to process it, and provide clear examples of how they can become part of history by making things better for everyone.[1]

Teachers who are apprehensive about introducing difficult subjects should first consider that students are already contemplating issues connected to race and trying to make sense of them more than we realize. Schools do not exist in a vacuum. They are part of the larger society in which our students immerse themselves every day. Students of every age are already getting myriad messages about race and inequality in our society. These messages are coming to them through their families, social media, popular culture, and the school curriculum. Furthermore, middle school, high school, and even college students are at critical stages of development where they are coming to understand the stratification within our society. These students begin to wonder about where they fit in the pecking order and the specific impact these issues may have on their life. They are already thinking about these issues whether we realize it or not and whether or not they are able to articulate their thoughts. For these reasons, there is no need to fear that we are "introducing" students to these issues. Our students have already heard the language, the insults, the slurs, and various references. What we find, however, is that most students do not understand where these things came from and why they persist. Furthermore, they may not understand why certain words are so loaded and how students like them could be part of efforts to change the culture around them. I argue that school should be a place where students receive the information that helps them understand and make sense of all the messages they are receiving.

As educators we must find ways to ground them in history if our goal is to raise awareness and instill a willingness to affect change. We don't do our students any favors by shielding them from the truth. In fact, we do them a huge disservice when we sugarcoat the facts of history. Still, I don't want to make light of the fact that dealing with things as they are can be frightening for teachers who are unsure of what the immediate outcomes of such conversations may be. I strongly suggest that teachers form learning communities composed of colleagues who are grappling with similar challenges; this would allow colleagues to share various strategies for presenting difficult subjects such as the history and legacy of slavery in the United States. Team teaching is another useful strategy. It is often helpful to have a second pair of eyes to make sense of what is happening and to monitor any dynamics that may need to be interrupted and addressed. I also encourage teachers to utilize the different modalities discussed in this volume to present these issues outside the standard textbook. I've found that the use of slave narratives, discussed in Cynthia Lyerly's essay in this volume, can be powerful for students and really brings history alive for them. For example, one such collection, *Born in Slavery: Slave Narratives from the Federal Writers' Project, 1936–1938*, contains more than 2,300 first-person accounts of slavery and photographs of former slaves. I have found that using personal stories brings the history of slavery out of the abstract and encourages the development of empathy as students gain a new understanding of the human cost of slavery. Teachers should also include the voices of abolitionists so that students have a firm understanding that from the outset there have always been socially conscious white and black people who were against the institution of slavery and who put their own lives at risk to end what they saw as an affront to humanity.

When teaching slavery, teachers likely will become aware that many of our students have no concept or frame of reference to understand that the institution of slavery is inextricably tied to the genesis of the nation and that it has had an impact long after its legal demise in 1865. To introduce students to these issues, I use the writing and oratory of James Baldwin. Most students have never heard of Baldwin but instantly find him curious and engaging, with a moral authority that comes only from speaking from what one has seen and experienced. The famous debate between James Baldwin and William F. Buckley filmed at Cambridge University in 1965 is readily available on YouTube and Vimeo. I have found that it is a powerful catalyst for meaningful dialogue with students about the experiences of African Americans and other subjugated peoples within the US context. Additionally, Baldwin's novels and essays, among them *Go Tell It on the Mountain* (1953) and *Notes of a Native Son* (1955), are powerful works that allow students to connect the facts of history to lived experiences of human beings.

Teachers also need to create a safe space for students to confront controversial or hurtful topics. If we don't do the work of creating safe spaces for student to process the information and work through a full range of emotions, they will simply become defensive and shut down. If we are willing to do the "shattering," then we must be willing to go the distance with students, hurting with them, picking up the pieces, and building something new together. I am reminded of a story told by one of my history professors in graduate school who earlier in his career failed to make these connections and lost his job as a high school teacher. While teaching a class of mostly African American students, he included in one lecture the point that many of our cultural heroes, including John F. Kennedy, Abraham Lincoln, and John Lennon, were flawed human beings. In discussing Martin Luther King Jr., he mentioned the wiretapping done by the FBI that allegedly captured the civil rights leader engaging in illicit sexual activities. Without providing space for students to make sense of the shocking revelation, the students went home distraught and upset. Students complained to their parents, and he was fired the next day. My professor realized in the years that followed that he hadn't thought through the jarring impact that would follow from disrupting his students' view of who Martin Luther King was. He hadn't conceived of how he would create space for students to make sense of this information and come to their own conclusions as to whether they believed it to be true. Indeed, he hadn't really examined his motivation for telling his students in the first place.

Even though they may not voice it, students are sitting with the questions "Why are you telling me this? What is your intention? What do you want me to do with this information now that I have it?" When we've done the work of building trust and creating community within our classrooms, the answers to those questions become clear and students develop their capacity to stay in the conversation. One technique to engender trust among students and to create safe spaces for them to engage is called "teacher as text." Teacher as text involves offering up your own personal narratives for the purpose of modeling for students the level of dialogue you hope to engage in. Your being transparent will allow students to feel they can be transparent as well. For example, when presenting content on the lasting impact of slavery, I share my own attempts to make sense of this history throughout the years. I talk about being the only African American student in my fourth-grade class and all the embarrassment, anger, and other emotions I felt when the subject of slavery was first introduced. I share stories of how my teachers, some skillfully and others less so, attempted to deal with these issues. I have found that sharing these stories makes it easier for students to make sense of what they might be feeling. Often they are very eager to share their own stories and perspectives. When students let their guard down and the dialogue becomes rich and dynamic, it allows us to see where there might still be gaps in their knowledge that need to be addressed. I recall one lesson where I wanted students to understand how recent slavery was when viewed through a generational lens. I listed my birth year (1968), followed by my father's (1931), followed by my grandfather's (1905), followed by my great-grandfather's, sometime in the 1870s. When I asked the students to tell me when slavery ended in the United States, I was met with blank faces. I was shocked to discover that my students, who were mostly white and female, had no idea when slavery had happened and ventured guesses ranging from the 1700s to the 1930s. I'm not certain that the responses would have been much different had my class been mostly students of color. This experience, along with many similar ones, has grounded my belief that we must give students the historical context that has shaped their current reality. Without that core understanding, so many other things related to the evolution of education in the United States will not make sense to them.

Part of creating a safe classroom includes managing feelings of guilt or shame about the past. White students, in particular, struggle under this burden when learning about aspects of history for the first time. One student in my urban education class told me that he had taken a multicultural education class with another professor and that it was a horrible experience. When I asked him why, he replied, "Instead of Multicultural Education the course should have been called White People Are Bad." This student expressed what I believe many white students feel when confronted with issues of race and the notion of privilege. While I understand where students are coming from, to stay in a place of guilt over dynamics you had no hand in creating is a waste of time and precious energy. As a person of color, at times I have little patience for guilt, misplaced or otherwise, yet I understand it is a real thing, and therefore I approach it with compassion.

I find that laying out a simple premise—namely, we didn't do this— in clear terms helps students get past any sense of personal guilt they may experience. We were born into this mess, and various forms of structural oppression are built on foundations that have been in place for centuries. This point—"we didn't create these systems of oppression in which we find ourselves"—is quickly followed by another statement: "We all have a responsibility for considering how we might be part of upholding these systems and we must commit ourselves to the work of undoing these systems." As a person of color, I don't present these ideas as something that white people need to do exclusively. I point out that I have my own assumptions, biases, blind spots, and areas of privilege that I need to constantly interrogate, and I invite them to join me in a lifelong journey of striving to become a reflective, contemplative person. I find that not prioritizing whiteness in this way makes for a more dynamic dialogue by stressing that we are all in this together and that we are all working together to find solutions. It's not a matter of pointing out to people all the ways that they may be racist but rather acknowledging as a starting point that we will all find racism within ourselves. This is part of being human and existing in a society that unfortunately is still struggling with these issues. To remove these elements from our hearts and minds as well as our pedagogy requires a deep scrubbing. The scrubbing process is composed of being reflective, interrogating our assumptions, and doing whatever it takes to fill in gaps in our knowledge when we find ourselves ignorant—a place we will all find ourselves at one time or another.

I learned from experience not to be surprised or intimidated by rage-filled outbursts from students who may be having their core understandings challenged and dismantled for the first time. I am reminded of an experience I had several years ago while working as a project director at New York University's Metro Center for Urban Education. I was part of a team that was sent to do a diversity workshop in a school district in upstate New York that was having issues with disproportionality. One of the teachers, a middle-aged white woman, explained that she wanted to learn more about African Americans and asked me how she could accomplish this. I began to share with her the titles of several books that would enhance her understanding of her African American students and the motivations behind some of the behaviors she had witnessed in the course of her own teaching.[2] The teacher at once became angry, saying, "You mean if I want to learn about Black culture I have to read a goddamn book?" I responded swiftly, "Yes, you must read and when you are done reading, read some more! Ask people about their experiences. Fill in the gaps in your knowledge!"

Creating a safe place, therefore, also requires knowing that there will always be more to understand and more to learn. We never arrive, and all of us will make mistakes. It is important that, while being vigilant, we also be gentle with ourselves and others. The "self-work" that I am describing is important as a starting point to our discussion because we can't possibly ask our students to engage around difficult aspects of US history if we have not engaged deeply with those topics ourselves. Our inexperience, discomfort, and fear will be communicated to our students in every nuance of our interactions with them, and our discourse will fall flat because of its lack of integrity.

Telling the truth and creating a safe place to discuss history as it happened are critical. Students should have an appreciation of what came before them, where they are now, and, most important, how they can be an integral part of making society more fair and just for everyone. Other essays in this book suggest resources and strategies to make students aware of the tragedy that was slavery and all the ways in which people are still discriminated against. We also must show students where there are opportunities for them to have a positive impact on society and to help it move forward. Inviting and encouraging students to be part of making society better is a critical component that many educators miss when talking about the past. We must consider the emotional and psychological impact our content can have for our students and ask this question: "Now that they have the information, what are they going to do with it?" We must allow our students to react, examine multiple perspectives, and consider how the future that they will be part of creating will be different. In my work teaching aspiring educators, I take students through all the difficult chapters of American history from slavery and Jim Crow to *Brown v. Board of Education*, the desegregation of the Boston public schools, and the current realities of the achievement gap that affects students of color. I do this so that they will understand why multicultural education is important and how they in their chosen professions will be part of making things better. If I didn't make the connections among past, present, and future, it would be virtually impossible for students to engage in difficult dialogues, and these dialogues might prove to be divisive. By dealing head on with things as they were, as they are, and how we hope they will be, we make the classroom a place where, despite our differences, we understand that we are all in this together, with the collective potential to truly make a difference.

We need our students to understand the worst aspects of our history so that we can ensure as a society that these things never happen again.

We need students to know that history has been profoundly influenced by the efforts of courageous men and women of all races in all places and times. We need students to be able to envision how they can be part of continuing efforts to undo the lasting impacts of slavery and various forms of oppression.

NOTES

1. My thinking around these issues is informed by the work of multicultural educators such as Sonia Nieto and Gloria Ladson-Billings. See S. Nieto and P. Bode, *Affirming Diversity: The Sociopolitical Context of Multicultural Education* (Boston: Pearson Education, publishing as Allyn & Bacon, 2012), and G. J. Ladson-Billings, *Crossing over to Canaan: The Journey of New Teachers in Diverse Classrooms* (San Francisco: Jossey-Bass, 2001). Both write extensively about the dangers of sanitizing history and thereby denying students the opportunity to engage with history as a complex, multidimensional, and living thing to which they can and should find ways to contribute. Additionally, I'm indebted to Patricia Gurin and Ratnesh Nagda, who have written extensively about the power and value of intergroup dialogue. See P. Gurin, B. Nagda, and X. Zuniga, *Dialogue across Difference: Policy, Theory and Research on Intergroup Dialogue* (New York: Russell Sage Press, 2013). Finally, contemporary Buddhist writers have infused my approach with core understanding of contemplative approaches to education, compassion, and the interconnectedness of all human beings. See T. N. Hahn, *The Miracle of Mindfulness* (Boston: Beacon Press, 1976), and T. Hart, "Opening the Contemplative Mind in the Classroom," *Journal of Transformative Education* (2004).

2. R. Majors and M. Billson, *Cool Pose: The Dilemmas of Black Manhood in America* (New York: Simon & Schuster, 1992), and P. A. Noguera, *The Trouble with Black Boys and Other Reflections on Race, Equity and the Future of Public Education* (San Francisco: Jossey-Bass, 2008).

PART TWO

Teaching
Specific Content

Teaching the Origins
of Slavery in the Americas

ERIC KIMBALL

The development of the system of race-based slavery in the Americas is one of the most difficult topics to discuss with students. Why did the maritime Atlantic European powers—Portugal, Spain, the Netherlands, France, and Great Britain—ultimately choose to utilize large numbers of enslaved Africans in their American colonies? The word "choice" matters. A major point to emphasize with students is that these European powers made the *choice* to use slaves. A second point for furthering students' understanding is that there was nothing "inevitable" about the use of slave labor, in particular African slave labor, as the primary plantation workforce. A third point is that the pioneering colonizers, the Spanish and the Portuguese, moved from a system in the Americas based on Indian slaves to one based on African slaves. (Again, choices were made.) A fourth point is to contrast this with the English experience. England moved from a system based on a mix of family and indentured labor, alongside some limited Indian slave labor, to one based on African slave labor in the Caribbean, the Chesapeake, and the southern colonies. (Once more: choices were made.) If all of these facts are not emphasized to students, the eventual decision to use African slaves in each case appears "normal" or "natural" or "inevitable" when it was none of those things. This is perhaps the most important issue to emphasize: using slaves was a decision made by conscious individuals.

Scholars disagree about both the impact and the timing of racial ideologies with regard to the eventual decision to rely primarily on African slave labor. There is, however, broad agreement that such

43

ideologies were a factor. Therefore, instead of saying "racism caused slavery" or "slavery caused racism," we can usefully employ Ira Berlin's paradigm to see the mutually reinforcing power of both factors. Thus, to paraphrase Berlin, "racism made slavery and slavery made racism."[1]

Students struggle to understand and analyze racialized ideas, racial ideologies, and racism. I always stress that racial ideology is illogical—by definition—because there is no such thing as race as a biological reality. Race is a historical and sociological construction that has changed over time. Moreover, our own contemporary use of race further complicates our understanding. To illustrate all of this and to start discussions with students, teachers can ask students to look up the legal term "white" as used by the US Census Bureau. Students will find the following definition: "A person having origins in any of the original peoples of Europe, the Middle East, or North Africa."[2] Plenty of useful class discussions (Africans are white?! What constitutes an "original people"?) can revolve around just this legal definition!

Another useful teaching exercise concerning powerful words involves some of the most basic reference terms we use: "African," "European," and "Indian." They are all deeply problematic because they sustain "the myth of continents."[3] This means these words imply a fixed, stable identity agreed to by all those individuals who lived in a particular place we have defined as continents.[4] Teachers can use maps and ask students: where does Europe begin and Asia end? What about the Americas? Were the Xhosa the same as the Akan? Were the English the same as the French? Were the Pequot the same as the Shawnee? Of course not, but through our usage we make them so, and by analyzing the bigger terms (African, European, and Indian) we can understand how they reflect political realities of power as much as historical constructions.

Another important "word" discussion to have is about "slavery." Teachers might begin by having students close their eyes and think of a "slave" and then write down what they "see." Most likely they will imagine a male African American from the early part of the nineteenth century in the southern United States: a cotton-plantation field worker. However, teachers can then contrast this by deconstructing the root word "slave" in English, which is "slav." This will help to emphasize that a long-standing trade in slaves in the pre-1492 world, and in particular in the Mediterranean region, originated with the purchase of people from the Slavic regions of Europe, not people from Africa. This slav/slave trade was conducted by Venetians and Genoese operating across the Baltic Sea region, with Constantinople (as the Christian conquerors called it, or Istanbul as it is known today) as the critical transport site.[5] This is important, as the word "slave" was found across many European languages: "esclave," "esclavo," "skalve," "sclavus," "slav." In no case did it directly indicate "African" or someone from Africa.[6]

To arrive at this historical decision-making series of moments, one can and should emphasize context. Taken either separately or together, however, the topics of race and slavery are complex, and what follows is only a cursory overview of one possible teaching emphasis that stresses the long context of slavery, beginning in the ancient Mediterranean world and on through the medieval era and then into the Atlantic world of the fifteenth century, followed by a comparative case study of English labor decisions in Virginia and Massachusetts.

Putting Atlantic Slavery in a Wider Context

Historically found everywhere across the globe, slavery is an institution mentioned among the oldest available records from ancient Sumeria.[7] Slavery was practiced in ancient China. Ancient Greece and Rome were slave societies, and slavery was legal and widespread among some African and Native American societies long before their contact with Europeans. In addition, both the Bible and the Qur'an sanction slavery. Highlighting passages in these religious texts will help students understand the long trajectory of slavery throughout Africa and Eurasia and realize that all three central monotheistic religions— Judaism, Christianity, and Islam—actively supported slavery through most of their historical past.[8]

Dealing with the ancient origins of slavery raises the issue of why certain people were deemed enslavable. Some scholars believe that in the case of classical antiquity, race and racism do factor into the explanation, while others do not and instead discuss "proto-racism"— though this distinction with the prefix "proto" (as opposed to just calling it "racism") is highly debatable.[9] Despite this controversy, students should know that Aristotle stated in *Politics* that "slavery is a natural institution and therefore 'good and just.'" The historian Robert Finley remarked that slavery in ancient Greece and Rome still involved racialized thinking, even though such thinking involved "the absence of skin-color stigma." As Finley noted, for "most Greeks and Romans slaves as a class were inferior beings, inferior in their psychology, *by their nature.*" Thus, by this way of thinking, whole groups, "Jews, Syrians, Lydians, Medes, indeed all Asiatics, are 'born to slavery.'"[10] Greeks and Romans often made slaves of their war captives, along with buying slaves through regular commercial activities.

For centuries slaves operated the galley ships of the Mediterranean. These maritime slaves had their counterparts in nearby islands, as the first sugar plantations were established in the Christian islands of Crete and Cyprus and owners there imported a range of slaves in the fifteenth century: "Greeks, Bulgarians, Turkish prisoners of war, and Tartars."[11] Technically, Christians were not supposed to enslave other Christians, but on Cyprus and Crete plantation owners sought to maximize production and profit, so the particular religion and/or origin of the slaves— Christians, Muslims, Slavs, Africans, and so on—was irrelevant. One point to stress to students, however, is that *neither the powering of galley ships nor the cultivation of sugar required slavery.* There was nothing "natural" or "necessary" about turning humans into commodities for maximizing profits.

The big shift away from the Slavic slaving ports and toward West Africa began after 1453, when the powerful Muslim Turks closed off the Black Sea port region, the traditional access point for Europeans acquiring "slavs"/slaves. This occurred just as the Portuguese were exploring the coast of West Africa. Portugal's goals included establishing direct trading routes to acquire gold, possibly making anti-Muslim alliances with new African allies, and spreading Christianity. Initially they tried to raid for slaves, but they lacked the maritime knowledge and military technology to overcome powerful West African nations. Thus, within a few decades after the 1440s the Portuguese moved from raiding to trading. Again, here we can stress that decisions were made: trading rather than enslaving, peace over war. This did not mean that racial ideas were not prominent; the Portuguese, in fact, still held onto the medieval concepts of race.

Medieval Ideas about Race

Just as our own confused racial ideas continue—as in the earlier example of the US Census definition of "white"—so too the medieval era contained confusing, contradictory, and complicated ideas about race. During the medieval era language and customs were viewed as essential components of a culture.[12] This culture, in turn, created ideas about ethnicity, and ethnicity was at this time another term/concept for race. Furthermore, medieval concepts of race and nation were tightly linked and blurred. Thus, "the medieval situation was one where 'race' almost always meant the same thing as 'ethnic group,'" and "communities were differentiated by language and customs, the latter including law and religion."[13] Finally, it is very important to remember that all of this "race thinking" occurred *prior* to both the new trading relations established by the Portuguese with sub-Saharan African nations in the mid-fifteenth century and the "discovery" or "invasion" of the Americas in 1492.

Invaders from Europe who colonized the Americas brought a whole range of concepts that supported discriminatory and racialized thinking: "Geographical, climatic, and ethnographic ideas that formed the basis of European visions of the world beyond their frontiers. Among these ideas were the attitudes of superiority that accompanied distinctions between 'Christians' and 'infidels' (Jews and Muslims) or between civilized English and Germans, and 'barbarians' on the periphery such as the Irish, Welsh, and Baltic peoples."[14] In addition, a broad range of other influences were present in the medieval Mediterranean world of the future colonizing powers, including the idea of wildness, which would be applied by the English to the Irish and Native Americans and "could represent either the goodness of natural man or the dangers of animal nature, and both images were reinforced by European experiences in the Middle Ages."[15] In sum, European invaders did not arrive in the Americas (or sub-Saharan West Africa) without some ideas that served as precedents for what we would later call racism.

Thus, the medieval era was one of profound racialized thinking among the maritime Atlantic European powers. The Portuguese held such ideas as they pushed southward along the West African coastline in the mid-fifteenth century. Simultaneously, as the Christian forces of Ferdinand and Isabella retook territory from Muslims and unified the land into Spain, they also sought to racially purify their new state through the forcible conversion and then, later, the expulsion of all Jews and Muslims.[16] This was the context of the Columbian voyage of 1492.

Another Ancient Precedent: Anti-Semitism

Prejudice, persecution, and hostility toward Jews were widespread throughout Europe in the pre-Columbian era. Students should be made aware of how pervasive this sentiment was, including in England. Since 1290 Jews had been officially banned from living there. This policy was not officially overturned until 1655–57. Predating even the order in 1290, "anti-Jewish beliefs in their classical religious form—the Jew as Christ-killer, as the servant of Satan, as the eternally damned outcast—were as widely diffused in England as they were on the Continent."[17] Thus, the newer racialized ideas of the medieval era and the expanding universe into which American Indians and sub-Saharan Africans would be added joined concepts in which Jews were already racialized. This is part of the longer history of racial ideas and ideologies that must be understood to analyze the colonizers' behavior in the Americas following 1492.

Early Precedents: Atlantic Islands

The Atlantic islands—the Azores, Madeira, and the Canary Islands—were "rediscovered" and claimed by both the Portuguese and the Spanish. Madeira was colonized in 1425, the Azores in 1440. Wheat, wine, and sugar became staple exports of both locations. Eventually the two empires divided the islands; the Portuguese kept the Azores and Madeira, and Spain took the Canaries. While the Azores and Madeira were uninhabited, the Canary Islands were populated by a people Europeans called the Gaunches. King Duarte I of Portugal asked for and received the pope's blessing in conquering and colonizing the island. Duarte said, in 1436, that "the nearly wild men who inhabit the forests are not united by a common religion, nor are they bound by the chains of law, they are lacking in social discourse, living in the country like animals." He got his papal support for war and for the enslavement of the Guanches.

Prince Henrique (called "Prince Henry the Navigator" by later English propagandizers) launched two expeditions to conquer the islanders.[18] The Guanches had no defenses against European diseases. Those who survived a microbial invasion of measles, mumps, chicken pox, small pox, bubonic plague, and tuberculosis stubbornly resisted the military campaigns launched against them. The Portuguese were not able to conquer the Guanches. Spain also claimed the islands and, with its army of 1,100 men, armed with steel armor, horses, and cannon, achieved the final surrender of the Guanches in 1493 and enslaved the survivors. By 1497, Portugal yielded its claim to Spain.

What factors help to explain Portuguese and Spanish actions to invade, decimate, conquer, and enslave? One justification both powers invoked came from the concept of a holy war or a just war. This was defined as a war against the infidel or pagan in the name of Christ, authorized by the pope or another high church official. An enemy had put itself outside the protection of Christianity by committing sacrileges or refusing to accept the teachings of Christ. A head of state could declare a "just war" using the same rationale. For example, in 1452, Pope Nicholas II gave the Portuguese permission to attack—and enslave—Muslims in North Africa under this doctrine. In another case, in 1493, the pope divided the "pagan" world of the Americas to be conquered between Spain and Portugal. Religion became a demarcation factor that allowed for the "enslavability" of those who rejected or resisted Christianity.

Later, during the American invasion, both the Spanish and the Portuguese used the "just war" principle as a legal justification to wage war and enslave Native Americans. The Portuguese also used the "just war" concept as a justification for the continued use of Indian slaves in Brazil. Furthermore, both Iberian powers used the idea that they were bringing Christianity and civilization to the inferior peoples of the Americas. All of the varied nations of the Americas would become subsumed into one category for the enslavers—"Indians"—and instantly another word was used synonymously to refer to them: "savages." It was a word the Spanish and Portuguese had used to describe both Africans and slaves back in Europe. It is important to stress to students, however, that for the Spanish and Portuguese the first choice for slaves in the Americas were Indians—not Africans.

Another issue to clarify is that during the many wars among the Christian powers (e.g., those between Spain and England or between England and France), there would be killing but not enslavement. This fact alone is worth emphasizing to students, who often wonder why the English did not enslave the French or vice versa, especially if labor demands alone were the primary factor in explaining the expansion of slavery in the Americas. Thus, while an economic explanation is part of the answer, ideas about race—who is "enslavable" and who is not—are clearly another important explanation. Moreover, the complicated relationship between class and race brings us to the case of English colonization. Here we can explore how elite colonizers' first choice for labor in any of their colonies was not slaves but servants.

The English First Choice: Indentured Servants

English elites first tried to use indentured servants in their colonies, whether in Virginia (1607), Barbados (1627), or Massachusetts (1630).[19] This replicated a familiar labor system in England whereby a large, mobile group of young men provided the bulk of the agricultural labor force.[20] In this way the English initially tried to reproduce a system they already knew, but they quickly ran into challenges. As a result, in two of the three examples (Virginia and Barbados), those with the means and money to do so switched from indentured servants to enslaved Africans as the primary labor force.

Labor in England

In England, "the majority of all hired labor in pre-industrial England was provided by 'servants in husbandry'—youths of both sexes, normally between the ages of 13 and 25, who lived and worked in the households of their masters, typically on annual contracts."[21] Transportation costs to the American colonies were high, and most emigrants could not afford the passage, so they signed contracts (indentures) to pay for the trip. Such transactions—contractual labor—represented continuity on the part of the English and a replication of their customary and preferred labor system.

Following the successful cultivation of tobacco in Virginia and the subsequent "boom" in production, more servants—and very few slaves—were imported. Yet some local planter elites contemplated Indian slave labor to supplement the indentured servants. For these elite Virginians, local Indians were enslaved as a matter of official policy—as when they tried to resist English encroachment: "during the Anglo-Powhatan war of 1622–1632, official directives mandated Indian slavery."[22] Indians captured but not killed were either enslaved locally or shipped abroad into slavery in the West Indies. Furthermore, unlike the "negotiated status" of some Africans at this time in Virginia, there was no uncertainty about the buying, selling, and keeping of Indian slaves.[23] Still, the combination of Indian resistance and the declining Native population meant that local Indians would be an insufficient source for English planters with the money and desire to purchase them.

For nearly seventy years following the establishment of Jamestown in 1607, despite the attempts to add enslaved Indians and a few enslaved

Africans (discussed later), indentured servants constituted the vast majority of the labor force. One might usefully explore with students contemporaries' remarks about the poor treatment of servants in the English colonies during these years.[24] At the core of English settlers' treatment of their servants were class-based views that underpinned elite concepts of servants and poor people in general. For example, William Bullock described Virginia's servants in 1649 as "idle, lazie, simple people" who would "rather beg than work." Servants often were also called criminals; they were described as "being either unfit for labor" or "had so mis-behaved themselves by Whoreing, Thieving, or other Debauchery, that none would set them to work." Many servants were poor, others had lost one or both parents, and both civil and religious authorities in England viewed shipping these individuals off to the colonies as a positive act. As James Horn notes, "Governments of the day were quite content to support measures that rid the country of its poor."[25]

Because of these views about the character of servants, in the early years, in places like Virginia, settlers viewed servants as commodities, to be bought, sold, branded, traded, and used as the masters desired or directed. There were important differences between indentured servitude and enslavement, however. Under the law, English servants had rights as free-born English subjects, whereas slaves had no rights. Servants were bound for a limited time; slaves were bound until death or manumission. Servants did not automatically transfer their servitude status to their children, but slaves did. And, finally, though some indentured servants were coerced and tricked, ultimately an indenture was a contract, fixed in terms that provided for an end date of laboring service. The typical contract was four or five years, though many "masters"—which was the legal term—often conspired to extend them by any means possible. At the end of the contract, indentured servants had a right to their "freedom dues," which frequently included some combination of land, tools, and clothes. By contrast, slaves did not sign contracts, because, again, slaves did not possess rights. Certainly masters considered both servants and slaves objects or commodities and listed them on property inventories as such. Also, given the conditions under which many individuals became indentured servants, it is important to emphasize that this form of contract labor was deeply exploitative and that many servants were tricked into service and treated poorly and that they barely survived under conditions that some servants themselves compared to those of slaves. Ultimately, teachers should stress that there were three critical differences between the two: the voluntary nature of indentured servitude, the lack of status transfer between generations, and the possession of rights under indenture. These factors must be compared to and contrasted against the involuntary nature of enslavement, the inherited condition of slavery, and the total lack of rights of the enslaved.

Masters in Virginia transitioned from importing indentured servants to purchasing enslaved Africans after Bacon's Rebellion in 1675–76.[26] The aspiring planter Nathaniel Bacon, trying to overthrow the colonial governor and needing supporters, offered freedom to enslaved Africans and indentured servants who would support him. Following his defeat, planters viewed enslaved Africans as both safer and more profitable than servants; after all, slaves never received "freedom dues" and had no legal rights; in addition, their children became the "property" of their masters. In addition, an increasing percentage of Virginia's colonial population was living longer, so for planters the initial extra cost of enslaved Africans became more financially attractive. Thus, colonial elites in Virginia consciously chose to make a calculated transition toward large-scale slavery.

By 1670, Virginians had imported approximately 880 Africans and 53,000 indentured servants. Given white Virginians' preference for indentured servants, the question then becomes how and why there were any enslaved Africans at all in Virginia before Bacon's Rebellion. Several primary sources, including a colonial census of 1619, colonial laws, slave voyage arrivals, and a letter by John Rolfe (of Pocahontas fame) all are useful in exploring the vexed story of Africans in early Virginia. The question of when the first Africans arrived, their subsequent status, and the degree to which the English did or did not possess some racial ideas about these particular Africans or Africans in general have become some of the most debated, investigated, and controversial topics in early American history. The year 1619 has largely remained the standard chronological start date for investigations, since that is the year in which John Rolfe wrote, in a letter, what is (now) considered an infamous sentence stating that "About the latter end of August, a Dutch Man of Warr . . . brought not any thing but 20. and odd Negroes." Ask your students to read the entire paragraph or the entire letter, and one thing will become immediately obvious: Rolfe's observation and discussion of the "Negroes" appears rather ordinary and no further commentary regarding them is provided at all. Such a discussion of Rolfe's letter with students will help illuminate just how "ordinary" the process of seeing enslaved Africans was as early as 1619 for English elites like Rolfe.[27]

But why did Rolfe view this as rather unremarkable? There were no large-scale plantations in England filled with vast numbers of enslaved Africans. Scholars seeking explanations for this and trying to explain the relative ease with which elite colonists in Virginia seamlessly switched from indentured servants to enslaved Africans have created what has been called "the Origins Debate."[28] Ira Berlin observed that "the literature on the status of the first black people to arrive in the Chesapeake is extensive, formidable, and inconclusive, in large measure because the incomplete evidence and the *ambiguous language* of 'slavery' and 'servitude' has become entangled in an all-encompassing discussion of the origins of racism in British North America." Whatever "ambiguity" existed over the status of African Americans in Virginia in 1619, it was over by 1705, when an elaborate and definitive slave code was passed.[29] Teachers can go over these laws with students and examine the slow but steady clarification of practices related to slavery in Virginia.[30]

Yet there are other approaches to this question of English racism and slavery. One approach is to consider that in 1641, more than a half-century before Virginia, Massachusetts clearly legalized slavery.[31] Indeed, unlike the slow, piecemeal process of legalized slavery in seventeenth-century Virginia that has been the source of much historical investigation, the quick, unequivocal process in Massachusetts has barely registered in the vast literature on race and slavery. Why? Perhaps because of what happened later in Virginia but also because slavery and racism in the context of the area that later became the United States are continuously framed as "southern" phenomena. And this framing only continues to perpetuate what Joanne Pope Melish calls "the myth of New England," and, as Richard Slotkin reminded us, "a people unaware of its myths is likely to continue living by them."[32] So, let us briefly examine and complicate the general narrative power of that southern framework by altering the geographic location of analysis with a specific learning exercise.

Teachers can have students examine the specific passages in the Body of Liberties that legalized slavery in Massachusetts.[33] As a "popular bill of rights," the document was "rooted in English law and precedents" and, of course, in the Bible.[34] The issue of slavery was addressed in article ninety-one: "There shall never be any bond slaverie, villinage or Captivitie amongst us unles it be lawfull Captives taken in just warres, and such strangers as willingly selle themselves or are sold to us."[35] The precision of the wording reveals a familiarity with the process of enslavement by New Englanders of Native Americans and the purchasing of slaves in Africa. The "just war" provision was clearly aimed at legalizing the enslaved Pequot Indians (and other future Indian slaves) who had been acquired in the Pequot War of 1637. The section on "strangers . . . sold to us" encompassed Africans, who, once defined as outsiders, that is, "strangers" to the community, could be purchased as slaves.

Enslaved Africans first arrived in Massachusetts via the *Desire*. Built in 1636 in the newly established port town of Salem, Massachusetts, the 120-ton vessel left in July 1637 with a human cargo for sale.[36] Fifteen young Pequot Indian boys and two women, who had survived the New Englanders' genocidal war against their nation, found themselves on board and headed to sea. Originally bound for Bermuda, Captain William Peirce had sailed to Providence Island in the West Indies, where another group of Puritans had settled in 1630. Seven months later, Massachusetts governor John Winthrop tersely noted in his journal that Captain Peirce had returned and "brought some cotton, and tobacco, and negroes."[37] Teachers might consider comparing Winthrop's private journal entry to Rolfe's letter to see how they both treat the arrival of "negroes" and display total ease at the commodification of human beings from Africa.

Another important consideration is that Indians had been exchanged for Africans, and thus the *Desire* was also a slave ship. As such, it provides a framework for understanding New England's history very different from that asserted by the ship typically associated with the region: the *Mayflower*. Teachers can emphasize the *Desire* contract over the "Mayflower Compact" as exemplifying New England's colonial history.

Obviously, the commodification process began long before Winthrop's brief notation regarding "some cotton, and tobacco, and negroes." He, like John Rolfe, had no doubt that Africans and African Americans were commodities. Yet, men like Winthrop reserved additional space in this mental category for another group of people: as the *Desire*'s voyage makes clear, Indians were also commodified. How did this process of commodification originate and progress such that the enslavement and exchange of two different groups of people was understood and recorded not as something extraordinary but as something rather ordinary? This essay has tried to provide some answers and teachable suggestions by stressing the long historical trajectory of racial ideas, which reach back to the ancient world, through the Mediterranean, and ultimately to the Atlantic, alongside an emphasis upon the conscious choices of those who created these systems of slavery in the Americas.

NOTES

1. Ira Berlin, *Many Thousands Gone: The First Two Centuries of Slavery in North America* (Cambridge, MA: Belknap Press of Harvard University Press, 1998). The paraphrased quotation is drawn from Berlin's prologue and epilogue.

2. US Census, http://quickfacts.census.gov/qfd/meta/long_RHI525211 .htm. This is the legal definition used by the US government and was used in the 2010 census.

3. Martin W. Lewis and Kären Wigen, *The Myth of Continents: A Critique of Metageography* (Berkeley: University of California Press, 1999).

4. Ibid.

5. Philip D. Curtin, *The Rise and Fall of the Plantation Complex: Essays in Atlantic History* (Cambridge: Cambridge University Press, 1990), provides an excellent discussion, as does Orlando Patterson, *Slavery and Social Death: A Comparative Study* (Cambridge, MA: Harvard University Press, 1982), 150–57.

6. David Brion Davis, *Inhuman Bondage: The Rise and Fall of Slavery in the New World* (New York: Oxford University Press, 2006), 49.

7. Ibid., 32.

8. For the Bible, one typical passage from Leviticus 25:44 is fairly representative: "Both thy bondmen and thy bondmaids which thou shalt have shall be of the heathen, which are round about you; of them shall ye buy bondmen and bondmaids." See also Exodus 21:1–6 for others. Jewish slavery is discussed in Catherine Hezser, *Jewish Slavery in Antiquity* (New York: Oxford University Press, 2006), and she concludes (on page 1): "for ancient Jews just as for Greeks and Romans slavery was an everyday experience whose existence was taken for granted." For Islam, "the Qur'an assumes the existence of slavery. It regulates the practice of the institution and thus implicitly accepts it." See Bernard Lewis, *Race and Slavery in the Middle East: An Historical Enquiry* (New York: Oxford University Press, 1990), 5. Under the "rules" of jihad (holy war), unbelievers could be—and often were—enslaved. Lewis provides some textual examples from the Qur'an on page 6. On a related point, the so-called biblical Curse of Ham was a widely invoked justification that involved all three faiths

over time and has its own complicated history: David M. Goldenberg, *Curse of Ham: Race and Slavery in Early Judaism, Christianity and Islam* (Princeton, NJ: Princeton University Press, 2005).

9. Benjamin Isaac, *The Invention of Racism in Classical Antiquity* (Princeton, NJ: Princeton University Press, 2004), argues in favor; Miriam Eliav-Feldon, Benjamin Isaac, and Joseph Ziegler, eds., *The Origins of Racism in the West* (Cambridge: Cambridge University Press, 2009), provides useful summaries in support and critique of Isaac. Obviously my use of the phrase "classical antiquity" follows the scholarly conventions of that field of study and regrettably omits large areas of the world, including India, the rest of Asia, and the Americas.

10. Moses Finley and Brent D. Shaw, *Ancient Slavery and Modern Ideology* (Princeton, NJ: Markus Wiener, 1998), 187 (italics mine).

11. J. H. Galloway, "The Mediterranean Sugar Industry," *Geographical Review* (April 1977): 190.

12. My discussion of the medieval era comes from Robert Bartlett, "Medieval and Modern Concepts of Race and Ethnicity," *Journal of Medieval and Early Modern Studies* (Winter 2001): 39–56.

13. Ibid., 53.

14. Stuart B. Schwartz, ed., *Implicit Understandings: Observing, Reporting and Reflecting on the Encounters between Europeans and Other Peoples in the Early Modern Era* (Cambridge: Cambridge University Press, 1994), 9. Schwartz is summarizing the work of Seymour Phillips, "The Outer World of the European Middle Ages," contained in this edited volume.

15. Ibid.

16. Teachers might want to highlight this by using the 1492 Edict of Expulsion regarding Jews, found online at http://www.sephardicstudies.org/decree.html.

17. Todd M. Endelman, *The Jews of Georgian England, 1714–1830: Tradition and Change in a Liberal Society* (Ann Arbor: University of Michigan Press, 1999), 86. For more on the expulsion and resettlement, see Todd M. Endelman, *The Jews of Britain, 1656–2000* (Berkeley: University of California Press, 2002), 15–35.

18. For the creation of this myth see P. E. Russell, *Prince Henry "the Navigator": A Life* (New Haven: Yale University Press, 2000), 1–2.

19. This list of early English colonies is obviously not comprehensive.

20. David Galenson, "The Rise and Fall of Indentured Servitude in the Americas: An Economic Analysis," *Journal of Economic History* 44, no. 1 (March 1984): 1–26.

21. Ibid., 2–3.

22. C. S. Everett, "'They Shalbe Slaves for Their Lives': Indian Slavery in Colonial Virginia," in Alan Gallay, ed., *Indian Slavery in Colonial America* (Lincoln: University of Nebraska Press, 2009), 69.

23. There is considerable debate among scholars regarding the status of some Africans in Virginia at this time, a topic discussed later in my essay. The phrase quoted is from Everett, "'They Shalbe Slaves,'" 69.

24. James Horn, *Adapting to a New World: English Society in the Seventeenth Century Chesapeake* (Chapel Hill: University of North Carolina Press, 1994), 266–76, provides a good discussion and sample of these.

25. Ibid., 31, 64. The old-English spelling has been retained.

26. Edmund Morgan, *American Slavery, American Freedom: The Ordeal of Colonial Virginia* (New York: W. W. Norton, 1975), remains the classic account of this process.

27. John Rolfe, "A Letter to Sir Edwin Sandys," January 1619/1620, in Susan M. Kingsbury, ed., *The Records of the Virginia Company of London, Volume III* (Washington, DC: US Government Printing Office, 1933), 243. In another version of this same letter, edited by Captain John Smith, the event was recorded slightly differently: "About the last of August came in a dutch man of warre that sold us twenty Negars." John Smith, *Works, 1608–1631*, ed. Edward Arber (Westminster: Archibald Constable, 1895), 541. See also Engel Sluiter, "New Light on the '20. and Odd Negroes' Arriving in Virginia, 1619," *William and Mary Quarterly* 54, no. 2 (April 1997): 395-98; and John Thornton, "The African Experience of the '20. and Odd Negroes' Arriving in Virginia in 1619," *William and Mary Quarterly* 55, no. 3 (July 1998): 421-34. Peter Kolchin's hugely popular and oft-assigned *American Slavery, 1619–1877* (New York: Hill & Wang, 1993; rev. 2003) is only one of countless examples that uses 1619 as the starting point. Teachers and students can access Rolfe's letter online via the Library of Congress: http://www.loc.gov/teachers/classroommaterials/presentationsandactivities/presentations/timeline/colonial/virginia/rolf.html.

28. For the "Origins Debate," which has focused until quite recently entirely in the Chesapeake region, see Alden Vaughan, "The Origins Debate: Slavery and Racism in 17th Century Virginia," *Virginia Magazine of History and Biography* (July 1989): 311-54.

29. Berlin, *Many Thousands Gone*, 386 note 2 (italics mine), 116.

30. Teachers can access a helpful list of the laws online via the Virtual Jamestown website: http://www.virtualjamestown.org/slavelink.html.

31. In 1641 Massachusetts legalized slavery in the Body of Liberties, a set of laws that governed the colony and that are discussed further in the essay.

32. Joanne Pope Melish, *Disowning Slavery: Gradual Emancipation and "Race" in New England, 1780–1860* (Ithaca: Cornell University Press, 1998), xi–10; and Richard Slotkin, *Regeneration through Violence: The Mythology of the American Frontier, 1600–1860* (Norman: University of Oklahoma Press, 1973), 4–5.

33. For the full text of the Body of Liberties see "A Coppie of The Liberties of the Massachusets Colonie in New England [facsimile]," in William H. Whitmore, *Colonial Laws of Massachusetts* (Boston: City Council of Boston, 1890),

1–170. An online version may be accessed at http://history.hanover.edu/texts/masslib.html.

34. For a brief history of the origins of and influences on the Body of Liberties, see Edmund S. Morgan, *The Puritan Dilemma: The Story of John Winthrop*, 2nd ed. (New York: Longman, 1999), 148–55.

35. The next line of this "right" seemingly provides some possibility for some "rights" a slave might possess: "And these shall have all the liberties and Christian usages which the law of god established in Israell concerning such persons doeth morally require." This was, however, left open to interpretation. Furthermore, the question of who might be enslaved was ultimately left to government officials: "This exempts none from servitude who shall be Judged thereto by Authoritie."

36. John Winthrop, *Winthrop's Journal*, vol. 1, *1630–1649*, ed. James Kendall Hosmer (New York: Charles Scribner's Sons, 1908), 187. Teachers can utilize online versions of Winthrop's journal via the Internet Archive. Teachers can also share this letter: John Winthrop to William Bradford, July 1637, in John Winthrop, *The Winthrop Papers*, vol. 3, *1631–1637*, ed. Allyn Bailey Forbes (Boston: Massachusetts Historical Society, 1943), 455–58.

37. Winthrop, *Winthrop's Journal*, 1:260. As noted in the preceding note, teachers and students can access this primary source online.

Slavery
in the New Nation

Human Bondage in the Land of Liberty

PAUL FINKELMAN

When Thomas Jefferson wrote the Declaration of Independence in 1776—asserting that all people were "equal" and were "endowed" with "certain unalienable Rights" including "Life, Liberty and the pursuit of Happiness"—slavery was legal in every one of the thirteen newly independent states. During and immediately after the Revolution, Massachusetts (1780) and New Hampshire (1783) ended slavery, while Pennsylvania (1780), Rhode Island (1784), and Connecticut (1784) passed laws to gradually end slavery. Under these statutes the children of all slave women would be born free. Thus, slavery would literally die out. By 1804 two new states, Vermont (1791) and Ohio (1803), had entered the Union with constitutions prohibiting slavery, while New York (1799) and New Jersey (1804) had passed gradual abolition acts. Meanwhile, slavery grew and expanded in the South, and two more slave states, Kentucky (1792) and Tennessee (1796), entered the Union. By the middle of Jefferson's administration the United States was clearly "half slave and half free." But, politically and economically, the United States was clearly a slaveholders' republic. It would remain that way until the Civil War.

When explaining the nation's founding, teachers should stress that *the protection of slavery in the Constitution* was clearly one of the legacies of the founding generation. The proslavery nature of the Constitution and the political domination of the nation by slave owners illustrate the power of slavery after the Revolution.

The Constitution

Teachers can highlight the central role that slavery played in the key moments of the nation's founding. For example, from the beginning of the Constitutional Convention, in May 1787, until the final signing of the document, on September 17, delegates grappled with the place of slavery in the new government. Throughout the Convention southerners persistently demanded special protections for slavery as well as enhancement of their political power because of their slaves. Some northerners objected to the proslavery concessions, but by and large the delegates from the slave states got what they wanted. After the Convention, the leader of the South Carolina delegation, General Charles Cotesworth Pinckney, proudly and correctly told his state legislature: "In short, considering all circumstances, we have made the best terms for the security of this species of property it was in our power to make. We would have made better if we could; but on the whole, I do not think them bad."[1] Pinckney, like other southern supporters of the Constitution, could point to numerous clauses in the document that protected slavery and gave the slave states enormous political advantages.

Southern supporters of ratification were quick to recognize those provisions of the Constitution that protected slavery and enhanced the power of the slave states. Similarly, northerners who opposed the Constitution easily focused on most of the proslavery provisions of the document.[2] Students today, however, may not recognize all—or even any—of the proslavery provisions of the Constitution. This is in part because the words "slave" and "slavery" do not appear anywhere in the original constitution. Indeed, the word "slavery" appears in only one place in the Constitution—in the Thirteenth Amendment, which was ratified in 1865 to abolish the institution. The Framers were careful not to use the word in the document, and thus throughout the main body of the Constitution slaves are referred to as "other persons," "such persons," or, in the singular, as a "person held to Service or Labour." However, the omission of the word "slavery" should not mislead students of the Constitution about its proslavery nature.

Throughout the debates the delegates talked about "blacks," "Negroes," and "slaves." But the final document avoided these terms. The change in language was clearly designed to make the Constitution more palatable to the North. In a debate over what became the commerce clause, the delegates from the Carolinas and Georgia vigorously demanded that the African slave trade remain open under the new Constitution. Gouverneur Morris, who represented Pennsylvania,[3] furious at this immoral compromise, suggested that the proposed clause read: the "Importation of slaves into N. Carolina, S—Carolina & Georgia" shall not be prohibited. Connecticut's Roger Sherman, who voted with the Deep South to allow the trade, objected not only to the singling out of specific states but also to the term slave. He declared that he "liked a description better than the terms proposed, which had been declined by the old Congs[4] & were not pleasing to some people." George Clymer of Pennsylvania "concurred" with Sherman. In the North Carolina ratifying convention James Iredell, who had been a delegate in Philadelphia, explained that "the word *slave* is not mentioned" because "the northern delegates, owing to their particular scruples on the subject of slavery, did not choose the word *slave* to be mentioned." Thus, southerners avoided the term because they did not want unnecessarily to antagonize their colleagues from the North. As long as they were assured of protection for their institution, the southerners at the Convention were willing to do without the word "slave."[5]

Despite the circumlocution, slavery was sanctioned throughout the Constitution. To demonstrate slavery's presence in the Constitution, teachers may ask students to read the original document and highlight those elements that signal the presence of slavery in the new republic. Before beginning this project, instructors can decide whether to tell their students about the founder's omission of the words "slave" or "slavery" from the document. After students complete this assignment in groups or individually, instructors will lead a discussion of the Constitution and slavery. Many students may easily point to five provisions that dealt directly with slavery:

- *Article I, Section 2, Paragraph 3.* The three-fifths clause provided for counting three-fifths of all slaves for purposes of representation in Congress. This clause also provided that, if any "direct tax" was levied on the states, it could be imposed only proportionately, according to population, and that only three-fifths of all slaves would be counted in assessing each state's contribution. However, most delegates at the Convention doubted that such a head tax would ever be imposed.

- *Article I, Section 9, Paragraph 1.* Popularly known as the "slave trade clause," this provision prohibited Congress from banning the "Migration or Importation of such Persons as any of the States now existing shall think proper to admit" before the year 1808. Awkwardly phrased and designed to confuse readers, this clause prevented Congress from ending the African slave trade before 1808 but did not require Congress to ban the trade after that date. By limiting Congress's ability to end the international slave trade, the clause was a significant exception to the general power granted to Congress to regulate all commerce.
- *Article I, Section 9, Paragraph 4.* This clause declared that any "capitation" or other "direct tax" had to take into account the three-fifths clause. It ensured that, if a head tax were ever levied, slaves would be taxed at three-fifths the rate of whites. The "direct tax" portion of this clause was redundant, because that was provided for in the three-fifths clause.
- *Article IV, Section 2, Paragraph 3.* The fugitive slave clause prohibited the states from emancipating fugitive slaves and required that runaways be returned to their owners "on demand."
- *Article V.* This article prohibited any amendment of the slave importation or capitation tax clauses before 1808.

Taken together, these five provisions gave the South a strong claim to "special treatment" for its peculiar institution. The three-fifths clause also gave the South extra political muscle—in the House of Representatives and in the electoral college—to support that claim. Because presidential electors are allocated by the number of seats each state has in the House, the three-fifths clause affected presidential elections.

Numerous other clauses of the Constitution supplemented the five clauses that directly protected slavery. Some provisions that indirectly guarded slavery, such as the prohibition on taxing exports, were included primarily to protect the interests of slaveholders. Others, such as the guarantee of federal support to "suppress Insurrections" and the creation of the electoral college, were written with slavery in mind, although delegates also supported them for reasons having nothing to do with slavery. The most prominent indirect protections of slavery were:

- *Article I, Section 8, Paragraph 15.* The domestic insurrections clause empowered Congress to call "forth the Militia" to "suppress Insurrections," including slave rebellions.[6]
- *Article I, Section 9, Paragraph 5.* This clause prohibited federal taxes on exports and thus prevented an indirect tax on slavery via the imposition of a tax on the staple products of slave labor, such as tobacco, rice, and eventually cotton.
- *Article I, Section 10, Paragraph 2.* This clause prohibited the states from taxing exports or imports, thus preventing an indirect tax on the products of slave labor by a nonslaveholding state.
- *Article II, Section 1, Paragraph 2.* This clause provided for the indirect election of the president through an electoral college based on congressional representation. This provision incorporated the three-fifths clause into the electoral college and gave whites in slave states a disproportionate influence in the election of the president.
- *Article IV, Section 3, Paragraph 1.* This clause allowed for the admission of new states. The delegates to the Convention anticipated the admission of new slave states (as well as free states) to the Union.
- *Article IV, Section 4.* The domestic violence provision guaranteed that the US government would protect states from "domestic Violence," including slave rebellions.
- *Article V.* By requiring a three-fourths majority of the states to ratify any amendment to the Constitution, this Article ensured that the slaveholding states would have a perpetual veto over any constitutional changes.[7]

Finally, teachers should point out that some clauses did not inherently favor slavery and were not necessarily considered to affect slavery when they were debated but ultimately protected the institution when interpreted by the courts or implemented by Congress after the adoption of the Constitution. It would be wrong to argue that these illustrate the proslavery nature of the Constitutional Convention. However, these clauses do illustrate the way the Constitution set a proslavery tone, which enabled Congress and the courts to interpret seemingly neutral clauses in favor of slavery. Such clauses also directly challenge William

W. Freehling's argument that the Framers were inherently antislavery and that "The impact of the Founding Fathers on slavery . . . must be seen in the long run not in terms of what changed in the late eighteenth century but in terms of how the Revolutionary experience changed the whole of American antebellum history."[8] If we look at the "long run" impact of the Constitution on "American antebellum history," we find that the following clauses were used to protect slavery, not to harm it.

- *Article I, Section 8, Paragraph 4.* This clause empowered Congress to regulate naturalization of noncitizens, and under this clause Congress prohibited the naturalization of nonwhites, even though it is likely that some of the new states, especially those that granted suffrage to blacks, would have also allowed foreign-born blacks to become citizens. Congress would in fact prohibit the naturalization of people of African ancestry until after the Civil War and did not allow the naturalization of east Asian and south Asian immigrants until the mid-twentieth century.
- *Article I, Section 8, Paragraph 17.* The federal district clause allowed Congress to regulate institutions, including slavery, in what became the national capital. Under this clause Congress allowed slavery in Washington, DC. During the convention southerners expressed fear that the national capital would be in the North.
- *Article III, Section 2, Paragraph 1.* The diversity jurisdiction clause limited the right to sue in federal courts to "Citizens of different States," rather than inhabitants. This clause allowed judges to deny slaves and free blacks access to federal courts.[9]
- *Article IV, Section 1.* The full faith and credit clause required each state to grant legal recognition to the laws and judicial proceedings of other states, thus obligating free states to recognize laws creating and protecting slavery.
- *Article IV, Section 2, Paragraph 1.* The privileges and immunities clause required that states grant equal privileges and immunities to "citizens" of other states. In *Dred Scott v. Sandford* (1857) the Supreme Court affirmed a long-standing position of the southern states that free blacks were not "citizens" under the Constitution and that the slave states were therefore free to deny privileges and immunities to them.[10]
- *Article IV, Section 3, Paragraph 2.* This clause allowed Congress the power to regulate the territories. In 1820 Congress used this clause

to limit slavery in the territories north and west of Missouri, but in *Dred Scott v. Sandford* the Supreme Court ruled that the clause authorized Congress to protect slavery in the territories but not to ban the institution.[11]

Besides specific clauses of the Constitution, the structure of the entire document ensured against emancipation by the new federal government. Because the Constitution created a government of limited powers, Congress lacked the power to interfere in the domestic institutions of the states.[12] Thus, during the ratification debates only the most fearful southern antifederalists opposed the Constitution on the grounds that it threatened slavery. Most southerners, even those who opposed the Constitution for other reasons, agreed with General Charles Cotesworth Pinckney of South Carolina, who crowed to his state's house of representatives: "We have a security that the general government can never emancipate them, for no such authority is granted and it is admitted, on all hands, that the general government has no powers but what are expressly granted by the Constitution, and that all rights not expressed were reserved by the several states."[13]

Slavery under the New Constitution

Pinckney was, of course, right. The Constitution protected slavery at almost every turn. As a "domestic institution" of the states, the national government had no power over slavery in the states where it existed. But the national government could and was required to support slavery in a variety of ways.

In 1787 no new slaves were coming into the United States. During the Revolution, all the states had prohibited the African trade because almost all slaves were imported on British vessels. After the Revolution the Deep South states planned to reopen the trade when the postwar economy improved. At the Convention the delegates from South Carolina insisted on a provision to prevent Congress from ending the trade in the near future. In one debate Charles Pinckney, General Charles Cotesworth Pinckney's younger cousin, asserted that South Carolina would "never receive the plan if it prohibits the slave trade."[14] Citing ancient Rome and Greece, he declared that slavery was "justified by the example of all the world." Any threat to the slave trade would "produce serious objections to the Constitution which he wished to see adopted."

The senior Pinckney made the same point, declaring that failing to protect the slave trade would be "an exclusion of S. Carola [sic] from the Union." He emphatically declared: "S. Carolina and Georgia cannot do without slaves."[15]

The result was Article I, Section 9, Clause 1 of the Constitution, technically called the "migration or importation clause" but better known as the slave trade provision, which prohibited Congress from ending the African slave trade until 1808.[16] Starting in 1808 Congress could ban the African slave trade but was not obligated to do so. Many delegates to the Convention had reason to doubt that Congress would end the trade in 1808. In 1787 most of the delegates at the Philadelphia Convention assumed that the Deep South would grow more rapidly than the North. Had they been correct in their analysis, then by 1808 Mississippi and Alabama might have been in the Union, but Ohio might have still been a territory. Furthermore, states like Georgia and North Carolina would have had substantially larger populations. Had this occurred, it is not unreasonable to believe that in 1808 there would have been sufficient congressional support for the trade to prevent its end. As it was, South Carolina and Georgia did not reopen the trade until 1803, but in the next five years slavers brought more than sixty thousand new slaves from Africa. Had the population moved south and west, instead of north and west, it is likely that the trade would have continued for many more years.

In 1800 the nation's capital was moved to Washington, DC, on land ceded to the national government by Virginia and Maryland. No one ever questioned that slavery would be legal in the new city. The government used slaves to build the Capitol, the president's mansion (later called the White House), and all sorts of other government buildings. Southern senators and congressmen brought their slaves with them, as did southern members of the Supreme Court. Thomas Jefferson brought some of his slaves to Washington to serve him when he became president in 1801. With the exception of eight years—during the administrations of John Quincy Adams and Martin Van Buren—slaves would serve in the White House from 1801 until 1850.

Congress did not pass any laws to create slavery in the national capital. The land used for Washington, DC, was taken from Maryland and Virginia, and the laws regulating slavery in those states were incorporated into the laws governing the District of Columbia. Thus, in the shadow of liberty and democracy slaves were auctioned off to the highest bidder; they were marched in chains through the streets of the capital; they were sent to the local sheriff for punishment. In the 1830s abolitionists in Washington, DC, were arrested for the mere possession of antislavery literature. Slaves worked in the hotels, boarding houses, and restaurants that served government officials, visitors, and foreign dignitaries. Diplomats from Europe quickly learned that the new "free" country contained a considerable number of people who were clearly not free.[17]

In 1793 Congress passed the first Fugitive Slave Law,[18] which provided for the return of slaves who escaped from bondage to the emerging free states. Federal judges and US marshals were tasked with helping to recover the human property of southern masters. But Congress refused to even consider laws to protect free northern blacks from kidnapping, and the House refused to even hear petitions from free blacks who complained that their relatives—their own children—had been kidnapped and taken south.

Students should understand that slavery also impacted foreign relations. During the American Revolution tens of thousands of slaves had escaped to territory occupied by the British. Many of them had joined the British army as soldiers or civilian workers. When the war ended, most of these former slaves evacuated the United States with the British. In Jay's Treaty (1795), the United States secured an indemnity for these former slaves who were living in various parts of the British Empire as free people. John Jay was pleased with this outcome, but Thomas Jefferson complained because he wanted the slaves themselves returned. In 1800 the United States, under President John Adams, was on the verge of giving diplomatic recognition to the new Republic of Haiti. Yet when Jefferson became president in 1801 the United States broke off all diplomatic negotiations with Haiti, and Jefferson soon imposed an embargo on all trade with the island. Jefferson also encouraged France to retake Haiti even though, if France had been successful in this, it is unlikely that Napoleon would have sold Louisiana to the United States. In 1806 Congressman John Wayles Eppes, Jefferson's son-in-law, declared he would "pledge the Treasury of the United States that the Negro government should be destroyed." On this issue Eppes was clearly the spokesman for his father-in-law, the president.[19] Under President James Madison the United States embarked on a war with Indians in Florida, known as the First Seminole War, in part to recover slaves who had escaped to live in freedom with the Seminole. In the 1830s and 1850s the United States would fight the Second and Third Seminole Wars, in part for the same purpose.

In 1787 the Congress under the Articles of Confederation passed the Northwest Ordinance, which allowed for the sale of lands in the national territories of the Old Northwest (the present states of Ohio, Indiana, Illinois, Michigan, and Wisconsin, as well as eastern Minnesota). The law prohibited slavery in all territory north and west of the Ohio River. The Ordinance is often taught as an early example of anti-slavery legislation. The reality, however, was that slavery's status in the Northwest Territories was more ambiguous. From 1787 until 1816, slavery persisted in what became Indiana, and slaves would be held in what became Illinois until the 1840s. At no time did the national government ever attempt actually to end slavery in the region or order the emancipation of any individual slaves. Moreover, a number of congressional committees proposed various repeals of the ban on slavery. The ban stood, and eventually the Old Northwest would be turned into free states. But, while banning slavery in the northwest, Congress allowed slavery to spread into the southwest.

Had the United States not acquired new lands, there might have been no debates over the status of slavery in the territories after 1787, because the Northwest Territory would have eventually been carved up into free states and the Southwest Territory (which included present Tennessee, Alabama, and Mississippi) would have been divided into slave states. But in 1803 President Jefferson bought the Louisiana Territory, which already had an estimated twenty-eight thousand slaves but only twenty-two thousand free people. In 1812 Louisiana entered the Union as slave state. In 1819 Missouri also sought to enter the Union as a slave state, but the northern majority in the House of Representatives objected, arguing that Missouri was north of the southern boundary of the Ohio River and thus should come in as a free state, under the provisions of the Northwest Ordinance. After nearly two years of debate, the southerners won, as Missouri entered the Union as a slave state under what is known as the Missouri Compromise or the Compromise of 1820. Under this series of laws, Missouri entered the Union as a slave state, with the proviso that slavery would be banned in all territory north and west of Missouri. In the Compromise of 1850 Congress failed to apply this rule and allowed slavery in all of the territories acquired from Mexico (except California, which became a free state), even though many of those territories were north of the southern boundary of Missouri.[20] In the Kansas-Nebraska Act of 1854, Congress repealed the ban on slavery in the Missouri Compromise and allowed slavery in what would later become Kansas, Nebraska, the Dakotas, and parts of Montana, Colorado, and Wyoming. Meanwhile, in 1844 Congress had annexed Texas, adding yet more land for slavery.

The laws allowing slavery into the West, as well as proslavery legislation such as the Fugitive Slave Law of 1850, were passed by very close votes in the House of Representatives. While the North had a majority in the House, there were always a few northerners willing to vote with the South on these issues. But if there had not been scores of congressmen from slaveholding states who owed their seats to the three-fifths clause, the slave states could not have prevailed in these debates.

Slavery and Political Power in the New Nation

Students can investigate the enduring power of slaveholders by researching which presidents before 1860 owned slaves. This exercise will allow students to understand that from the ratification of the Constitution, in 1788, until the Civil War began, in 1861, southern slave owners (often with the help of a few northern allies) dominated the national government and national politics. From 1788 until 1850 only three northern, nonslaveholders (John Adams, John Quincy Adams, and Martin Van Buren) were elected president, and each served only one term.[21] This contrasts with the forty years of two-term slave owners—Washington, Jefferson, Madison, Monroe, and Jackson—and the ten years of the 1840s when Harrison, Tyler, Polk, and Taylor held the office. The Constitution did not require that the South dominate politics, but the structure helped. In 1800 Thomas Jefferson defeated John Adams by six electoral votes. Students should be reminded that a state's electoral votes were based on the size of each state's delegation in the House of Representatives and that allocation of seats in the House was based on the three-fifths clause. A cross-curricular classroom exercise comparing the slave and free populations of southern states will allow students to determine the number of representatives and electors that the system of slavery granted to the South. If completing this project for the election of 1800, students will see that the application of the three-fifths clause to the allocation of seats in the House of Representatives provided Jefferson's majority in the electoral college. Thus, without the three-fifth clause and its application to the electoral college, the nonslaveholding Adams would have defeated the slaveholder Jefferson.[22]

Except for a few years in the 1820s, there was a southern, slave-holding majority on the Supreme Court from 1800 to 1860, even though a majority of the nation lived in the North.[23] From 1801 until 1864 a slave owner served as Chief Justice. No active opponent of slavery was put on the Court after John Jay served as Chief Justice in the 1790s. In the 1840s and 1850s Justice John McLean was moderately antislavery, but this was a result of his changing views. President Andrew Jackson appointed him to the Court on the assumption he would support slavery. There were a few other justices who expressed antislavery views from time to time, such as Smith Thompson and Joseph Story. But these few moderate opponents of slavery contrast with the vigor-ously proslavery and vigorously antiblack views of Justices Peter Daniel, John Campbell, Philips Barbour, and most of all, Chief Justice Roger B. Taney.

Most of Speakers of the House were southerners, as were most leaders of the Senate. Cabinets were disproportionately southern. More important, extreme proslavery politicians like John C. Calhoun, Able Upshur, Howell Cobb, and Jefferson Davis served in important cabinet positions, but no antislavery politicians served in a cabinet from the 1790s until the Lincoln administration.[24]

In sum, the politics of the American government reflected the pro-slavery Constitution created in 1787.

The Special Case of Thomas Jefferson

No one better illustrates the contrast of liberty and slavery than Thomas Jefferson. Examining his actions and writings provides a powerful lens into the contradiction between freedom and slavery that existed in the new nation. As the primary author of the Declaration of Independence, Jefferson articulated the essence of American values—equality and the rights to life, liberty, and the pursuit of happiness. But in his public career, his intellectual achievements, and his private life, Jefferson was a staunch defender of slavery and racism.

As the governor of Virginia during the Revolution, he refused to allow the enlistment of free blacks or the emancipation of slaves so that they could fight in the Continental Army, even when the British invaded Virginia and the state was in desperate need of soldiers. During the war he drafted a code for slaves and free blacks that was particularly harsh. While decreasing the number of capital crimes for whites, he wanted to increase the number for blacks. He would have jailed visiting free black sailors and arrested and exiled former slaves when their owners voluntarily freed (manumitted) them. Under Jefferson's proposed law, Virginia slaves who were freed would have to leave all their family and friends. He also proposed that white women who had children with black men be exiled. If these women refused to leave the state, they would be outlawed.[25] Such laws were too harsh for the rest of the legislature, which refused to pass them. At the same time, as chair of the committee to revise the state's law he refused to allow a bill to come to the floor that might have gradually brought an end to slavery in Virginia. He even opposed laws that would allow masters to voluntarily free their slaves, although such a law passed when he was not in the legislature.

In his book *Notes on the State of Virginia*, Jefferson asserted that he had never found a black who "had uttered a thought above the level of plain narration; never seen an elementary trait of painting or sculpture." He found "no poetry" among blacks. Jefferson argued that blacks' ability to "reason" was "much inferior" to whites', while "in imagination they are dull, tasteless, and anomalous" and "inferior to the whites in the endowments of body and mind." Jefferson conceded blacks were brave, but this was due to "a want of fore-thought, which prevents their seeing a danger till it be present." Jefferson admitted some qualms at reaching a "conclusion [that] would degrade a whole race of men from the rank in the scale of beings which their Creator may perhaps have given them." But, qualms or not, he suspected blacks might be "originally a distinct race, or made distinct by time and circumstances" and that because of this they were "inferior to the whites in . . . body and mind." He reached these conclusions while he was surrounded by slaves who were skilled carpenters, blacksmiths, joiners, and chefs and who in other ways showed enormous ability, even though they were denied any education. According to Jefferson, blacks even lacked basic human emotions: "Their griefs are transient" and their love was more like lust, lacking "A tender delicate mixture of sentiment and sensation."[26] With views such as this, Jefferson had no moral qualms about selling scores of his slaves away from their closest relatives. He could justify this in his own mind because he believed blacks were incapable of feeling love the way whites could. Such a stark analysis from the author of the Declaration of Independence makes *Notes* a powerful teaching resource.

When discussing these texts, students will become aware that Jefferson's negrophobia was profound.[27] A scientist and naturalist, he nevertheless accepted and repeated absurdly unscientific and illogical arguments about the racial characteristics of blacks, speculating that blackness might come "from the colour of the blood" or that blacks might breed with the "Oran-ootan."[28] His assertion that black men preferred white women was empirically unsupportable. The reverse was more likely the case, as he surely knew. Many white men, including his late father-in-law, maintained sexual liaisons with their enslaved women. Indeed, within a few years after he wrote these words, Jefferson would himself begin a sexual relationship with his own slave (who was also the half-sister of his late wife), Sally Hemings.

Jefferson's reputation as the nation's leading philosopher on freedom meant that in the early republic many looked to Jefferson for guidance about the issue of slavery. Unfortunately, Jefferson refused to ever take a public stand against slavery and in private correspondence counseled others to support, not oppose, slavery. In 1814 Jefferson's neighbor Edward Coles resolved to free his own slaves and take them to Illinois. He asked Jefferson to endorse this act. But instead, Jefferson urged Coles to change his mind. He told Coles that people "of this color" were "as incapable as children of taking care of themselves." Free blacks were "pests in society by their idleness, and the depredations to which this leads them." Jefferson feared their "amalgamation with the other color." Refusing to endorse manumission, Jefferson implored Coles to continue to care for his slaves. Merging his lifelong affection for states rights with his hostility to free blacks, he urged Coles to "reconcile yourself to your country and its unfortunate condition."[29]

In 1784 Jefferson proposed a ban on slavery in the western territories, but it would not take place until 1800, thus giving masters sixteen years to populate the Ohio Valley with their slaves. This is the closest Jefferson ever came to trying to stop the spread of slavery. During the Missouri Compromise debates of 1819 and 1820 he refused to support a ban on slavery in the West and instead condemned those who debated it, asserting they were about to "perpetrate [an] act of suicide on themselves, and of treason against the hopes of the world" and that they were "committing treason against the hopes of mankind" for even debating slavery.[30] As already noted, as a diplomat he fought hard to force the British government to return former slaves who had gained their freedom by fighting in the American Revolution against the slaveholding patriots like Jefferson. As president he offered to provide food and munitions to a French army if Napoleon would invade Haiti and crush the black rebellion there. A free black nation at the doorstep of the United States was more than the author of the Declaration of Independence could bear.

Teachers can note that Jefferson's private relationship with slavery was equally dismal. He owned between four hundred and five hundred slaves in his lifetime. Between 1784 and 1794 he sold at least eighty-five slaves to raise money for his extravagant lifestyle. He also sold slaves as a form of punishment, exiling them from their families. But this was consistent with his view that slaves did not love as white people did. While holding all of these views and showing no regard at all for black families or emotions, Jefferson maintained a sexual relationship with his slave Sally Hemings. He fathered children with her and kept most of those children in bondage until he died. At his death he freed his remaining children and some of Sally's brothers but not Sally herself.

Jefferson would have exiled white women for having children with blacks, but he had no qualms about fathering children with a black woman himself. He wrote about liberty while buying and selling people most of his adult life. He proclaimed equality but wrote that no black could ever be his equal—even those who were his own children. He was a founder of the new Republic, while at the same time a founder of scientific racism. He was a founding father of a nation "conceived in liberty and dedicate to the proposition that all men are created equal,"[31] while he was personally fathering children whom he held as slaves. In his life and his politics, it was in the end Jefferson who committed "treason against the hopes of the world" by failing to use his considerable talents and energies to fight the monstrous institution that supported his lifestyle and both corrupted and dominated the politics of the new land of liberty.

NOTES

1. Jonathan Elliot, *The Debates in the Several State Conventions on the Adoption of the Federal Constitution*, 5 vols. (1888; reprint, New York: Burt Franklin, 1987), 4:286. For a more elaborate discussion of the issues in this essay, see Paul Finkelman, *Slavery and the Founders: Race and Liberty in the Age of Jefferson*, 3rd ed. (New York: Routledge, 2014).

PART TWO: TEACHING SPECIFIC CONTENT

2. Curiously no northern opponents of the Constitution discussed the fugitive slave provision of the Constitution, although southern supporters of the Constitution such as James Madison used it as an argument for ratification in their states. The authors of the Federalist Papers, who were in favor of ratification, completely ignored the provision because it was not likely to help them persuade New Yorkers to vote in favor of the Constitution.

3. Morris was actually from New York, where his family owned a substantial amount of land in what is today the Bronx, as well as large tracts of land in Morris County, New Jersey. He was in Philadelphia when the legislature was preparing to host the Convention, and his prominence led the state legislature to choose him as a delegate. His grandfather, Lewis Morris, had been chief justice and then governor of the New York colony, and his brother, also Lewis Morris, had been a signer of the Declaration of Independence.

4. This is an abbreviation for "Congress." It is a reference to the Second Continental Congress and the Congress under the Articles of Confederation.

5. Max Farrand, ed., *The Records of the Federal Convention of 1787*, rev. ed. (New Haven: Yale University Press, 1966), 1:561; 2:415; Elliot, *Debates in the Several State Conventions*, 4:176.

6. The abolitionist Wendell Phillips considered this clause, and the one of Article IV, Section 4, to be among the five key proslavery provisions of the Constitution. Wendell Phillips, *The Constitution A Pro-Slavery Compact; or, Selections from the Madison Papers*, 2nd ed. (New York: American Anti-Slavery Society, 1845), vi.

7. Had all fifteen slave states remained in the Union, they would to this day be able to prevent an amendment on any subject. In a fifty-state union, it takes only thirteen states to block any amendment.

8. William W. Freehling, "The Founding Fathers and Slavery," *American Historical Review* 77 (1972): 81–93, quotation at 82.

9. The proslavery implications of this clause did not become fully apparent until the Supreme Court issued its opinion in *Dred Scott v. Sandford*, 60 US (19 Howard) 393 (1857). There the Court held that even free blacks could not sue in diversity in federal courts.

10. *Dred Scott v. Sandford*, 60 US (19 Howard) 393 (1857). Throughout the antebellum period the slave states refused to grant privileges and immunities to free blacks from other states or countries. Most of the slave states prohibited free blacks from even entering their jurisdictions. In *Elkison v. Deliesseline*, 8 F. Cas. 493 (1823), Justice William Johnson refused to strike down such a law in South Carolina, although he believed it to be unconstitutional. For more on this problem see Paul Finkelman, *An Imperfect Union: Slavery, Federalism, and Comity* (Chapel Hill: University of North Carolina Press, 1981), 109n; Paul Finkelman, *Slavery in the Courtroom* (Washington, DC: Government Printing Office, 1985), 256–63, and my articles "States Rights North and South in Antebellum

America," in Kermit Hall and James W. Ely Jr., eds., *An Uncertain Tradition: Constitutionalism and the History of the South* (Athens: University of Georgia Press, 1989), 125–58, and "The Protection of Black Rights in Seward's New York," *Civil War History* 34 (1988): 211–34.

11. In *Dred Scott* Chief Justice Taney held unconstitutional the Missouri Compromise, which banned slavery in most of the western territories.

12. Under various clauses of the Constitution the Congress might have protected, limited, or prohibited the interstate slave trade (Article I, Section 8, Paragraph 3), slavery in the District of Columbia or on military bases (Article I, Section 8, Paragraph 17), or slavery in the territories (Article IV, Section 3, Paragraph 2). None of these clauses permitted Congress to touch slavery in the states. Some radical abolitionists argued that under the guarantee clause, Article IV, Section 4, Congress had the right to end slavery in the states. See William Wiecek, *The Sources of Antislavery Constitutionalism in the United States, 1760–1848* (Ithaca: Cornell University Press, 1978), 269–71. The delegates in Philadelphia did not debate these clauses with slavery in mind, although the commerce clause was accepted as part of a bargain over the African slave trade.

13. Pinckney quoted in Elliot, *Debates in the Several State Conventions*, 4:286. Patrick Henry, using any argument he could find to oppose the Constitution, feared that, "among ten thousand implied powers which they may assume, they may, if we be engaged in war, liberate every one of your slaves if they please" (Elliot, *Debates in the Several State Conventions*, 3:589). Ironically, the implied war powers of the president would be used to end slavery, but only after the South had renounced the Union.

14. Farrand, *Records of the Federal Convention of 1787*, 2:263–65.

15. Ibid., 2:371–75.

16. Congress actually passed a ban on the slave trade in 1807, but it could not go into effect until January 1, 1808. See Paul Finkelman, "Regulating the African Slave Trade," *Civil War History* 54 (2008): 379–405.

17. Paul Finkelman and Donald R. Kennon, eds., *In the Shadow of Freedom: The Politics of Slavery in the National Capital* (Athens: Ohio University Press, 2011).

18. The history of the adoption of this law is found in Finkelman, *Slavery and the Founders*, 102–32.

19. Charles C. Tansill, *The United States and Santo Domingo, 1798–1873: A Chapter in Caribbean Diplomacy* (Baltimore: Johns Hopkins University Press, 1938), 104–5. See also Finkelman, *Slavery and the Founders*, 178–82, 215–16.

20. Paul Finkelman, "The Appeasement of 1850," in Paul Finkelman and Donald R. Kennon, eds., *Congress and the Crisis of the 1850s* (Athens: Ohio University Press, 2012), 36–79.

21. William Henry Harrison was a resident of Ohio when elected in 1840, but he was a lifelong slave owner and came from a wealthy slave-owning family in Virginia.

22. Census data for 1800, including the slave and free population, is available on census.gov.

23. Some biographers of Chief Justice Roger B. Taney mistakenly claim he did not own any slaves while on the Court. It is true he freed some of his slaves in the years before he went on the Court, but he always owned some slaves. Equally important, he came from a slaveholding family and slaveholding culture and was always deeply hostile to the rights of free blacks. A quarter-century before his opinion in *Dred Scott v. Sandford* (1857) asserting that free blacks could not be citizens of the United States, Taney took the same position in a memo written to President Andrew Jackson while serving as his attorney general.

24. Alexander Hamilton and John Jay were founders of the New York Manumission Society and deeply opposed to slavery. Both served in Washington's administration.

25. "Outlawed" is a legal term that would have allowed such women to be arrested and jailed (or even shot) without trial.

26. Thomas Jefferson, *Notes on the State of Virginia*, ed. William Peden (Chapel Hill: University of North Carolina Press, 1954), 138–43.

27. This issue is discussed at length in Finkelman, *Slavery and the Founders*, 193–280. Jefferson's discussion of slavery and race in *Notes on the State of Virginia* are found in Query XIX and Query XVIII.

28. Jefferson, *Notes on the State of Virginia*, 138–39.

29. Thomas Jefferson to Edward Coles, August 25, 1814, in Merrill Peterson, *The Portable Thomas Jefferson* (New York: Penguin Books, 1975), 546.

30. Thomas Jefferson to John Holmes, April 22, 1820, in Paul Leicester Ford, *The Works of Thomas Jefferson*, 12 vols. [Federal Edition] (New York: G.P. Putnam's Sons, 1904–5), 10:157–58.

31. Abraham Lincoln, Gettysburg Address.

Blood-Stained Mirrors

Decoding the American Slave-Trading Past

SOWANDE' MUSTAKEEM

On May 21, 2010, members of the Texas State Board of Education adopted a more conservative approach to the social studies curriculum offered within the Texas public school system. Among the piles of amendments proposed to affect future textbooks, student achievement tests, and, more important, the education of 4.8 million Texan students over a ten-year period were proposals to ban the use of the term "slave trade" and to replace it with "Atlantic triangular trade."[1] Some could argue that students will gain a more global view by interlinking this operative trade to a larger Atlantic trading system. By subsuming the buying and selling of other human beings for profit under the general term "Atlantic triangular trade," however, teachers can avoid any real engagement with the nation's historical involvement in this commercial traffic of men, women, and children, focusing instead on the more general movement of raw materials and manufactured goods. The long-term effects of such an amendment for Texas students still remain to be seen. This is merely one example of a national trend emerging in schools across the United States. Textbooks and curricula employ similar tactics to erase the history of the slave trade by relegating it to conversations centered on economics and commodities or by avoiding the subject altogether.

The slave trade is a window to the country's own complicated past. In many cases this history has been watered down and creatively woven into a brief discussion of plantation slavery, followed by a quick move to explain when and how those enslaved became free. In this narrative, the slave trade is best remembered by many as a period when Africans sold other Africans to foreign traders who boarded them on big ships that sailed across winding, watery routes leading to America. Once the ships docked overseas, those held captive were sold and made property of plantation owners. On the surface, this captures the essence of the trade, although it carefully avoids probing any of the horrors of the slaving process. Many students know all too little about the lives ruptured and the separations and losses inflicted by the trade. Nor do they understand the incredible greed anchored within the trans-Atlantic slave trade. Many are commonly taught about the slave trade with maps comprised of separate continents linked by colorful lines and arrows moving in a triangular pattern tracing the global movement of goods. These simple arrows linking Africa, Europe, the West Indies, and the Americas obscure stories of human connections forged through the slave trade—manipulation, loss, devastation, murder, sickness, and death. Equally invisible in these colorful diagrams is the lure of profit and accrued wealth—no matter the financial or human costs incurred— that impelled innumerable merchants, private traders, seamen, and surgeons to participate in the buying of African people.

As historic kingdoms rose and fell across the interiors of West Africa, merchants in distant locales heard whispers of an explosive enterprise taking form. European merchants engaged in private chats and held meetings in secured offices, bars, and coffeehouses in hopes of enticing investors to the lucrative pursuits emerging out of Africa. Surviving sources leave muted how these investors justified profits wrung from the human tragedies of millions of men and women that made up the human merchandise bought and sold across much of the Atlantic world. We must therefore stress to our students that their invest-ments spawned an industry based on the bodies of African people that led to immense wealth, new industries, and, for many investors, a rise in social status.[2]

Students should know that the Portuguese were the first successful slave traders of the modern era. The Portuguese launched the initial engagement with African merchants for gold in 1441, and this, a few short years later, led to the gradual gifting of small groups of captives to Portuguese royalty. These initial human gifts became more desir-able, producing an incredible appetite for the purchase and importation of even more African people—men, women, and children—this time as labor. The constant circulation of monies, ships, and bodies led other nations—including Spain in the early 1500s, the Netherlands in the 1630s, and England and France in the mid-seventeenth century—to formulate mercantile companies protected by royal governments. These companies employed seamen to travel to western Africa in hopes of securing control of this burgeoning maritime slave empire. The seventeenth century represented a testing ground for slave sales, whereas the eighteenth century witnessed a dramatic transformation in commercial slavery. Many of the formerly lucrative charter companies proved ill equipped to fulfill the vast demand for bondpeople, thus permitting the slave trade to become the least regulated branch of commerce. Consequently, by 1730 investors saw the downfall of many formerly profitable monopolies and lost control of the trade to a growing base of private traders, including American slavers. These traders aggressively vied for a larger share of slaving profits, more than tripling the number of captives deposited into New World slave societies from close to two million during the seventeenth century to more than six million in the eighteenth century.[3]

The arrival of foreign white traders to the African coast brought more than the temporary docking of ships and crewmen. Over the centuries some governments established trading posts that were run by their official representatives. This presence, as well as the construction of slave dungeons that lined the coast, changed the physical landscape, led to a rise in mixed-race children, and altered the customs, laws, and processes of trade. The increased participation of private traders allowed eager entrepreneurs to finance ships and employees and thereby construct their own rules of trade. Countless merchants wrote letters to hired captains detailing expectations about their forthcoming West African ventures. These letters outlined behaviors expected of sailors on and off ship, detailing preferences for slave selections as well as requirements for overseas auction sales following the voyage. Although they were the working-class laborers of the sea, mariners were central to the entire slave-trading operation.[4]

Sea captains were well aware of the instructions provided, yet they adapted their own tactics in their dealings in Africa. No matter the increase of white foreigners, the most crucial partnerships were those that ship commanders established with local African rulers and brokers. The volumes of testimony given before the British House of Commons in the years before the slave trade was outlawed allow us to understand the contours of this trade.[5] Crewmen chartered vessels into often-crowded

African seaports loaded with different types of tobacco, silks, guns, alcohol, and other luxury goods. They used these items often to gain access to and to buy the most ideal bondpeople. Unavailable in West Africa, these exotic goods invariably created a need and dependency among Africans. Playing upon the illusion of friendship in private negotiations, slave-trading men discussed the state of the local slaving business and other global affairs over drinks and meals. Local rulers and foreign slave traders agreed upon terms, and rulers granted approval for sailors to purchase available slaves. The bondpeople at the center of these negotiations were kidnapped during inland raids, sold to pay debts, and in many cases accused of witchcraft; some were prisoners of war.[6] Once confined on the coast, some slaves were taken aboard ships for private display to different sea captains. Usually, however, African sellers held shoreline auctions to give docked buyers the opportunity to inspect larger groups of captives and to determine those most suitable for the plantation system.

Regardless of how bondpeople entered the trade, students must see that the violation and mistreatment perpetrated by the African slave trade forever altered their lives. Separated from their families and communities, often forced to march for days and weeks to the coast, captives were uncertain about their futures. On the coast they were thrown into darkened slave dungeons that only worsened the terror of their captivity. Tormented by offensive smells and the agonizing cries of other captives, they grew increasingly fearful of their looming fate as they saw other bondpeople leave and never return. The auction block system further exacerbated these traumatic experiences. Many women, men, and children were subjected to publicly degrading inspections as their bodies were poked, prodded, and roughly handled to ascertain their long-term value for overseas sales. As bids were made, parents were split from children, siblings and friends were broken apart, and the elderly were rendered unable to protect themselves or the young. During the sale, terms such as "prime" and "refuse" slaves gained greater meaning when buyers determined some bondpeople to be valuable while others were cast as worthless. Those unsold—infants, toddlers, the aged, the disabled—were many times given to other traders, beaten, or even killed because of their inability to secure foreign interest. The slave trade involved not only the mass filtration of people out of West Africa but also created a rapid dependence on foreign goods and money. The predatory atmosphere it fueled made every African person—regardless of status—susceptible to enslavement.

The slave trade operated for well over four centuries, involving a multitude of countries, languages, and practices, rendering it difficult to know precisely how many bondpeople were forced into the Atlantic slaving system. Scholars' estimates vary widely. Beginning with W.E.B. Du Bois's seminal 1896 work on the slave trade through to contemporary scholarship, estimates of the number of those sold range from as low as eight to eleven million people to as high as fifty to one hundred million people.[7] An easy and fully accessible set of digital sources that students, teachers, and parents can use to understand some of the intricate patterns within the slave trade is the online database housed at Emory University, which provides a useful interactive tool to quantify and trace the numbers of the people moved into Atlantic world slavery.[8]

With shoreline sales completed, crewmen ferried groups of captives offshore in small boats to waiting slave vessels. Pulled on board by other sailors, they were stripped of all clothing for fear of spreading contamination and disease during the voyage. All bondpeople were then separated by gender and placed into different holds of the ship. Adult male captives, often making up the largest part of the human cargo, were lodged in the bottom holding, while women and children were stowed in a separate part of the vessel, many times on the top deck. The gendered separation of female captives from their enslaved male counterparts placed them close to crewmen, which in turn subjected them to routine threats of rape, sexual harassment, and assault. All captives traveled the Atlantic aware of the probability of sexual assaults and other abuses. Yet adult women, young girls, and even pregnant females routinely became the sexual prey of many employed sailors who violated their bodies with little fear of repercussions for their seaborne actions.[9]

Slave traders assumed women and children would be docile. Women and children were thus typically unshackled throughout the passage—in contrast to black men, who traveled in chains, shackles, and leg irons. The day-to-day traumas common on ships took an unimaginable toll on bondpeople. Some captives nonetheless found creative means to resist their captivity. Iconic images arising most often from the nineteenth-century illegal slave trade portray angry black men engaged in shipboard rebellions against white crewmen. One such image that is readily available online is the "Death of Captain Ferrer" aboard the *Amistad*. Although absent from the renderings, enslaved women similarly engaged in physical combat during the Middle Passage. Some females, aware of their access to artillery stored on top deck, snuck guns down below to awaiting men. Others served as spies and corralled other captives to wage war with a small army. Tasked with the transport and preservation of their boarded human cargo, crewmen were required to protect their slaving interests by reprimanding and reforming any disobedient slaves. In so doing, they relied heavily upon violent punitive measures, including floggings and beheadings. The cat-o'-nine-tails (for whippings) and the speculum oris (for forced feedings) were two instruments the crew employed on virtually every slave ship.[10]

Students are often most curious about ship revolts, which took place on one out of every three ships, yet many times they are unfamiliar with any other forms of resistance on slavers. Captives refused medicine, instituted hunger strikes, acted belligerent, and even aborted children. Not every captive responded to his or her enslavement through openly violent means. As such, slave ship sailors were forced to contend with bondpeople who attempted and in many cases succeeded in hanging themselves, jumping overboard, clawing at their throats to cut their necks, and even swallowing their tongues to impose self-strangulation. Different types of captives—young and old, sick and healthy, female and male—acted out in these ways. Their shipboard experiences often go unremarked in contemporary narratives and dialogues.

A focus on resistance, while interesting and important, obscures the fact that slave ships were sites of layered suffering, in large part because of the presence of illness and death. A wide range of diseases and medical problems arose from the isolated conditions of traveling at sea. Confined naked bodies swaying on ships endured splinters and other incredibly damaging wounds. The captives were exposed to dangerous amounts of excrement, urine, mucus, and blood that filtered into the floorboards and planks, creating a permanent stench throughout the entire vessel. Different worms, vermin, and rats scattered about ships, spreading toxins as they moved silently among the sailors and captives. Those responsible for the medical treatment of ailing slaves—slave ship surgeons or designated seamen—similarly contributed to the contaminated world of slavery at sea by moving from body to body without washing their hands or cleaning their instruments. Diseases such as scurvy, smallpox, dysentery, consumption, cholera, measles, and yaws among many others claimed the lives of a significant number of bond-people forced onto slave ships.[11] Students must be taught that the Middle Passage was not just about transporting humans as commodities. Crewmen held captives in a constant state of degradation that fore-shadowed a similar world of violence and exploitation that they would later face once displaced into plantations.

Teachers can explore themes of resistance and disease during the slave trade by examining two journal entries from an iconic figure in slave trade history, John Newton, who served as a ship captain. His 1754 words briefly recount shipboard instances affecting the vessel's passage, while also sketching the human landscape of life, pain, and death in the Middle Passage. The sources contain difficult but critically important content. Teachers will, of course, need to take care that the sources' instructional potential is not lost in students' initial shocked reaction. To that end, teachers should probe students on exactly what we learn about the slave trade from these log entries. Students can work in groups, with partners, or perhaps individually to interrogate these documents. What Newton etched largely for business purpose provides a direct link to the slaving past. Asking questions such as "How do these sources inform our understanding of the slave trade experience for both females and males?," "How is enslaved resistance portrayed?," "What is Captain Newton's perspective on these incidents?," and "How are slave ship sailors portrayed in the document?" will help students to both create and gain a more nuanced interpretation of these primary sources.

> *Monday 24 June.* Buryed a girl slave (No 92). In the afternoon while we were off the deck, William Cooney seduced a woman slave down into the room and lay with her brutelike in view of the whole quarter deck, for which I put him in irons. I hope this has been the first affair of the kind on board and I am determined to keep them quiet if possible. If anything happens to the woman I shall impute it to him, for she was big with child. Her number is 83.
>
> *Thursday 27 June.* When we were putting the slaves down in the evening, one that was sick jumped overboard. Got him in again but he dyed immediately between his weakness and the salt water he had swallowed, tho I imagine he would have lived but a little while being quite worn out.[12]

Once on shore, imported slaves were cleaned, oiled, and relocated to local jails and pens in preparation for auction sales. Farmers, doctors, lawyers, bankers, and politicians scoured newspapers and met with local brokers to participate in sales of newly arrived Africans. Slaves were often put to work growing crops such as cotton, tobacco, sugar, and indigo, but some slaveholders were interested in a bondperson's ability beyond the fields, including swimming and diving, horseracing, playing music, divining, conjuring, blacksmithing, and midwifery. Buyers made offers that ruptured ties that shipmates had forged at sea. Mothers were torn from their children, and friends and loved ones were likewise separated, never to see each other again. Captives were forced to endure a relentless life of slavery toiling on someone else's land, cooking food for others, and raising another family's children. Those unable to find immediate buyers—children, the very old, diseased or disabled captives—were sent to "vendue" or what some called "refuse sales," where they were held until sold through clearance sales.

The buying, selling, and constant importation of African people functioned as a normal and necessary part of American society over time. As a vital enterprise, the slave trade spanned several centuries; we can never truly determine the amount of wealth amassed from this intricate web of commerce and capitalism. Investors in some cases averaged profits of between 20 and 50 percent from a completed slaving voyage. Moreover, the monies that circulated during the slave trade fueled economies, spawned new industries, increased participants' social status, and, most of all, created a racialized social order. While precise details of the movement of people, goods, ideas, and monies through the trans-Atlantic slave trade are unknown, there are many sources available for classroom adoption. Many of these resources are discussed in the notes to this chapter. Further, within the remainder of this essay I provide possibilities for teaching slavery and the slave trade to this new generation of young thinkers, based on my own successes and challenges, that can serve as a useable template for other instructors.

Knowing the heartbreaking and rather painful emotions the slave trade can invoke, how does a teacher get students to grapple with the slaving past? How do you teach a subject that is at once inaccessible and yet looming ever close, haunting American society? As the recent Texas curricular change has already revealed, the easiest answer is to avoid it outright, ban it from textbooks and classroom discussions, exclude it from comprehensive exams, and purposely forget to include it in a lecture so as to spare the students from confronting such agony. The truth is that our unwillingness as a nation to look into the historical mirror and collectively acknowledge the history of the slave trade fuels racism today. I cannot profess that I have developed any insightful new theory or pedagogy for confronting this history, yet I have faced trials and challenges that have allowed me to become more flexible in my approach to the classroom to increase the learning on all sides. Although merely one of many other possible methods, the one I employ continues to generate heightened student interest in discussing not just black history but what many deem a stain in American history.

For the first two years at my university I offered a course titled "Gender, Health, and Resistance: Comparative Slavery in the African Diaspora," for which I was lucky to get anywhere from six to eight students each time that I taught it. The first class was primarily female and the second was composed largely of African American students. I was confused and unsure of what to do in order to entice other students to be a part of what I saw as necessary historical dialogues. I soon learned from other colleagues that these challenges were not unique to my university and that many American students avoid the topic of slavery if given a choice. One semester I was granted an opportunity to develop and pilot a sophomore seminar for the history department. I titled the new course "Slavery and Memory in American Popular Culture." Much to my surprise, students vied to become enrolled in the class. I soon learned that a single statement within my course description noting the incorporation of "literature, public history, art/poetry, visual culture, movies and documentaries, as well as contemporary music including reggae and hip hop" had became the unexpected tool in my marketing success. This fact was evidenced by its popularity both times that I taught the course. Teaching at a time when those in the humanities are finding it harder to attract students, I realized very quickly that providing a history class that incorporates students' cultural understandings generates far more excitement about learning about the past. There are four key areas—course resources, field trips, class visitors, and, critically important, popular culture—that encouraged creative new ways of making the study of slavery more engaging and culturally relevant.

Determining what students would read and watch throughout the semester was a crucial factor in generating substantial interest. My primary rubric was to keep it simple, accessible, and, most of all, interesting. I relied upon expected slave trade sources such as a useful clip of the slave trade featured in the film *Amistad*. I also used several well-known history monographs, although I kept these to a minimum, preferring instead to quickly expose students to different themes of slavery through an array of articles, essays, and book chapters.[13] Students were curious and enthusiastic about a 1993 film by the Ethiopian director Hallie Gerima called *Sankofa*; the classic 1976 science fiction novel *Kindred*, by Octavia Butler; and the 2008 PBS documentary *Traces of the Trade: A Story from the Deep North*.[14] They became enthralled by grappling with two questions both the movie and book subconsciously posed to audiences: What if you were sent back into slavery, and how would you cope with learning that your family was involved in perpetuating and benefiting from the slave trade? Each source prompted questions and passionate conversations on slavery. Students confronted these questions in different ways, but most beneficial for them was the comfortably open and supportive classroom environment that allowed them to share thoughts, feelings, and frustrations with this history.

To encourage creativity in another way, I also varied the learning spaces to better show how education can operate within and beyond the classroom. I created an assignment requiring the students to travel as a class to explore two museums in the local St. Louis area. During the course, Tavis Smiley's corporate-sponsored exhibit "America I AM" was on tour at the Missouri History Museum. The exhibit explored the broader history of blacks in American history, including plantation slavery and the slave trade. I felt that by attending the exhibit the students would gain a greater sense of public history, museum culture, and the politics of historical memory.[15] To provide a local point of contrast, the students also traveled to the Griot Museum of Black History, a smaller local St. Louis venue that sustains itself through donations, grants, and any additional labor the two black female owners provide for its upkeep.[16] There the students gained significant exposure to the histories of black St. Louis; particularly valuable to the course was the incredible replica of the Middle Passage that offered a 3-D-like visual of confined bodies, interracial violence, rodents, and sickness on a slave ship. Teachers who do not have access to these types of public resources can create a similar dialogue by "virtually" visiting a number of large and well-respected museums with significant online presences, including the Liverpool International Museum of Slavery. The smaller Griot Museum also offers online tours of some of its slavery exhibits.[17]

The varied outcome of these trips affirms the unpredictability of teaching even as both sites offered valuable experiences and generated a rather passionate classroom dialogue on the role and limits of public history. Several students expressed deep frustration with the Smiley exhibit, arguing that it sidelined the horrors of the slave trade. They also felt that the corporate influence created a "feel good black history" traveling exhibit. Students found themselves sympathetic and appreciative of the grassroots localized history the Griot Museum offered. As a result of their collective frustration, I devised an assignment in which each student was asked to write a letter to Tavis Smiley and give a "museum review" from his or her collegiate perspective. The point of this assignment was to teach students to go beyond their frustrations and to respectfully confront problems while offering tangible solutions to make something better. Less than a month later, Smiley sent a signed thank-you card to the class for the letters, and the students were honored to receive a note from a nationally recognized public intellectual. During my second stint teaching the course, the class traveled with me to a local predominantly black college, Harris Stowe State University. My students and their peers from another class at HSSU participated in a workshop that I cohosted with a colleague there to provide an unprecedented educational arena to dialogue on the meaning of slavery for twenty-first-century college students. This same idea could be adopted on a secondary level to promote collective learning through projects or forums that look to forge greater institutional affiliations by bringing students together for these important racially necessary conversations.

I commonly push students to learn outside the classroom while also bringing the scholarly world into theirs through in-class visits. Two colleagues on the faculty at my university who write and publish about the history of slavery visited the class and spoke during one semester. The students were surprisingly curious about a career based largely on writing and teaching about slavery. The second time that I taught the course, my students had a significantly different guest interaction. At the beginning of the semester I was informed that one of the authors of a class text, Thomas DeWolf, a descendent of the prominent slave-trading DeWolf family, was coming to campus.[18] As the visit drew closer, the students were excited about the different questions they hoped to pose and discuss, having watched the PBS film *Traces of the Trade* and read the scholarly essay "'She Must Go Overboard and Shall Go Overboard': Diseased Bodies and the Spectacle of Murder at Sea," which synergistically helped to recount a black woman's murder at sea during a slaving voyage. During his visit, however, the students felt their guest avoided any deep engagement with his family's connection to the slave trade. Much to their dismay, he focused his attention instead on sharing stories of race from his youth rather than listening to the students' twenty-first-century curiosities and even frustrations that emerged as they grappled twice weekly with this painful slaving past. Perhaps because of the unfavorable interaction, the students became even more passionate about the need for cross-generational and interracial dialogues about learning slavery and the slave trade on both the national and the local levels, within and beyond the classroom environment.

The final and most successful way I made my course relevant was the infusion of popular culture and contemporary music to better bridge the gap between the past and the present. Prior to the start of the most recent class, I required all enrolled students to see Quentin Tarantino's Hollywood film *Django Unchained*, then still in the theaters. Taking special note of the audience's reaction, each student wrote a two-page paper discussing the movie's impact and any criticisms the student had. Given the nature of the assignment, this set a culturally open tone for the class, and the conversations were exciting and devoid of any first-day discomfort.

In many ways, the infusion of popular culture made both classes particularly innovative. Political and journalistic slipups as well as the outcry that swept through social media in connection with the hoax video game "The Slavery Game" in 2011 made for extremely engaged classroom sessions.[19] In particular, students enjoyed critically analyzing a cultural constant in their everyday lives—music. Knowing the power of music to transcend age, race, gender, sexuality, and status, I created diverse group pairings and encouraged them to locate not only *if*, but *where* and *how* slavery is musically remembered in contemporary society. My first class had more freedom with the artists and songs they selected and presented to their peers. Feeling, however, that some students' musical selections bordered on uncreative last-minute attempts to fulfill the assignment, I imposed on the second class a more structured assignment that required them to decode a preselected 2000 hip hop album, *Reflection Eternal*, produced by the hip hop artists and producers Talib Kweli and Hi Tek. Moving beyond intoxicating rhythms and beats, I wanted students to engage Kweli's sociohistorical and political commentary. Often viewed by many as a "conscious hip hop artist,"

Kweli lyrically prompts audiences to think beyond any familiar "corner" or urban street narrative. Instead, listeners were able to glimpse an innovative twenty-first-century effort to bridge the gaps between Africa and America, as well as the Middle Passage and corporate slavery, and to musically confront other hard-hitting social and cultural trends emerging at the time of the album's release. Lyrics from the song "Africa Dream" connect the past with the present through creative similes: "Like slaves on a ship talking about who got the flyest chain." Given this untapped and rather invisible body of rich material, at least for academics, I invited students to engage the album beyond mere listening and to write a five- to seven-page paper critically engaging where and how these hip hop artists memorialized the history of slavery through their music.[20] Making no assumptions about students' familiarity with the album or about any deeper understanding of the evolving variations of hip hop, this assignment facilitated a deeper exchange and a genuine excitement among younger generations about aspects of an active slaving past. Taking this pedagogical leap proved successful on multiple levels, not because I kept a close watch on the changes in hip hop and youth culture but because this assignment signaled that I, as a teacher, was not only willing to meet the students where they were at both culturally and musically but also that I validated creativity and fun learning. I also allowed them to teach me in the process. Students in both classes unanimously expressed heightened appreciation for the assignment, if only because it allowed them to hear how good music can recall history over tracks laced with creative beats and melodic rhymes. While music is rarely incorporated into the history classroom, it has endless potential to spark passion, creativity, and deeper engagement in students. This excitement is desperately needed, especially when discussing a topic as difficult as slavery.

Although subtle, the haunting history of slavery is everywhere in American society. Looking toward the future, we can no longer hold to the traditional ways of teaching students based on textbooks, monotonous diagrams, and outdated documentaries. We instead have to actively pursue and integrate current news that becomes teachable, such as the 2012 slavery math case in Georgia or the recent frenzy in social media related to the underwater sculpture park in Grenada commemorating the slave trade.[21] Many may frown upon the use of hip hop as a viable educational tool, yet recent controversies related to Lil Wayne's sexualized invocation of Emmett Till in a song and even Kanye West's release of his controversial album *New Slaves* underscore the value of using pop culture as well as the lure of pop icons in getting students to engage and critique the incredible power contemporary musicians hold as transmitters of history and culture.[22] Creatively preparing students to engage the multitude of ways that the past can influence the present will have a far greater impact on the conversations, friendships, and connections among any class of peers, regardless of differences. As educators, perhaps even more amidst these racially uncertain times, many of us remain hesitant about our own engagement with the best ways to discuss the history of slavery, the slave trade, and essentially race. Yet, we can impart longer lasting seeds in opening the minds of future generations by prompting students to pull back the curtains and come face to face with the tarnished mirrors of America's slaving past.

NOTES

The author wishes to dedicate this essay to the memory of Dean James E. McLeod, who supported development of this course through Arts and Sciences to make the humanities even more engaging for future undergraduates. I would most especially like to thank all the students in two Washington University classes, the Fall 2011 and Spring 2013 "Sophomore Seminar: Slavery and Memory in American Popular Culture," that collectively sparked passionate dialogues, prompted difficult questions, and insisted on the greater need for honest conversations related to race and twenty-first-century discussions of slavery and memory. I remain convinced that the future remains bright.

1. See Lois Elfman, "Texas State Board of Education Approves Controversial Social Studies Curriculum Changes," *Diverse Issues in Higher Education*, May 24, 2010; and Terrence Stutz, "Texas State Board of Education Approves New Curriculum Standards," *Dallas Morning News*, May 22, 2010.

2. On the origins of the trans-Atlantic slave trade, see Hugh Thomas, *Slave Trade: The Story of the Atlantic Slave Trade, 1440–1870* (New York: Simon & Schuster, 1997); and Robin Blackburn, *The Making of New World Slavery: From the Baroque to the Modern, 1492–1800* (New York: Verso, 1997).

3. See Stephanie Smallwood, *Saltwater Slavery: A Middle Passage from Africa to American Diaspora* (Boston: Harvard University Press, 2008); and William Pettigrew, *Freedom's Debt: The Royal African Company and the Politics of the Atlantic Slave Trade, 1672–1752* (Chapel Hill: University of North Carolina Press, 2013).

4. For more on the worlds of merchants and seamen, see David Cecelski, *The Waterman's Song: Slavery and Freedom in Maritime North Carolina* (Chapel Hill: University of North Carolina Press, 2001); David Hancock, *Citizens of This World: London Merchants and the Integration of the British Atlantic Community,*

1735-1785 (Cambridge: Cambridge University Press, 1997); Daniel Vickers and Vince Walsh, *Young Men and the Sea: Yankee Seafarers in the Age of Sail* (New Haven: Yale University Press, 2007); Emma Christopher, *Slave Ship Sailors and Their Captive Cargoes, 1730-1807* (Cambridge: Cambridge University Press, 2006); Daniel Mannix and Marcus Cowley, *Black Cargoes: A History of the Atlantic Slave Trade, 1518-1865* (New York: Viking Press, 1969); Marcus Rediker, *Between the Devil and the Deep Blue Sea: Merchant Seamen, Pirates, and the Anglo-American Maritime World, 1700-1750* (New York: Cambridge University Press, 1989); Kenneth Andrews, *Trade, Plunder, and Settlement: Maritime Enterprise and the Genesis of the British Empire, 1480-1630* (New York: Cambridge University Press, 1984); Marcus Rediker and Peter Linebaugh, *The Many Headed Hydra: Sailors, Slaves, Commoners, and the Hidden History of the Revolutionary Atlantic* (Boston: Beacon Press, 2001); Joseph Miller, *Way of Death: Merchant Capitalism and the Angolan Slave Trade, 1730-1830* (Madison: University of Wisconsin Press, 1996).

5. Sheila Lambert, ed., *House of Commons Sessional Papers of the Eighteenth Century*, 4 vols. (Wilmington, DE: Scholarly Resources, 1975).

6. For more on the operation of the slave trade within Africa see Miller, *Way of Death*; Robin Law, *The Slave Coast of West Africa, 1550-1750: The Impact of the Atlantic Slave Trade on an African Society* (Oxford: Clarendon Press, 1991); John Thornton, *Africa and Africans in the Making of the Atlantic World, 1400-1800* (New York: Cambridge University Press, 1992); Anne C. Bailey, *African Voices of the Atlantic Slave Trade: Beyond the Silence and the Shame* (Boston: Beacon Press, 2005); Anthony J. Barker, *The African Link: British Attitudes towards the Negro in the Era of the Atlantic Slave Trade* (London: Frank Cass, 1978); Blackburn, *The Making of New World Slavery*; Joseph Inikori, "The Import of Firearms into West Africa, 1750-1807: A Quantitative Analysis," *Journal of African History* (1977): 339-68; Walter Rodney. "Upper Guinea Coast and the Significance of the Origins of Africans Enslaved in the New World," *Journal of Negro History* (1969): 327-45; and Walter Rodney, "African Slavery and Other Forms of Social Oppression on the Upper Guinea Coast in the Context of the Atlantic Slave Trade," *Journal of African History* (1966): 431-43.

This argument based on the importance of slave ship sailors is in direct line with the work of recent scholars, including Rediker and Christopher; however, my analysis of the slave trade builds upon these scholars' ideas while departing by centering questions of both gender and health in this history. See Sowande' Mustakeem, "'I Never Have Such a Sickly Ship Before': Diet, Disease, and Mortality in Eighteenth-Century Atlantic Slaving Voyages," in "Ending the Trans-Atlantic Slave Trade," special issue, *Journal of African American History* 93 (Fall 2008): 474-96; and Sowande' Mustakeem, "'She Must Go Overboard and Shall Go Overboard': Diseased Bodies and the Spectacle of Murder at Sea," *Atlantic Studies* 8, no. 3 (2011): 301-16.

7. These calculations represent a broad span within scholarly interpretation. One could argue that following Du Bois's 1896 publication—he argued that close to fifty million Africans were forced into trade—the estimations continued to get far more conservative, with numbers as low as ten million suggested by several scholars almost a hundred years later in the historiography. For further estimations of bondpeople transported and sold into the Americas across centuries see especially Blackburn, *The Making of New World Slavery*; Eric Williams, *Capitalism and Slavery* (Chapel Hill: University of North Carolina Press, 1944); and Phillip Curtin, *The Atlantic Slave Trade: A Census* (Madison: University of Wisconsin Press, 1972).

8. Teachers can access this unique online database at the following site: http://www.slavevoyages.org/. A possibly unique class assignment combines three disparate sources to help interweave statistical data with social histories of the slave trade while exposing the limits and successes of different historical methods. One could begin by researching the data provided through the Trans-Atlantic Slave Trade Database related to the sail of the Rhode Island vessel *Polly* in the 1790s (see TSTD #36560). Once the data are accessed, students could be tasked with placing information gained on the ship's sail and the human cargo forced aboard in conversation with the work of two historians on this same slave trade case. See Marcus Rediker, *The Slave Ship: A Human History* (New York: Viking Press, 2007), 343–56; and Mustakeem, "'She Must Go Overboard and Shall Go Overboard.'"

9. For further information on sexual violence, bodily perceptions of black females, and treatment of ailing females see Sowande' Mustakeem, "'Make Haste and Let Me See You with a Good Cargo of Negroes': Gender, Power, and the Centrality of Violence in the Eighteenth Century Atlantic Slave Trade," in Glenn Gordinier, ed., *Gender, Race, Ethnicity, and Power in Maritime America* (Mystic, CT: Mystic Seaport Museum, 2008), 3–21; Jennifer L. Morgan, "Some Could Suckle over Their Shoulder," *William and Mary Quarterly* 54, no. 1 (1997): 167–92; Saidiya Hartman, "Venus in Two Acts," *Small Axe* 12, no. 2 (2008): 1–14; and Mustakeem, "'She Must Go Overboard and Shall Go Overboard.'"

10. For primary-source accounts regarding the disciplining of bondpeople within the trans-Atlantic slave trade, see Alexander Falconbridge, *An Account of the Slave Trade on the Coast of Africa* (London: J. Phillips, 1788); and Bernard Martin and Mark Spurrell, eds., *The Journal of a Slave Trader (John Newton) 1750–1754, with Newton's Thoughts upon the African Slave Trade* (London: Epworth Press, 1962). Teachers may also want to consider the tremendously valuable online database The Atlantic Slave Trade and Slave Life in the Americas, hosted through the University of Virginia. This database compiles close to 1,300 slavery images from primary-source materials (books, maps, historical artifacts) across the world in an online portal format to assist educators in visually reconstructing

the history of bondage for classroom and public discussions. This site can be accessed at: http://hitchcock.itc.virginia.edu/Slavery/search.html.

11. The medical history of the slave trade is still a curiously untapped area of scholarship and is deserving of new narratives. For further reading on this critical period in medical understanding generated aboard slave ships, see Philip Curtin, "Epidemiology and the Slave Trade," *Political Science Quarterly* 83, no. 2 (June 1968): 190–216; Richard Sheridan, "The Guinea Surgeons on the Middle Passage: The Provision of Medical Services in the British Slave Trade," *International Journal of African Historical Studies* 14, no. 4 (1981): 601–25; Richard H. Steckel and Richard A. Jensen. "New Evidence on the Causes of Slave and Crew Mortality in the Atlantic Slave Trade," *Journal of Economic History* 46 (1986): 57–77; Hartman, "Venus in Two Acts"; Mustakeem, "'She Must Go Overboard and Shall Go Overboard'"; and Mustakeem, "'I Never Have Such a Sickly Ship Before.'"

12. See Martin and Spurrell, *The Journal of a Slave Trader, John Newton, 1750–1754.* This published source is available in most public libraries, allowing teachers to deepen their discussion of slavery.

13. For a poetic visual of a slave auction, I use the poem "Bid 'Em In" by Oscar Brown; see https://www.youtube.com/watch?v=Tu3j7rPscpY. Additional sources often integrated into the course include the following: "A Prince among Slaves," Unity Productions Foundation, 2007; Christopher, *Slave Ship Sailors and Their Captive Cargoes*; Rediker, *The Slave Ship*; Mustakeem, "'I Never Have Such a Sickly Ship Before'"; Smallwood, *Saltwater Slavery*; Vincent Harding, *There Is a River: The Black Struggle for Freedom in America* (New York: Harcourt Brace Jovanovich, 1981); Mustakeem, "'She Must Go Overboard and Shall Go Overboard'"; Antonio T. Bly, "Crossing the Lake of Fire," *Journal of Negro History* 83, no. 3 (1998): 178–86; Thomas Foster, "The Sexual Abuse of Black Men under Slavery," *Journal of the History of Sexuality* 20 (September 2011): 445–64; Angela Davis, "Reflections on the Black Women's Roles in the Community of Slaves," *Massachusetts Review* 13 (Winter–Spring 1972): 81–100. On the theme of sexuality and slavery, see Trevor Burnard, *Mastery, Tyranny, and Desire: Thomas Thistlewood and His Slaves in the Anglo-Jamaican World* (Chapel Hill: University of North Carolina Press, 2003); chapter 3 of Daina Ramey Berry's *Swing the Sickle for the Harvest Is Ripe: Gender and Slavery in Antebellum Georgia* (Urbana-Champaign: University of Illinois Press, 2007; and chapter 3 in James Sweet's monograph *Recreating Africa: Culture, Kinship, and Religion in the African-Portuguese World, 1441–1807* (Chapel Hill: University of North Carolina Press, 2006).

14. Hallie Gerima, *Sankofa* (Myphedud Films, 1993); Octavia Butler, *Kindred* (Boston: Beacon Press, 1979); and Katrina Brown, Alla Kovgan, and Jude Ray, *Traces of the Trade: A Story from the Deep North* (California Newsreel, 2008).

15. See http://www.tavistalks.com/events/signature-events/america-i-am/america-i-am.

16. See http://www.thegriotmuseum.com.

17. Of the museum exhibitions my students interacted with, one was local and one was national. In many ways, the students' experience provides a glimpse into a shared learning opportunity afforded through public history. The digital expansion of information and, most of all, access is currently at a point of alteration and expansion, if merely because of the growth of virtual museum experiences online. Available time and monies will of course dictate how extensive such online exhibits can be; however, educators can still teach slavery through public history by keeping close tabs on offerings and even pressuring museum curators to provide an online portal so that everyday people can gain access to the past. Some relevant museums include not only the Griot Museum of Black History (http://www.thegriotmuseum.com/) but also the Liverpool International Slavery Museum (http://www.liverpoolmuseums.org .uk/ism/); the National Great Blacks in Wax Museum in Baltimore, Maryland (http://www.greatblacksinwax.org/); and the Charles H. Wright Museum of African American History in Detroit, Michigan (http://thewright.org/). To be sure, one could argue not only that the highly acclaimed "Slavery in New York" exhibit hosted at and through the New York Historical Society in 2005 symbol-ized public discourse on the history of slavery at a prestigious and nationally respected institution but also that the online exhibit generated by the NYHS similarly fostered much discussion. See Adele Oltman, "The Hidden History of Slavery in New York," *The Nation*, November 7, 2005, http://www.thenation .com/article/hidden-history-slavery-new-york. In many ways this exhibit signaled a new platform for historical transmission and historical exposure, but it could also point to the growth in universities' efforts to address the history of slavery through the establishment of centers devoted specifically to uncovering this shameful past. Examples include the Brown University Center for the Study of Slavery and Justice (http://www.brown.edu/initiatives/slavery-and-justice/) and the Gilder Lehrman Center for the Study of Slavery, Resist-ance, and Abolition (http://www.yale.edu/glc/index.htm). Most recently has come the news that the oldest black library in the United States, the Schomburg Center for Research in Black Culture, will also be establishing an intellectual space for scholars and the general public to delve into the history of the Atlantic slave trade. For further information, see Felicia R. Lee, "Schomburg to Create Center to Study Slave Trade" *New York Times*, June 12, 2014.

18. See Thomas Norman DeWolf, *Inheriting the Trade: A Northern Family Confronts Its Legacy as the Largest Slave Trading Dynasty* (Boston: Beacon Press, 2009).

19. On the faux "Slavery the Game" video game see http://www.youtube .com/watch?v=9HsVK92epoU; on John McCain's ties to slavery see http://

living.jdewperry.com/2008/10/mccains-family-ties-to-slavery/; on Michelle Bachmann's controversial view on the founding fathers and slavery see http://www.politico.com/news/stories/0611/57907.html; on Fox News' argument regarding bondpeople being armed during slavery see http://thinkprogress.org/politics/2013/01/11/1435261/pro-gun-advocate-arming-black-people-would-have-prevented-slavery/.

20. The two classroom assignments based largely on hip hop could easily be expanded to include other musical genres. One could encourage students to focus a project, for example, solely on reggae to explore how the history of Caribbean slavery is publicly remembered through music. One final suggestion would be the incorporation of poetry and rap. Most times I rely on Oscar Brown's 1970s poem "Bid 'Em In" (see https://www.youtube.com/watch?v=Tu3j7rPscpY) because of the contemporary poetic visual it provides of a slave auction and bidding for bondpeople, especially in reference to the breeding potential of black females. Going further, however, educators could easily encourage creativity by tasking students with coming up with a poem, skit, or rap acted out for their peers or even a larger audience. The success of this will depend heavily on a deeper understanding of the history of slavery and the slave trade; otherwise, it can easily run the risk of modern-day interpretations that conflate the past by equating contemporary discourses on twenty-first-century human trafficking with the often unimaginable circumstances anchored in the forcible sale and movement of African descended people during the legal slave trading era.

21. "'Slavery' Math Problems Fallout Prompts Ga. Teacher to Resign," http://www.huffingtonpost.com/2012/01/18/slavery-math-problems-pro_n_1214028.html; for more on the "Viccisitudes" Grenada sculpture see http://www.underwatersculpture.com/sculptures/viccisitudes/.

22. On the Lil Wayne controversy see http://www.xxlmag.com/news/2013/05/future-believes-lil-wayne-raised-awareness-of-emmett-till-with-controversial-lyric/; on the Kanye West album release see http://4resh.com/2013/05/29/la-bey-new-slaves.

Slavery and
the Northern Economy

CHRISTY CLARK-PUJARA

Over the past twenty years, scholars have placed increasing emphasis on recognizing the North's complicity in southern slaveholding. These efforts have challenged the concept of slavery as solely a southern institution, breaking down simplistic dichotomies of an antislavery North and a proslavery South. Yet, outside academic scholarship, public knowledge of the importance of the business of slavery in the northern financial and manufacturing systems is relatively slim. American slavery has become almost synonymous with the American South, disregarding the fact that northern colonists and citizens invested heavily in it. The history of slavery and freedom in North America is fundamentally skewed without a full accounting of the role that northerners played in the development and maintenance of slave societies in the West Indies and in the American South. The West Indian trade, the trans-Atlantic slave trade, and the textile industry were essential parts of the northern economy. Like other northerners, Rhode Island's farmers, tradesmen, merchants, and manufacturers played a central role promoting and maintaining the institution of slavery. Like other northerners, New Yorkers bought, sold, transported, and traded slave-grown products. Slaveholders throughout the Americas were dependent on the collective activities of northern colonies and states like Rhode Island and New York to provide them with markets, slaves, food, goods, and clothing.

The institution of slavery was integral to the northern economy from the late seventeenth century through the nineteenth century. In a mutually sustaining cycle across regions, white northerners invested and participated in the economy of slaveholding. The business of slavery included all economic activity directly related to the maintenance of slaveholding in the Americas, specifically the buying and selling of people, food, and goods. All the northern colonies and states invested and participated in business of slavery, but Rhode Islanders and New Yorkers were the most deeply entrenched and are therefore salient examples of how the northern economy depended on the institution of slavery. Rhode Islanders dominated the North American trade in African slaves, were dependent on a bilateral trade with West Indian planters, and manufactured slave-grown cotton. New York relied on the commodities trade, especially cotton, to become a financial center of the United States. From the colonial period through the antebellum era, the institution of slavery was part of—not apart from—the northern economy.

During the colonial and post-Revolutionary periods, the Atlantic slave trade and West Indian trades sparked secondary and subsidiary industries that employed a multitude of northerners, especially New Englanders.[1] By 1775 nearly 80 percent of New England exports went to the British West Indies and not to other parts of what was to become the United States.[2] The business of slavery allowed New England to become an economic powerhouse without ever relying on a staple crop.[3] The business of slavery continued to play a critical role in the northern economy following the American Revolution as the northern textile industry depended entirely on slave-picked cotton. In fact, the profits from the West Indian trade and the North American trade in African slaves funded the industrial revolution in the United States.[4]

The West Indian and Trans-Atlantic Slave Trades

Teaching about slavery and the northern economy requires acknowledging the many ways that individuals, towns, and entire regions depended on the institution of slavery. Northern merchants, tradesmen, and farmers supplied plantations throughout the Americas with basic necessities, which allowed planters to devote their energies to slave management and the production of crops: sugar in the West Indies, tobacco in the Chesapeake, and rice in the Coastal Low Country. Northern colonists planned and financed Atlantic slave-trading voyages; they brought slaves, food, lumber, and household goods to plantations in the West Indies and the American South. In return they received cash and molasses, the key ingredient for rum. This trade was essential to the survival and success of the northeastern colonies.[5]

Nowhere was this trade more important than in Rhode Island, in the cities of Newport and Providence and in the rural towns of Narragansett Country in southern Rhode Island. Farmers in the Narragansett Country put more than one thousand enslaved men and women to work cultivating food and raising livestock for West Indian trade. Enslaved people bred horses, cattle, and sheep; manufactured dairy products (butter and cheese); and grew small amounts of Indian corn, rye, hemp flax, and tobacco.[6] The West Indian trade then carried these products from Newport to the sugar islands.[7] The return route from the islands and the American South to Newport gave southern farmers and merchants a market for slave-produced goods: sugar, cotton, ginger, indigo, linen, woolen clothes, iron, and especially molasses. Rhode Island distilleries refined slave-produced molasses into rum—the colony's number one export—which Rhode Island traders then used to purchase slaves in the Atlantic slave trade.

In addition to their participation in the West Indian trade, Rhode Islanders dominated the North American trade in African slaves. Throughout the eighteenth century, local traders controlled more than 60 percent of the American trade in African slaves.[8] During the colonial period, Rhode Islanders sent 514 slave ships to the coast of West Africa; during the same period, the rest of the colonies combined sent only 183 slaving voyages (see table 1).[9] The southern colonies sent less than 1 percent of all the slave ships that left from North America. Throughout the first half of the eighteenth century, Rhode Island traders sold 66 percent of their slaves in the West Indies, 31 percent in North America, and 3 percent in South America.[10]

Numerous Rhode Islanders worked in the slave trade. Teachers can ask students to look at images of eighteenth-century ships and docks and think about the kinds of jobs made available by the slave-trading industry. Moreover, what subsidiary industries developed out of the Atlantic slave trade? Preparing even the smallest sloop or ship required a small army of laborers, businessmen, and tradesmen. Sail makers, carpenters, joiners, riggers, caulkers, and painters built ships. Distillers fermented molasses into rum, and coopers made barrels to transport the liquor that was traded for slaves. Insurance underwriters, warehouse clerks, and city trade officials kept the records of the trade. Scores

Table 1. Slave ships that disembarked from British North American colonies (Number of slaves transported to the Americas)

	1701–25	1726–50	1751–75
Rhode Island	8 (948)	123 (16,195)	383 (41,581)
New England (excluding RI)	4 (363)	36 (4,575)	82 (11,485)
New York	4 (355)	3 (407)	28 (3,318)
Carolinas	1 (48)	3 (415)	17 (2,195)
Virginia	1 (144)	2 (247)	2 (667)
Total	18 (1,858)	167 (21,839)	512 (59,246)

of unskilled laborers loaded and unloaded slave ships.[11] Sailors manned the vessels, and slave-trading voyages required additional crew to control and manage the "human cargo." The sloop *Adventure*, for example, sailed out of Newport in 1773 with eleven men, twice the number needed for a sloop bound for commodities trade with other colonies or England.[12]

Slave-trading voyages also helped Rhode Island merchants sell their goods. The *Adventure* left Rhode Island with 24,380 gallons of rum, enough to purchase several dozen slaves. Enslaved women cost an average of 190 gallons each, and men averaged 220 gallons. *Adventure* reached Africa in five weeks, but it took the captain four months of cruising to acquire sixty-two slaves, along with rice, pepper, palm oil, and gold dust. Fifty-eight slaves survived the trans-Atlantic voyage, and they were sold in Grenada for between £35 and £39. The ship's owners received a 5 percent return on their investment.[13] Such voyages were common in Rhode Island. Slave-trading voyages produced profits of from 2 to 10 percent; most voyages yielded returns of 5 or 6 percent, and while these profit margins may seem low by contemporary investment standards, investments in the Atlantic slave trade "were less risky and more liquid (that is capital could be extracted) and needed less time to garner returns than all other forms of possible investment in the eighteenth century."[14]

Many Rhode Island merchants were also traders and slaveholders. The slaveholding merchant and slave trader Aaron Lopez was one of Rhode Island's most successful businessmen. Teachers can use the example of Aaron Lopez to demonstrate the multiple ways in which

Table 2. Lopez-Rivera slaving voyages

Name of Ship	Captain	Date of Departure and Return	Ports where slaves were sold
Brig *Grayhound*	William Pinneger	November 2, 1761–January 7, 1763	Charleston, South Carolina
Sloop *Spry*	William Pinneger	July 16, 1764–May 22, 1766	Barbados, Jamaica, and New York
Brig *Africa*	Abraham All	May 3, 1765–July 11, 1766	Kingston
Sloop *Betsey*	Nathaniel Briggs	July 22, 1765–August 21, 1766	Kingston
Brig *Sally*	Nathaniel Briggs	August 21, 1766–July 1767	St. Kitts
Brig *Africa*	Abraham All	October 20, 1766–January 9, 1768	Kingston
Brig *Hannah*	Nathaniel Briggs	May 3, 1768–May 4, 1769	South Carolina and Barbados
Sloop *Mary*	William English	June 4, 1770–Spring 1771	Barbados
Ship *Cleopatra*	Nathaniel Briggs	July 1770–January 11, 1771	Barbados
Ship *Cleopatra*	Nathaniel Briggs	June 16, 1771–May 27, 1772	Barbados
Brig *Ann*	William English	November 27, 1772–Winter 1773	Kingston
Ship *Africa*	Nathaniel Briggs	April 22, 1773–July 24, 1774	Jamaica
Ship *Cleopatra*	James Bourk	June 30, 1773–August 1774	Jamaica
Brig *Ann*	William English	Spring 1774–March 1775	Jamaica

northern merchants' careers intersected with slavery. Lopez began his career as a partner in a candle-making business with his brother Moses Lopez and his uncle Jacob Rodriguez Rivera. Lopez and Rivera employed slaves to render whale head matter for spermaceti candles.[15] In 1761 Lopez sent out the first of his slaving voyages, carrying flour from Philadelphia, beef from New York, and, most important, 15,281 gallons of rum from local distilleries. Over a fourteen-year period Lopez was responsible for transporting an estimated 1,116 slaves from West Africa to the West Indies and the American South. Between 1761 and 1774, Lopez sent fourteen slave ships to the west coast of Africa (see table 2), a fraction of the more than two hundred voyages he sponsored between 1760 and 1776.[16] So, although Lopez was primarily involved in intercolonial trade, not slave trading, it was the West Indian trade that sustained his enterprises by providing him with molasses—the key ingredient for rum, his leading good. In others words, while most of Lopez's trading business was concentrated on American imports and exports, it was his trade with the West Indian sugar islands that sustained his continental business because the rum he bartered was made out of West Indian molasses—a by-product of slave-produced sugar.

The Textile Industry

New Yorkers, like Rhode Islanders, were invested in slaveholding and the business of slavery in the Americas; Rhode Islanders transported slaves, while New Yorkers transported and sold slave-grown goods. Colonists and citizens in the North could not produce a profit or sustain themselves by relying solely on agricultural enterprises; consequently, they turned to commerce. Conversely, colonists and citizens in the South devoted nearly all of their efforts to staple crop production. Few southerners imported slaves, processed the raw material produced by enslaved people, or transported the finished product. White northerners and southerners needed each other; their economic success depended on cooperation. The institution of slavery in the Americas required a proslavery consensus among most whites— northern and southern.

By being mindful of slavery's importance in the North, instructors can incorporate discussions of the institution across a broad spectrum of content. For example, New York City, one of the biggest and richest cities in the world, owed much of its establishment, rise, and wealth to slavery. In 1621 the Dutch West India Company "settled" New Amsterdam (present-day Manhattan) and five years later imported eleven African slaves. These "company slaves" were put to work building Fort Amsterdam. They also "built roads, cut timber and firewood, cleared land, and burned limestone and oyster shells to make the lime used in outhouses and burying the dead." In other words, they performed essential labor, building both the settlement and its infrastructure.[17]

New York's early dependence on slavery continued as the city matured. In the nineteenth century, New Yorkers' wealth was tied to southern slave labor. By the mid-nineteenth century, American slaves were growing cotton for the world, and New Yorkers were buying, selling, and shipping it. By 1860 cotton represented more than half of all US exports. Lower Manhattan was populated with cotton brokers, bankers, merchants, shippers, auctioneers, and insurers who profited from that export.[18] New York banks extended massive lines of credit to plantation owners so that they could buy seed, farming equipment, and slaves. Southern farmers insured their plantations and slaves through firms in the city. New York was also home to water and rail transportation companies that shipped cotton from the South to the North and abroad.

The cotton trade allowed for an array of investments in the city; hundreds of New York businessmen made their fortunes in cotton, and, in turn, they made New York the commercial and financial center of the United States. Among the most famous cotton businessmen were the Lehman brothers. The three brothers were cotton brokers in Montgomery, Alabama, before they moved to New York and helped to establish the New York Cotton Exchange. Alexander Stewart, a cotton merchant, opened the country's first department store in New York in 1848.[19]

While New York was center of the cotton trade, New England was the epicenter of the textile industry. The textile industry represents an additional link between the economies of the North and the South. Over the nineteenth century, the textile industry transformed northern towns. In 1816 large-scale textile factories employed 1 percent of the New England workforce; thirty-six years later, in 1852 the industry employed 14 percent of the labor force. By 1860 New England was home to 472 cotton mills.[20] These textile factories were often the sole employers in towns throughout the region and were a direct link between New England wealth and southern slaveholding.[21] Enslaved

African Americans in the southern United States produced the bulk of the world's cotton and almost all of the cotton consumed by the US textile industry during the antebellum era (1820–65). In fact, abolitionists described the business relationship between northern industrialists and southern planters as the union of "the Lords of the Lash and the Lords of the Loom," because the textile industry was dependent on slave-grown cotton.

Although it was a small segment of the textile industry as a whole, the kersey industry is a salient example of the cooperation between the northern and southern economics and is a symbol of southern ante-bellum slavery—a symbol manufactured in the North. Made in part from cotton picked by enslaved people, "negro cloth" was a colloquial term for kersey, a cheap, coarse, blended cotton-wool material made especially to minimize the cost of clothing enslaved African Americans.[22] Only enslaved people wore kersey; even the poorest whites did not. For enslaved African Americans, the kersey industry produced literally the fabric of their lives.

Rhode Islanders relied on southern slaves not only as a source of cotton but also as a market for "negro cloth." Nearly every northern state manufactured kersey, but Rhode Island mills were substantially invested in its production. Between 1800 and 1870, eighty-four kersey mills opened in Rhode Island, one at almost every river fall. By 1850, 79 percent of all Rhode Island textile mills manufactured kersey—the highest percentage in the United States. Twenty-two Rhode Island towns and cities manufactured kersey for more than sixty years, and more than eighty Rhode Island families owned part of a kersey mill during the antebellum era. In comparison, only about one-third of all the cloth produced at the Lowell mills in Massachusetts was destined for south-ern plantations.[23]

The Hazard family represents a useful example of the connections between Rhode Island textile manufacturers and the slaveholding South. Rowland Hazard Sr. and his sons, Rowland Jr., Isaac, and Jonathan, ran one of Rhode Island's most successful kersey mills manufacturing clothing for enslaved African Americans from 1810 to 1855. Hazard Sr. purchased a half interest in a mill on the Saugatuck River in 1802. Three years later, he acquired a carding machine and opened the Narragansett Cotton Manufacturing Company. At first, Hazard manufactured hand-spun gingham and linen. When he had a difficult time competing against other regional mills, he abandoned gingham and linen for kersey. The Hazard brothers transformed their father's small mill into a major operation supplying plantations throughout the South. For twenty-seven years they provided southern slaveholders with clothing, blankets, and shoes for enslaved people.

The Hazard brothers courted southern slaveholders aggressively and counted them among their friends. The letters that circulated among the Hazard brothers, their sales agents, and their clients reveal the close relationships the brothers developed with slaveholders and illuminates their unfailing commitment to a family business that depended on slave labor. For example, Isaac Hazard was introduced to the "kersey" market in South Carolina by the planter John Potter. Potter owned close to four hundred slaves and espoused the benevolent nature of slaveholding. Isaac accepted Potter's world view, writing to his brother Rowland Jr. that southern slaves "do not do a quarter so much work as the northern negroes or whites."[24] The Hazards eagerly sought out advice on how to improve the production of goods for the southern market. In 1829 Isaac Hazard inquired of a plantation owner, "Could we serve you in anyway [sic] it would give us pleasure and shall be pleased to have your views on the subject of manufacturing materials for plantations either as clothing or utensils, wherever anything may present itself to your views as mutually beneficial to the North and South."[25] The brothers even commented on the management styles of the planters. Isaac Hazard informed a sales agent: "We got an order today from J. H. Couper for 2900 yds of milled double Kersey. . . . The high character of J. H. Couper as a Planter and careful human manager of Negroes is well known."[26] The Hazard brothers admired Couper, who owned a cotton plantation in the Georgia Sea Islands. The comment on his human management skills indicates that northern textile manufacturers, like their southern clients, accepted slavery in the South as a given. By developing personal relationships with planters and catering to their needs, the Hazards secured a place for themselves in the kersey industry, as exemplified in the following letter from a distributor in New York: "The prospect of a very good business season here, has become quite certain. Many of our customers are already in, large supplies will be required. If you have any parcels of goods on hand, and you will send them to us, we make no doubt we shall be able to make very satisfactory account sales for you. We should be pleasured to receive a few bales of your Negro Cloth as we know they will do well."[27] Hazard kersey became a sought-after commodity. One customer wrote, "[T]he kersey you sent me wear so much better than any we have had before, that I want some more . . . you will please send me about one Hundred yards of the basest of those you sent me last year." The brothers also advertised directly to their customers. An 1836 advertisement in a New Orleans paper described their products and services to local planters. It worked. The Hazards were so successful that they sometimes had to outsource some of their orders.[28]

The Hazards' Narragansett Cotton Manufacturing Company, later renamed Peace Dale Manufacturing, was the lifeblood of its village. In 1823 Peace Dale village had just thirty residents, five houses, and one store. By 1830 Peace Dale Manufacturing employed eighty-one people, and by 1860 there were one hundred employees. In 1823, the mill was worth $6,000. Twenty-four years later it had grown to be worth $140,000. After a 1855 fire at the mill, the brothers switched to producing shawls and cashmere, which they had been producing in small amounts since 1844.[29] The brothers did not try to rebuild their kersey business, most likely because of the abundance of kersey mills in the state and the growing regional divide over slavery.

Students should learn that slaveholding and the business of slavery tied northern families' wealth to slaveholding for multiple generations. For example, the Hazard family began as small slaveholders who later invested in the business of slavery and then parlayed those investments into other businesses. In the 1690s Thomas Hazard II (1660–1746) purchased a large tract of land from the war-ravaged Narragansett Indians in rural Rhode Island. He and his son Robert (1689–1762) set their slaves to work cultivating grains and raising livestock for the southern and West Indian markets.[30] Although, Robert's son Thomas (1720–98) became a Quaker and denounced slaveholding, remaining committed to abolitionism even after his family threatened to take away his inheritance, the family's entrenched interest in southern markets led Thomas's son Rowland Hazard (1763–1835) to reestablished the family's connection with the business of slavery.[31] Rowland Hazard Sr. financed a mercantile firm in Charleston, South Carolina, that was primarily involved in trade with the West Indies. In 1802 Rowland Hazard Sr. used the capital from this venture to begin milling cotton and manufacturing textiles, eventually turning to the manufacture and distribution of kersey. Decades later, his sons used the profits they had made from the kersey industry to open a general store in Providence and to buy part ownerships in the Narragansett Pier and Wisconsin Central Railroads.

The business of slavery allowed the Hazards to invest in other lucrative businesses. To help students discover powerful examples like these, it is important to let them peruse primary sources and reach their own conclusions.

Resources for Teaching Slavery and the Northern Economy

For students to grasp white northerners' investments in the business of slaveholding, they must recognize that slaveholding was socially accepted, legally sanctioned, and widely practiced in the North. When the numbers of enslaved people in the North declined precipitously after the American Revolution, white northerners remained heavily invested in the business of slavery. It can be difficult to explain how and why northerners were so entrenched in the business of slavery because many students will have preconceived notions of the pre–Civil War North as the land of freedom, the antithesis of the slaveholding South, and some students may believe the pervasive narrative of the post-Revolutionary northern abolition movement. Abolitionists, those who called for an immediate or eventual end to slavery, were a minority in the North. Although the vast majority of white northerners opposed slavery's expansion into the new western territories, in the post-Revolutionary and antebellum periods most northerners were ambivalent about the abolition of slavery.[32]

To replace traditional narratives, teachers need to incorporate discussion of slavery across the chronology and geography of American history. Acknowledging the central role that northerners played in the maintenance of the institution of slavery throughout the Americas is essential to fully unpacking American slavery and the legacies it has left. Using the examples of the Lopez-Rivera slaving logs discussed earlier, students can be taught that in the colonial period the Atlantic slave and West Indian trades undergirded many local economies. By the eve of the Civil War, northern businesses, including insurance firms, railroad and shipping companies, and banks, depended almost entirely on slave-grown products, especially cotton, and on the cotton trade.[33] To understand the role that the plantation economy played in both the northern and the southern United States, students need contextualized definitions of the following: plantations, the West Indian trade, and the trans-Atlantic slave trade, as well as exposure to primary evidence of the connection between the northern economy and the institution of slavery.

The plantation was an agricultural enterprise at the center of the Atlantic economy, an unprecedented international economic system of labor management, capital, and investment. The mature plantation complex had seven major characteristics: (1) most of the labor was forced, consisting of bonded people and slaves; (2) outside the post-colonial plantations in the United States, plantations' populations were not self-sustaining; (3) plantations were capitalistic enterprises; (4) plantations had managers and supervisors overseeing fifty to several hundred workers; (5) plantations had federal features—the right to punish and control movement; (6) crops were grown to supply a distant market; and (7) outside the antebellum South the political control over the system lay in another continent and society.

The first plantations emerged in the Mediterranean (eleventh to thirteenth centuries) and the system later moved to the West African islands (fourteenth and fifteenth centuries). These early plantations focused on sugar cultivation and depended on European, African, and Middle Eastern bond laborers and slaves. The plantation system then moved to the Caribbean, South America, and North America (sixteenth to eighteenth centuries), where the climate led to more profitable and successful sugar production. Eric Kimball's and Laird Bergad's essays in this volume provide a more complete discussion of the evolution of plantations in the Americas. As the plantation economy began to take hold on islands and in continental colonial societies, planters grew to depend on the Atlantic slave trade for labor.[34]

The trans-Atlantic slave trade and the West Indian trade involved linked American and European routes that supplied European states and their American colonies with wealth and labor. The trans-Atlantic slave trade was a complex, extraordinary, and unprecedented movement of peoples and capital. Sowande' Mustakeem's essay in this volume includes more information on the trans-Atlantic slave trade. Although North Americans were late and minor players in the Atlantic slave trade as a whole, the West Indian trade was the lifeblood of the New England economy.[35] New Englanders were the essential middlemen in the Atlantic economy, supplying the sugar islands with food, household goods, and slaves. In return, they received cash, molasses, sugar, wine, and tobacco for both home consumption and re-export to England.[36]

After learning these contextualized definitions, students will better recognize how northerners relied on an economic system that promoted a white master class and subjugated people of African descent. By including discussions of the trans-Atlantic and West Indian legs of the familiar Triangle Trade, teachers can emphasize how slavery enriched specific regions and individuals in the North. The economic history of places like Rhode Island reveals how northerners were centrally involved in developing and maintaining of the institution of slavery.[37] Slave labor and the businesses of slavery in the northern colonies supported the development and maintenance of slave societies in the Americas.[38] This reality points to the necessity of including the roles of northern colonists and citizens when teaching the history of slavery in North America. The stories of the Champlin brothers and Aaron Lopez demonstrate how slave trading employed large numbers of Rhode Islanders and enriched its wealthiest merchants. The wealth and success of the Hazard brothers highlight how manufacturers supported and profited from the institution of slavery.

The Trans-Atlantic Slave Trade Database, the report of the Brown University Steering Committee on Slavery and Justice, and the African Burial Ground in New York City are three great tools that allow students to learn about the centrality of the institution of slavery in the North. These online sources clearly highlight the role of slavery in the northern economy and explicitly detail how individuals and families used slave labor and the business of slavery to create personal wealth. These types of sources provide students with concrete examples of how the institution of slavery led to wealth for many northern Americans and for the country at large.

The Trans-Atlantic Slave Trade Database collects the records of more than thirty-five thousand slaving voyages.[39] Students can use a number of variables to search the database, such as date of voyage, ship's country of origin, place where voyage began and ended, principal place of slave purchase and sale, vessel name, captain name, date, mortality rates, and percentages of men, women, and children. This type of source is particularly good at conveying the sheer magnitude of the slave trade and its global impact. Students could do region-based searches (places where voyages began, comparing, for example, Rhode Island to New York to South Carolina to England to Spain to the Netherlands) to get a sense of what colonies, states, and nations were most invested in the slave trade. Students can also search mortality rates for men, women, and children and consider whether and why there were demographic differences among these groups. This line of inquiry could elicit discussion about how the experience of slavery was different for different groups of people—men were usually held below deck, while women and children were often were kept above deck. There is a good discussion of the drawbacks of both situations in Marcus Rediker's *The Slave Ship: A Human History* and the introduction to Deborah Gray White's *Ar'n't I a Woman?*[40]

The report of the Brown University Steering Committee on Slavery and Justice, released in 2006, provides an accounting of the institution's early connections to slavery and to the slave trade in particular, a surprising revelation for a school that has long celebrated its abolitionist founders.[41] The report was commissioned by Ruth Simmons, the first black president and the first female president of an Ivy League university, and it confirmed what many black residents of Rhode Island had claimed for generations—that Brown University was built on the backs of black slaves. In the twenty-first century, Brown, like all the other Ivy League schools, is reckoning with a history that administrators, alumni, students, and Americans know little about.[42] The Lopez and Rivera company, one of the largest slave trading firms in New England, donated the wood for the college's first buildings. Some early donors honored their monetary pledges to the college by providing the labor of their slaves for a set number of days. Furthermore, the college's early Board of Fellows and Trustees was populated with slave traders, merchants who profited from slaveholding, and slave-trading professionals. The report details the business history of the Brown family and reproduces dozens of primary documents from the Brown family business. The committee published the report online in its entirety, including scanned images of original business records from the Brown family's candle, irons works, and shipping companies. The website also has community responses to the report in the form of newspaper editorials, opinion pieces, and local forum minutes. This type of source provides students with a rare opportunity to discuss the role of slavery in the northern economy and how our understanding of that role affects the present. There is a link to documents from a particularly ill-fated slave-trading voyage undertaken by the Browns in 1764: the voyage of the slave ship *Sally*. The documents include the letters, invoices, legal documents, ship's manifests, and trade books and memoranda. One of the inventories lists the tools, foodstuffs, medicine, and various weapons that were loaded onto the ship. The ship's account book lists when and where slaves were bought along the African coast as well as when and why enslaved people died during the Middle Passage. These types of documents can cultivate discussion about the dangers and the deadly realities of the Atlantic slave trade.

The African Burial Ground in New York City is among the most important urban archaeological projects undertaken in the United States.[43] In 1991 construction workers excavating land for a new federal building in Lower Manhattan discovered the skeletal remains of more than four hundred men, women, and children. Investigation revealed that during the seventeenth and eighteenth centuries enslaved and free Africans were buried in a six-acre burial ground outside the boundaries of the settlement of New Amsterdam. Over the centuries, the unmarked cemetery was covered by development and landfill. Today the site is a National Monument featuring a memorial commemorating and communicating the story of the African Burial Ground, a reminder that Africans and African Americans labored to build America's greatest city. The skeletal remains, housed at Howard University, reveal the hard labor and short lives of America's northern slaves. The Burial Ground is also a poignant reminder of how history can be lost. The rediscovery of New York's African Burial Ground redresses such loses. The "burial sheets," which are available online (via a "Learn about the Park/Education" link), are particularly engaging documents. The detailed burial sheets are summaries of what was found in specific graves. For example, the archeological notes indicate age, injuries, and sometimes cause of death; they also include materials that individuals were buried, such as pipes or beads. A discussion of the conditions of the human remains along with the types of artifacts that were buried along with the bodies can help students think about the enslaved as individuals.

These sources are vivid entryways to the ongoing contemporary debates about how the institution of slavery has shaped both the economy and race relations in the United States, as well as how we as a nation choose to commemorate or ignore its impact—North and South.

NOTES

1. See Elaine Forman Crane, *A Dependent People: Newport, Rhode Island, in the Revolutionary Era* (New York: Fordham University Press, 1985).

2. See Martin H. Blatt and David Roediger, *The Meaning of Slavery in the North* (New York: Garland, 1998); Anne Farrow, Joel Lang, and Jenifer Frank,

Complicity: How the North Promoted, Prolonged, and Profited from Slavery (New York: Ballantine Books, 2005), 49–50.

3. Small amounts of tobacco were grown in Rhode Island and Connecticut. Bernard Bailyn, "Slavery and Population Growth in Colonial New England," in Peter Temin, ed., *Engines of Enterprise: An Economic History of New England* (Cambridge, MA: Harvard University Press, 2000), 254–55; Gavin Wright, *Slavery and American Economic Development* (Baton Rouge: Louisiana State University Press, 2006), 14.

4. See Wright, *Slavery and American Economic Development.*

5. See Bernard Bailyn, *The New England Merchants in the Seventeenth Century* (Cambridge, MA: Harvard University Press, 1955); John McCusker and Russell Menard, *The Economy of British America, 1607–1789* (Chapel Hill: University of North Carolina Press, 1985); and John McCusker and Kenneth Morgan, eds., *Early Modern Atlantic Economy* (New York: Cambridge University Press, 2000).

6. Robert K. Fitts, *Inventing New England's Slave Paradise: Master/Slave Relations in Eighteenth Century Narragansett, Rhode Island* (New York: Garland, 1998); William Davis Miller, *The Narragansett Planters* (Worchester: American Antiquarian Society, 1934), 4, 20–41.

7. The sugar islands include Antigua, Jamaica, Barbados, Guadalupe, St. Thomas, Marincio, St. Lucia, St. Christopher, Surinam, and the Bay of Honduras.

8. Jay Coughtry, *The Notorious Triangle: Rhode Island and the African Slave Trade, 1700–1807* (Philadelphia: Temple University Press, 1981), 25; Farrow et al., *Complicity*, 95–119 and 53–54.

9. David Eltis et al., *The Trans-Atlantic Slave Trade: A Database on CD-ROM* (Cambridge: Cambridge University Press, 1999).

10. See Coughtry, *The Notorious Triangle.*

11. See Crane, *A Dependent People.*

12. The sloop was owned by Christopher Champlin (majority owner) and George Champlin. The Champlin family owned a large estate in the Narragansett, but they were also involved in commerce—and particularly slave trading.

13. The article is based on the original manuscript in the library of George L. Shepley, with notes and introduction by Professor Verner W. Crane of Brown University. Verner W. Crane, "A Rhode Island Slaver: Trade Book of the Sloop Adventure, 1773–1774" (1922), Shepley Library, Providence, Rhode Island.

14. Herbert Klein, *The Atlantic Slave Trade: New Approaches to the Americas* (Cambridge: Cambridge University Press, 2010), 100.

15. Stanley F. Chet, *Lopez of Newport: Colonial American Merchant Prince* (Detroit: Wayne State University Press, 1970), 24–30.

16. Virginia Bever Platt, "'And Don't Forget the Guinea Voyage': The Slave Trade of Aaron Lopez of Newport," *William and Mary Quarterly* 32, no. 4 (1975): 601–4, 608.

17. Leslie Harris, *In the Shadow of Slavery: African American in New York City, 1626–1863* (Chicago: University of Chicago Press, 2003), 13–20.

18. R. W. Bailey, "Those Valuable People, the Africans," in Blatt and Roediger, *The Meaning of Slavery in the North*, 13. Farrow et al., *Complicity*, 4–10.

19. Farrow et al., *Complicity*, 4–23.

20. Jacqueline Jones, *American Work: Black and White Labor* (New York: W.W. Norton, 1998), 160, and Bailey, "Those Valuable People, the Africans," 13.

21. Mary Blewett, *Constant Turmoil: The Politics of Industrial Life in Nineteenth-Century New England* (Amherst: University of Massachusetts Press, 2000); Jonathan Prude, *The Coming of Industrial Order: Town and Factory Life in Rural Massachusetts, 1810–1860* (Cambridge: Cambridge University Press, 1983); and Steve Dunwell, *The Run of the Mill* (Boston: David R. Godine, 1978).

22. Frederick Douglass was one of the first people to provide a detailed description of "negro cloth" and how it was allotted. Frederick Douglass, *Narrative of the Life of Frederick Douglass: An American Slave Written by Himself with an Introduction by Peter J. Gomes* (New York: Signet, 1997), 26.

23. Rowland Hazard Sr. was the first American to employ water power for carding wool and operating power looms. Tony Horowitz, "La Chanson de Roland: A Short History of Peace Dale Rhode Island" (student paper, January 23, 1977), Rhode Island Historical Society, Providence. Myron O. Stachiw, "'For the Sake of Commerce': Slavery, Antislavery, and Northern Industry," in Blatt and Roediger, *The Meaning of Slavery in the North*, 33–36.

24. Rowland Gibson Hazard to Isaac Peace Hazard, January 24, 1828 (Charleston), in the Isaac P. Hazard Papers, MSS 483, sg 5, Box 1, Folder 5, Rhode Island Historical Society Library, Providence.

25. Isaac Peace Hazard to J. H. Couper, Esq., January 5, 1829, in the Isaac P. Hazard Papers, MSS 483, sg 12, Box 1, Folder 26, Rhode Island Historical Society Library, Providence.

26. Isaac Peace Hazard to William Ravenel, July 9, 1829, in the Peace Dale Manufacturing Company Records, Baker Library Historical Collections, Harvard Business School, Boston.

27. Pickering Kendall Pope to Isaac Peace Hazard, August 1, 1825, in the Isaac P. Hazard Papers, MSS 483 sg 12, Box 1, Rhode Island Historical Society Library, Providence.

28. Winder Grouch (Cheneyville, Louisiana) to Rowland Gibson Hazard, April 26, 1840, in the Peace Dale Collection, Case 12, Folder 4, Baker Library Historical Collections, Harvard Business School, Boston; Isaac Peace Hazard to J. H. Couper, Esq., January 5, 1829, in the Isaac P. Hazard Papers, MSS 483, sg 12, Box 1, Rhode Island Historical Society Library, Providence; Susan Oba, "Mostly Made, Especially for This Purpose, in Providence, R.I.: The Rhode Island Negro Cloth Industry" (honors thesis, Brown University, 2006), 54–58.

29. "Rowland and Mary (Peace) Hazard Papers," Historical Note MSS 483, sg 4, Rhode Island Historical Society Library, Providence. See Caroline E. Robinson, *The Hazard Family of Rhode Island; Being a Genealogy and History of the*

Descendants of Thomas Hazard, with Sketches of the Worthies of the Family, and Anecdotes Illustrative of their Traits and also of the Times in which they Lived (Boston: Printed for the Author, 1896), 77–78. Horowitz, "La Chanson de Roland," 4–6. Also see "Historic and Architectural Resources of South Kingstown, Rhode Island: A Preliminary Report" (Providence: Rhode Island Historical Preservation Commission, 1984). The Peace Dale Manufacturing Company, Mss 446, 1742–1919, Baker Library Historical Collections, Harvard Business School, Boston.

30. The Narragansett Country, located along the southeastern coast of Rhode Island, was conducive to grazing large livestock and small-scale agriculture. Fitts, *Inventing New England's Slave Paradise*, 113, 121–40; Rhett S. Jones, "Plantation Slavery in the Narragansett Country of Rhode Island, 1690–1790: A Preliminary Study," *Plantation Society* 2, no. 2 (1986): 157; Irving H. Bartlett, *From Slave to Citizen: The Story of the Negro in Rhode Island* (Providence: Urban League of Greater Providence, 1954), 10; Christian M. McBurney, "The Rise and Decline of the South Kingstown Planters, 1660–1783" (honors thesis, Brown University, 1981), 55, 221–38; Miller, *The Narragansett Planters*, 20–41; Philip D. Curtin, *The Rise and Fall of the Plantation Complex: Essays in Atlantic History*, 2nd ed. (Cambridge: University of Cambridge Press, 1998).

31. Caroline Hazard, *Thomas Hazard son of Robt, Call'd College Tom: A Study of Life in Narragansett in the XVIIIth Century, by his Grandson's Granddaughter* (Cambridge, MA: Riverside Press, 1893).

32. David Grimsted, *American Mobbing, Toward Civil War* (New York: Oxford University Press, 1998), 34. See John Wood Sweet, "'More Than Tears': The Ordeal of Abolition in Revolutionary New England," *Explorations in Early American Culture* 5 (2001): 151–52. See also Leonard Richards, *Gentlemen of Property and Standing: Anti-Abolition Mobs in Jacksonian America* (New York: Oxford University Press, 1970).

33. Farrow et al., *Complicity*, 4–10; Bailey, "Those Valuable People, the Africans," 13.

34. Curtin, *The Rise and Fall of the Plantation Complex*, 1–28.

35. See Herbert Klein, *The Atlantic Slave Trade* (Cambridge: Cambridge University Press, 1998).

36. Margaret Ellen Newell, "The Birth of New England in the Atlantic Economy," in Peter Temin, ed., *Engines of Enterprise: An Economic History of New England* (Cambridge, MA: Harvard University Press, 2000), 11–69.

37. Farrow et al., *Complicity*, 49–50.

38. Temin, *Engines of Enterprise*, 253–59; John McCusker, *Rum and the American Revolution: The Rum Trade and the Balance of Payments of the Thirteen Continental Colonies* (New York: Garland, 1989); McCusker and Morgan, *Early Modern Atlantic Economy*; McCusker and Menard, *Economy of British America*.

39. See slavevoyages.org/.

40. Marcus Rediker, *The Slave Ship: A Human History* (New York: Viking, 2007); Deborah Gray White, *Ar'n't I a Woman? Female Slaves in the Plantation South* (New York: W. W. Norton, 1985).

41. See brown.edu/Research/Slavery_Justice/.

42. See Craig Steven Wilder, *Ebony and Ivy: Race, Slavery, and the Troubled History of America's Universities* (New York: Bloomsburg Press, 2013). In 2002, Yale University held a conference titled "Yale, New Haven, and American Slavery" to discuss local ties to slavery. The conference coincided with the release of the Hartford *Courant*'s special issue "Complicity: How Connecticut Changed Itself to Slavery"; three years later the same writers published *Complicity: How the North Promoted, Prolonged, and Profited from Slavery*. See http://news.yale.edu/2002/09/06/yale-new-haven-and-american-slavery-conference; Farrow et al., *Complicity*. In 2011 Harvard and Brown held a joint conference to investigate the history of capitalism and slavery in the region: http://www.brown.edu/web/slaveryconf/. And in 2013 Princeton University launched the Princeton and Slavery Project to investigate direct and indirect links between the university and the institution of slavery: http://dailyprince tonian.com/news/2013/10/seminar-explores-u-s-little-known-connection-to-slavery/; https://www.h-net.org/jobs/job_display.php?id=46703.

43. See http://www.nps.gov/afbg/index.htm.

Northern Slavery and Its Legacies

Still a New (and Unwelcome?) Story

JOANNE POPE MELISH

Teaching about northern slavery and emancipation remains an uphill battle. Almost everyone—students, teachers, the general public—comes to this history with the same set of assumptions about what American slavery was, where it was, how it ended, and what it meant. Collectively, these ideas constitute a sort of comprehensive mythology of American history and the place of slavery (and race) in it. This is a Manichean vision of the first 250 years of American history—the North as a white bastion of freedom, the South as a realm of black unfreedom and white tyranny. Most students believe that the only connection between the northern states and slavery was their opposition to it; northerners helped escaped southern slaves flee to freedom via the Underground Railroad. When sectional war finally erupted, sturdy northern soldiers (imagined to be white, until the movie *Glory* integrated the Union army) marched south to end slavery for good.

I used the term "still unwelcome" with a question mark in the title of this essay, but in fact the responses I have received when I have taught and lectured on northern slavery and the origins of northern racism in various venues around the country suggest that it is bewildering to many, unwelcome to some, and *too* welcome to others. While there have been exceptions, generally speaking white northern audiences are shocked and dismayed, while white southern audiences are often relieved and occasionally gleeful ("See? It wasn't just us!"); white audiences in other parts of the country are simply interested. Black northern audiences, on the other hand, find this history affirming. Most of them have had very vivid experiences of racist behavior on the part of some classmates and neighbors and found them inexplicable in the face of the relentless narrative of white northern benevolence they often have found in the classroom. Most black southern audiences are surprised but see this history as more evidence that African Americans are truly one people who share a common history of struggle.

What are the key elements in the mythology of the American North as a bastion of white freedom, how can we dispel them, and why is that important?

While many students and teachers remain convinced that the northern states had no connection whatsoever to the domestic use of slaves, most have learned that New England was involved in the Atlantic slave trade. They tend to see this involvement, however, as brief and tangential, a matter of serving as the middleman in someone else's nasty business. When I explain the extent of this involvement, they are shocked. They are even more shocked when I tell them that the first Africans were brought to the northern colonies in exchange for members of another group already enslaved there—Native people.

The first slaves in the New England colonies were not Africans but Indians, who became enslaved in a variety of ways. Before 1700 most Indians entered servitude by becoming prisoners of war. In 1637, at the end of the Pequot War, and again after King Philip's War in 1675, Massachusetts and Rhode Island authorities held mass auctions of Pequot, Narragansett, and Wampanoag captives. English colonists also kidnapped and enslaved or sold Indian noncombatants, from friendly tribes as well as foes. A third route to servitude for New England Indians was conviction for debt or crime; Indians who were unable to pay fines and claims were frequently sentenced to long terms of service. By 1700 Indians were serving in English colonial households throughout New England and the northern colonies.[1]

But Indians captured in the Pequot War and the Seven Years War proved to be inadequate to meet the burgeoning demand for labor in the so-called New World. In 1638 several Pequot captives were exchanged in the West Indies for enslaved Africans, who then were brought back to New England and sold as laborers. It was this trade—bodies for bodies—that actually inaugurated the Atlantic slave trade. By 1644

Massachusetts merchants had begun outfitting ships specifically for the purpose of trading rum and other products for enslaved laborers in Africa and transporting them to Caribbean sugar plantations.

Massachusetts remained the principal American slave trading colony until 1700, after which Rhode Island became the center of the American slave trade. Recent scholarship has corrected an earlier notion that only elite merchants and other wealthy colonists invested in slave trading; in fact, ordinary artisans and middling sorts bought shares in slave-trading voyages the way middle-class Americans today invest in stocks. The Atlantic slave trade undergirded the development of the banking and insurance industries, along with shipbuilding, iron-making (for ships' anchors and hardware as well as for iron pots as trade goods in Africa), sail-making, and other important industries, in the northern states, especially in New England and in New York. Christy Clark-Pujara's essay in this volume provides more information on slavery and the northern economy.

Congress made participation in the slave trade to foreign ports illegal for all American citizens in 1794, but the number of slaving voyages leaving New England ports actually increased in the 1790s.[2] Students are shocked to learn that in the nine months between the passage by the US Congress of the 1807 Act banning all US participation in the Atlantic slave trade and January 1, 1808, when the ban went into effect, the rate of importation of Africans in American boats reached an all-time peak. That is, far from responding to the 1807 Act as a moral wake-up call, Americans hastened to invest in the trade and to make as much money from it as possible in the short time allowed.[3] Even after that, we know that New England ships continued to carry slaves illegally at least through 1821. By the end of the legal trade, in 1808, North American vessels, more than half of them New England owned, had accounted for two thousand slave-trading voyages that had transported close to a quarter-million African slaves to the Americas.[4]

Even people who are aware of the role of New England in the slave and provisioning trades are convinced that the actual institution of slavery never took root in New England and the other northern colonies. Since most textbooks today do make some mention of northern slavery, most—but not all—younger students do know about its existence, but nearly all of them are certain that the actual use of enslaved labor was uncommon and incidental to the social, political, and economic development of the North. On the contrary, by the mid-1600s, every northern colony employed enslaved African laborers, working alongside enslaved and indentured Indians and indentured whites. In 1641 Massachusetts— not Virginia or South Carolina—became the first British mainland colony to give legal recognition to chattel slavery as a lifetime, hereditary status. In a little over ten years, the other northern colonies had followed suit. By the time of the American Revolution the enslaved population had reached around fifteen thousand in New England and forty-eight thousand in the northern colonies as a whole.

Perhaps most surprising to students and teachers alike is the fact that there were slaves in the Upper Midwest. But, they insist, what about the ban on slavery in the Northwest Ordinance that was signed into law in 1789 and organized the Northwest Territory? That ban did not emancipate slaves already living in the territory; there were about three hundred slaves, for example, in Detroit in 1796.[5]

Slavery was widespread in the northern colonies. Settlers at the middling and upper levels of society and in all occupations, from wealthy landowners and ministers to urban artisans and rural farmers, owned slaves. Africans and African Americans were most densely concentrated in towns and cities. In ports, they loaded and unloaded the boats and worked in shipyards, ropewalks, and other maritime industries. Frequently they were hired out as laborers or as sailors on merchant ships (and sometimes on slave ships). Urban slaves also performed domestic labor in the homes of middling and wealthy artisans, merchants, and elites. Slaves worked in saltworks, iron furnaces, candle works, and other manufacturing operations. Many hired out part of their own time or participated in trade in other ways and negotiated agreements with their owners to keep part of their earnings.

In a few small areas of southeastern Connecticut, southern Rhode Island, and the Hudson and Delaware Valleys, large plantations produced agricultural products and raised animals for export to the slave societies in the West Indies and to other mainland colonies. Most northern slaves, however, lived and worked on the farms clustered around small towns. As colonists near the coast moved westward in search of more or better land, they often brought one or two slaves with them. Therefore, even families living on the frontiers of settlement often had one or two slaves. On these rural farms, slaves worked alongside the white men and women of the household. Enslaved women performed household labor, cooking, washing, spinning, weaving, and caring for children. Enslaved men practiced carpentry, stone masonry, and other skilled tasks in the field and barn.

The particular conditions of northern slavery had important implications for the development of local cultures. The relative isolation of most African slaves in small numbers in the attics, cellars, and back rooms of their owners' houses made keeping African customs and practices alive difficult. But in the mid-1700s, the Africanity of northern slave culture was reinvigorated when the increasing demand for black labor led slavers to begin bringing slaves directly from Africa to the northern colonies. Evidence of this re-Africanization can be seen in the mid-eighteenth-century emergence of "Negro elections" in New England and "Pinkster" celebrations in the mid-Atlantic colonies—West African–based festivals in which the slaves elected a "Negro Governor" or a "Negro King." Slaveholders, thinking that their slaves were mimicking English colonial elections and imagining that such leaders could be useful, supported these celebrations with food, finery, and time off, unaware of their actual meaning. A classroom activity in which students in two groups, "slaves" and "slaveholders," are asked to compile lists of the potential advantages and dangers of these celebrations from each perspective can provide considerable insight into social relations and their tensions in slaveholding New England.[6] Many enslaved Africans who adopted Christianity incorporated African ideas and customs into their religious practices.

For Native people, living in servitude usually required the adoption, at least superficially, of European customs, but they sometimes were able to continue to participate in traditional cultural practices in Indian communities nearby. At the same time, many enslaved Indians formed families with enslaved Africans working in the same households. Together, Indians and Africans created a rich culture that blended Indian, African, and English customs and practices. It is important for students to realize that this history alters the narrative of the "disappearing" Indian. While disease, massacre, and dispossession indeed dramatically reduced the numbers of Indians in the northern colonies and states, Indians also disappeared into Anglo-American racial reassignment, as the descendants of Afro-Indian families became characterized as simply "black."[7]

One of the enduring myths of northern slavery is that slaves served primarily as "status symbols" in the homes of elite men, where they

performed "household labor." This idea needs to be unpacked carefully; the point is not that owning slaves was *not* a status symbol for the
rich—it was—but that this was only one small aspect of their value.
Students need to realize the complexity of northern slave ownership,
which, in turn, will teach valuable lessons in how to contextualize the
past before rendering judgments. Understanding northern slavery will
also show students how historical interpretations change over time.

First, many students are unimpressed by the difficulty of the "household labor" of northern slaves because they have no idea what that labor
entailed. It is important for them to understand that the household was
a productive unit in colonial America; one or two household slaves
might be responsible for caring for sheep, goats, pigs, chickens, a cow,
and draft animals, for planting, tending, and harvesting from herb, dye,
and vegetable gardens and fruit trees, for gathering and processing raw
fibers to turn them into woven and sewn clothing for the family, for
cutting, splitting, and stacking firewood, for cutting and milling lumber,
and for digging out stumps and stones and making stone walls.[8]

Then, students need to realize that evidence for the uses and significance of enslaved labor appears in several different kinds of colonial
documents, and examining only one of these can be misleading; indeed,
it led many earlier historians astray. Slaves appear as property in wills
and probate inventories, and these demonstrate that rich men owned
slaves—hence the "status symbol" argument. But wills are drafted by
men nearing the end of their lives; an examination of the journals of
younger men, who wrote of buying slaves to replace the labor of dead
sons, to augment the labor of living ones, and to replace their own labor
as they freed themselves to serve as doctors and ministers and lawyers
and judges, supports a different argument—that slaves made men rich.
A good example is Joshua Hempstead of New London, Connecticut,
who kept a daily journal from 1711 to 1758. For the first sixteen years
recorded in his journal, Hempstead owned no slaves and seems to have
spent about 70 percent of his waking hours working on his own farm.
But his purchase of a slave, named Adam, in 1727 inaugurated a variety
of productive activities for the market on Hempstead's part, as well as a
new career as an attorney, justice of the peace, and probate judge, which
regularly took him away from home. In the meantime, Hempstead
purchased another slave almost immediately following the death of
two adult sons in 1729.[9]

Teachers should also point out that some of the up-and-coming younger men like Hempstead who were availing themselves of enslaved labor to advance their fortunes, as well as the rich old men who had done so before them, were heavily represented among the social and political leaders of the American colonies. Students asked to research prominent northern Revolutionary-era leaders, such as John Jay of New York, first Chief Justice of the US Supreme Court and coauthor of The Federalist Papers, and Stephen Hopkins, governor of Rhode Island and author of the 1764 pamphlet "The Rights of the Colonies Examined," will be surprised to discover that these men and others owned slaves. A fruitful discussion question is whether and how it might be meaningful that many of the *northern* as well as southern Revolutionary-era leaders who designed and supported our framework of American political liberties at the local, state, and federal levels grew up taking for granted the "natural" right of whites to subordinate people of color. Paul Finkelman's essay in this volume also will help teachers to unpack these issues. This exploration gives new complexity to students' consideration of the oft-cited response of the British writer Samuel Johnson to the First Continental Congress's Declaration of Rights: "How is it that we hear the loudest *yelps* for liberty among the drivers of negroes?"

A corollary of the concept of northern "status symbol" slavery is the conviction that northern slavery was somehow "milder" than southern slavery. Here the problem is partly the seduction of numbers. Students compare the 48,000 slaves in the northern colonies at the peak of northern slavery before the Revolution with the 422,000 enslaved in the South at the same time, or (ahistorically) with the four million enslaved at the South's peak of slavery in 1860; or they compare the proportion of slaves in, say, New York (12 percent) with the proportion in South Carolina (60 percent); or they compare the relatively modest body of slave laws in the northern colonies with the much more extensive laws in the South, and they conclude that fewer slaves and fewer laws must indicate a milder form of slavery. But there are other numbers. The frequency with which ads for northern fugitive slaves appeared in local northern papers and the descriptions in those ads of the scars on fugitives' bodies do not tell a benign story. And what might "mild" slavery mean? On this point, students should be encouraged to consider what slavery may have meant to slaves themselves: What was being enslaved

"like"? Consider the poignant self-description of a group of slaves peti-
tioning the Massachusetts legislature in 1773 as people "who have had
every Day of their Lives embittered with this most intollerable Reflection, That, let their Behaviour be what it will, neither they, nor their
Children to all Generations, shall ever be able to do, or to possess and
enjoy any Thing, no, not even Life itself, but in a Manner as the Beasts
that perish. . . . We have no Property. We have no Wives. No Children.
We have no City. No Country."[10] Beyond the conditions protested in
this petition, there are other factors for students to consider. Teachers
may divide a class into three groups, asking them to imagine the daily
life of a single slave in a northern port city, a small town, and a farm-
stead on the fringes of northern settlement, respectively. How are they
alike? How are they quite different? Students can weigh factors such as
the terrible isolation and degrading lack of privacy of rural slaves versus
the possibilities for sociability with other nearby slaves in the other two
situations and the relative benefits and potential costs of close personal
relations in each of the three environments.

The ontological problem presented by slavery is the contradiction
of property in personhood. However, slaves were never in fact utterly
objectified in either their own or their owner's eyes, even though they
were bought and sold as commodities; too many slaveholders handed
over the care of their children to enslaved women for that to have been
the case. Rather, the lived contradiction was that there was no way to *be*
a "good slave." The most useful slave was one who could perform tasks
as well as the master or mistress, but the fiction of slavery rested on the
conviction that slaves were *not* the equal of white people. Hence slaves
had to be simultaneously just like and nothing like their masters and
mistresses and could be beaten or punished in distinctive ways for
failure in either direction. Similarly, they were entirely responsible for
but had no authority over important aspects of their owners' lives and
livelihoods. They were required to keep order in their own households
but had no authority over those households and could not keep them
together if the master wanted to sell a wife, a child, or a husband to
another master far away.

Slavery was less draconian in northern than in southern law, but in
fact in both places it was the very arbitrariness with which actual practice
followed or did not follow the dictates of law that made enslavement
terrible everywhere. Northern slaves could legally make arrangements
to hire themselves out and earn money to purchase their own freedom

and the freedom of their own families, as they could in some places and at some times in the South. Slaves also could legally own property almost everywhere in the North, something that was nominally illegal in most of the South but frequently allowed by owners who ignored laws to the contrary. Legal or not, however, the possession of money and property by slaves and agreements about them between owners and slaves rested solely on the good faith of the owner; the narratives of northern as well as southern slaves are replete with instances of the arbitrary confiscation of money and violation of agreements by slaves' owners. The security of each slave's life and relationships rested solely on the whim of her owner.

Northern slaves responded to their enslavement in many different ways. Some ran away—more men than women, because it was equally difficult for mothers to leave their small children behind and to run away with them in tow. Some resisted in subtle ways, breaking tools and working slowly; others resisted in more dramatic ways, occasionally burning down their owners' barns or houses or poisoning or bludgeoning their owners and their families. Most enslaved people simply endured.

If slavery, then, was such a ubiquitous institution in the North, why and how did it end? Many textbooks and some scholarly monographs still say that by 1800, slavery had been abolished in the North. While it is true that most—but not all—northern states had taken preliminary steps by 1800 to initiate some kind of process to end slavery, abolition was nowhere near accomplished by that date. Most students are stunned by the way in which slavery actually ended in "the free states"—a story well worth discussing in some detail.

As early as the seventeenth century, a growing chorus of voices began to denounce the slave trade and slavery as immoral, but political opposition to slavery grew very slowly. Enslaved people themselves were its most vigorous opponents, using freedom petitions and lawsuits to plead their cause in colonial assemblies and courts beginning in the early eighteenth century. By the 1770s, religious opposition from the Society of Friends (Quakers) had spread to a growing number of Puritan ministers, but it was the American Revolution that finally produced conditions under which abolition could begin to gain public support. Teachers can ask students to compare a pre-Revolutionary petition of 1773 from Massachusetts slaves to General Gage that protests the conditions of their enslavement and articulates their natural right to freedom with the 1777 petition of Prince Hall and other free blacks that explicitly refers to the Revolution and insists that "every principle from which America has acted in the course of their unhappy difficulties with Great Britain pleads stronger than a thousand arguments in favour of your petitioners . . . whereby they may be restored to the enjoyments of that which is the natural right of all men." Students will discover that enslaved and free people of color were fully conversant with Enlightenment principles of natural rights before they were formally articulated in the founders' documents but were also quick to seize upon the act of rebellion based on these principles as supporting their own claim to freedom.[11]

In practical terms, the economic disruption of the war eroded the profitability of northern slavery, but most students have been persuaded that it was the Revolutionary natural rights argument that convinced American patriots of their slaves' right to freedom. Students forget that Revolutionary ideology also emphasized property rights; in fact, the only forms of emancipation that northerners discussed in the Revolutionary era were those that would either compensate slave owners for their slaves or would free newborns, leaving adult slave property intact.

Other practical considerations led to the emancipation of some slaves. During the Revolution, the shortage of recruits for the Continental Army led Washington reluctantly to authorize the enlistment of slaves, and several states passed legislation emancipating slaves who would enlist; but here again, these statutes offered slave owners either monetary compensation or freedom from their own enlistment in return for their willingness to allow their slaves to serve.

Beginning in 1780, northern courts and legislatures began to take legal action against slavery, but these steps were tentative and in some cases had ambiguous results. A freedom suit brought by a slave named Quock Walker led to a 1783 Massachusetts court decision widely interpreted as affirming that the 1780 state constitution had effectively abolished slavery by guaranteeing that "All men are born free and equal," but the wording of this decision was ambiguous, and Massachusetts continued to tax slaves as property through 1785. In the First Federal Census of 1790, no slaves were recorded in Massachusetts, but one commentator reported that the census taker had discouraged household heads from reporting their slaves. The 1783 New Hampshire constitution was similarly interpreted by some to have made slavery illegal, but this wording, too, was ambiguous, and slaves were listed in the state census through 1840.

The first state to initiate abolition by passing legislation was Pennsylvania, in 1780, followed by Connecticut and Rhode Island in 1784. These were *post nati* acts, requiring children born to enslaved women to serve their mothers' owners until the age of majority (between eighteen and twenty-eight, depending on the gender of the child and the state), to compensate their owners for "raising them," after which they would be free. Slaves born before that date remained enslaved; Rhode Island and Connecticut did not officially act to make slavery illegal until 1842 and 1848, respectively. A citizenship act passed by New Hampshire in 1857 is widely interpreted to have ended slavery there. Pennsylvania never passed a final abolition act.

In 1799 New York, too, passed a *post nati* bill; then, in 1817, the legislature passed a second bill that would emancipate all remaining slaves—in another ten years. New Jersey passed a gradual bill in 1804 and then in 1846 abolished slavery entirely—and created a new category called "perpetual apprenticeship." The last eighteen perpetual apprentices in New Jersey were freed by the Thirteenth Amendment.

In the Northwest Territory, the new state constitutions of Ohio, Indiana, and Illinois (1802, 1816, and 1818, respectively) abolished slavery, but black laws and bond requirements deprived free blacks of most civil rights. In Illinois, blacks who broke the law could be sold at auction.

Throughout this period, as legislation and constitutional interpretations made it obvious that slavery was doomed, increasing numbers of slave owners began to emancipate their slaves individually; at the same time, more slaves began to run away and fewer owners bothered to advertise for their return. But enough northern slave owners, seeking to protect their investments, sold their slaves south to states where slavery remained legal that several state governments passed legislation forbidding owners from selling their slaves out of state.[12]

By the eve of the Civil War, there were only a few slaves and about 226,000 free people of color in the northern states. These free people struggled to improve their status and to demonstrate that they deserved all the rights and benefits of full citizenship. While they struggled to achieve equality for their own families, they continued to battle against the continuing enslavement of millions of their brothers and sisters in the South. This leads to another firmly held misconception—that it was a network of good Quakers and other white people that created the Underground Railroad to help fugitive slaves along the way to freedom further north. Of course, there were some white abolitionists who sheltered fugitive slaves (and famously fought against their re-enslavement). But, most commonly, southern slaves found refuge in the homes of northern free people of color. It is important for students to recognize that the Underground Railroad was a *black* and white network of safe houses. Free people of color formed Vigilance Committees to watch ports and railroad stations to spy out slave catchers and warn fugitives. It took exceptional courage for free blacks whose own freedom was endangered by the Fugitive Slave Law to engage in these dangerous and illegal acts. Teachers can find useful lesson plans, an interactive map of documented Underground Railroad sites, a searchable data base, and other documents at the National Park Service "Network to Freedom" website at its "Education" link. Another excellent online resource is the "Enabling Freedom—History" link on the website of the National Underground Railroad Freedom Center.[13]

As free blacks struggled to achieve economic success and political and social equality in the northern states, they faced intense hostility and discrimination. Whites became increasingly unwilling to hire free blacks to perform skilled work that routinely had been performed by slaves, preferring instead to hire less skilled native-born whites and a growing population of Irish immigrants. Because they were often poor and employed only infrequently, free blacks were vilified as "degraded." At the same time, black achievement was often ridiculed by whites in satiric broadsides with graphics and text that portrayed free blacks as pretenders to a citizenship and social status for which they were ineligible and unqualified. Schools and other public spaces and conveyances excluded blacks. A widespread move to "democratize" voting by eliminating property requirements, which had allowed black as well as white men who met the requirements to vote, and extending the franchise to all, *but only*, white men, effectively disfranchised all blacks in most northern states.

Free blacks in antebellum New England towns were increasingly subject to being rounded up and "warned out" as "strangers" who might become indigent and require town charity even though many of them had supported themselves without incident for years in the same towns. Legislatures in all of the northern states passed or considered passing "black laws" to restrict the influx of nonresident people of color into their states, and often these laws led to violent attacks on black communities and on whites who seemed to be encouraging black immigration. Supporters of the American Colonization Society, founded in 1816 to encourage free blacks to leave the United States altogether and "return" to Africa, described their condition as "one of extreme and remediless degradation, of gross irreligion, of revolting profligacy and, of course, of deplorable wretchedness," to quote one 1826 Colonizationist sermon. In large cities across the North, mobs of whites attacked black communities repeatedly throughout the 1820s and 1830s. Teachers may find the story of Prudence Crandall particularly helpful in encouraging students to explore the rise and extent of white hostility to blacks, even children, in the antebellum North. Crandall was a white Quaker who admitted one out-of-state black student to her girls' school in Canterbury, Connecticut, in 1833. This act ultimately led to a mob attack on her schoolhouse and to her arrest and imprisonment for violating the state's "Black Law," which made it illegal to operate a school for out-of-state African American students. Students can base their discussions on the various perspectives reflected in primary documents associated with the case, which are available at the website of the Gilder Lehrman Center for the Study of Slavery, Resistance, and Abolition.[14]

Where did this unfathomable degree of hostility come from? The rise of emergent racism as the legacy of northern slavery and emancipation is the most important part of this story.

The gradualness of the process by which people of color had become a free people meant that for more than fifty years, whites in the northern states could imagine that any black person they encountered *might* be a slave—and behave toward that person as though she *were* a slave. In other words, the gradualness of the emancipation process allowed northern whites to transfer a set of assumptions and practices developed over 150 years of slavery to a growing population of free people of color. The result was a virulent racism that escalated in the northern states throughout the antebellum period. This racism was also fueled by a kind of collective amnesia about the history of slavery in New England. Quite quickly after the passage of the *post nati* bills and the constitutional interpretations that inaugurated slavery's slow demise, New England political leaders began heralding their states as "the free states," highlighting the contrast between a society "built" on free labor and a slaveholding South that seemed to pose an ever greater political threat. The erasure of a local history of slavery had devastating consequences for people of color. Without a history of enslavement to account for the disproportionate poverty and illiteracy of free people of color, whites could explain these circumstances and justify discrimination against black people as "natural" consequences of blacks' own innate inferiority.

I encounter many students who believe that American racism is the enduring legacy of *southern* slavery. For the most part they acknowledge that there is widespread racism in the North, but they see that racism as accountable, as the sociologist Nathan Glazer once said, to the Great Migration of blacks in the early twentieth century—that somehow it came north with them. This idea is a tragic compound of several of the other myths and their corollaries: that there were no slaves, hence no blacks, in the North until after the Civil War; that racism is an outgrowth and unchanging vestige of one region's embrace of slavery, regrettably transferred to another. It is not. It is an ideology that emerged in both the North and the South, but differently, to maintain the power relations of slavery by other means in both places.

Two final points on teaching the history of northern slavery and emancipation: In broader courses on American slavery or American antebellum history, northern slavery is usually discussed first in the semester, before southern slavery, because its institutional life had peaked and faded before the cotton revolution fastened slavery irrevocably on the South. To avoid repetition, instructors are tempted to postpone discussion of elements common to slavery everywhere—slave mistreatment, the separation of enslaved families, the rape of enslaved women, and the many forms of slave resistance—until the focus has shifted to southern slavery. It is important to resist this temptation. Discussing these phenomena only in conjunction with southern slavery, even with abundant references to "northern slaves, too . . . ," reinforces the conviction that northern slavery was "mild" and that southern slavery was somehow the "real" slavery.

Finally, while teaching this material is important, teaching it comfortably is also important. Instructors who have not taught this subject before and who are not African Americans themselves sometimes express misgivings about how African American students will respond to this subject matter when they teach it. It is true that African American students encountering a white teacher of African American history for the first time are sometimes suspicious, even hostile. Many years of experience as a white woman teaching northern slavery and emancipation and African American history in general have taught me that for the vast majority of students, "authenticity" is not a matter of identity but a matter of knowing the subject and having confidence in that knowledge. Many African American students come to college having had the experience in high school of being taught a unit or even a term of African American history by a white teacher who really knew very little about the subject and was visibly uncomfortable with it. (It is still the case that in some high schools, many history courses are taught by specialists in something else, for example, coaching a sport.) So African American students have legitimate cause to be suspicious, and many of their chins will go up during that first class with a white instructor. It is unwise and unnecessary for the instructor to try to confront this suspicion, become defensive, or justify her legitimacy. If she simply makes it obvious from the outset that she is deeply knowledgeable and very enthusiastic about the subject, by the second or third class the chins will come down. Another strategy is to make sure that a large proportion of the assigned readings, especially primary sources, reflect African American voices. One of the best portrayals of the arc of a northern African American life from freedom in Africa through enslavement to hard-won freedom on American soil, with its own woes but also triumphs, is the narrative of Venture Smith. Students can read it online, and at about twenty-six pages it is brief enough for most classroom uses. A very powerful firsthand analysis of the racism that succeeded slavery in the North and how it affected free blacks is *A Treatise on the Intellectual Character and Civil and Political Condition of the Colored People of the U. States: and the Prejudice Exercised Toward Them*, written by an Afro-Indian named Hosea Easton in 1837. In a chapter titled "The Nature of Prejudice," Easton offers a no-holds-barred perspective on how white racism "makes the colored people subserve almost every foul purpose imaginable. Negro or nigger, is an opprobrious term, employed to impose contempt upon them as an inferior race, and also to express their deformity [in whites' estimation] of person. . . . These impressions received by the young, grow with their growth, and strengthen with their strength." *Our Nig*, one of the first novels published in the United States by an African American writer, also movingly conveys the horror of antebellum northern racism in fictional form. Its narrator, Frado ("our Nig," as most of the members of the white family to which she becomes an indentured servant characterize her), comments ironically on the conditions of her later life in Massachusetts: "Watched by kidnappers, maltreated by professed abolitionists, who didn't want slaves at the South, nor niggers in their own houses, North. Faugh! To lodge one; to eat with one; to admit one through the front door; to sit next one; awful!"[15] Using these last two sources in class is tricky, because the authors repeatedly use what many schools insist on euphemizing as "the n word" to vividly evoke the racism of their era. I believe that the value of showing clearly how racist language was deployed by whites and its emotional impact on those subjected to it far outweighs the danger of giving the word new substance or currency. In fact, reading these two texts in my classes has led black students on several occasions to want to talk about their own use of the term, and lively class discussions have ensued. Drawing on sources like these, anyone with a passionate interest in early American history and a conviction that slavery and emancipation are important parts of the story can successfully teach the history of northern slavery and emancipation. And teaching this material serves an important civic purpose. Helping students to understand the *historical* roots of persistent racial inequality in the American North—roots in slavery and its reluctant, ambiguous end—arms them to challenge the persistent claim that disadvantaged people of color are and always have been "naturally" unequal.

NOTES

1. On the enslavement of New England Indians, see Margaret Newell, "The Changing Nature of Indian Slavery in Colonial New England," in Colin Calloway and Neal Salisbury, eds., *Reinterpreting New England Indians and the Colonial Experience* (Boston: Publications of the Colonial Society of Massachusetts, 2004); and Margaret Newell, "Indian Slavery in Colonial New England," in Alan Gallay, ed., *Indian Slavery in Colonial America* (Lincoln: University of Nebraska Press, 2010).

2. For the 1794 law, see "A Chronology of Antislavery: The 18th Century" on the website of the University of Houston: http://www.digitalhistory.uh .edu/timelines/antislavery_chronology.cfm.

3. For a discussion of the increase in the number of slaving voyages as the 1808 deadline approached and also of the participation in the slave trade of the middling classes and artisans along with the wealthy, see Rachel Chernos Lin, "The Rhode Island Slave-Traders: Butchers, Bakers, and Candlestick-Makers," *Slavery and Abolition* 23, no. 3 (December 2002).

4. The best source of detailed information on the Atlantic slave trade is the Trans-Atlantic Slave Trade Database at http://www.slavevoyages.org/tast /index.faces. See David Eltis, "The Volume and Structure of the Transatlantic Slave Trade: A Reassessment," *William and Mary Quarterly*, 3d Series, 58 (January 2001), for some very useful tables drawn from the first iteration of the database. (The numbers have been subsequently revised and expanded slightly in the actual database, but the tables remain useful.)

5. To place northern slavery in continental perspective, see Ira Berlin, *Many Thousands Gone: The First Two Centuries of Slavery in North America* (Cambridge, MA: Belknap Press of Harvard University Press, 1998). For a somewhat dated look at northern slavery per se, see Edgar McManus, *Black Bondage in the North* (Syracuse: Syracuse University Press, 1973).

6. For discussion of northern "Negro elections," see Shane White, "'It Was a Proud Day': African Americans, Festivals, and Parades in the North, 1741–1834," *Journal of American History* 81 (June 1994): 13–50; see also Melvin Wade, "Shining in Borrowed Plumage: Affirmation of Community in the Black Coronation Festivals in New England, 1750–1850," *Western Folklore* 40 (July 1981): 211–31.

7. For a discussion of the "disappearance" of Indian people into the characterization "black," see Ruth Wallis Herndon and Ella Wilcox Secatau, "The Right to a Name: The Narragansett People and Rhode Island Officials in the Revolutionary Era," *Ethnohistory* 44, no. 3 (Summer 1997): 433–62.

8. See chapter 4, "Slave Occupations," in Lorenzo J. Greene, *The Negro in Colonial New England* (New York: Columbia University Press, 1948).

9. For Hempstead's story, see Allegra di Bonaventura, *For Adam's Sake: A Family Saga in Colonial New England* (New York: Liveright Publishing Corporation, a Division of W. W. Norton, 2013); see also Joanne Pope Melish, *Disowning Slavery: Gradual Emancipation and "Race" in New England, 1780–1860* (Ithaca, NY: Cornell University Press, 1998), 21–23, 33, 47.

10. "Felix" (unknown), Slave Petition for Freedom, January 6, 1773. This petition is readily available on several online sites.

11. Petition for Freedom to Massachusetts Governor Thomas Gage, His Majesty's Council, and the House of Representatives, May 25, 1774; Slave Petition for Freedom to the Massachusetts Legislature. These petitions, too, are readily available on several sites online.

12. For a discussion of how slavery slowly ended in the northern states and how much resistance there was to abolishing it, see Arthur Zilversmit, *The First Emancipation: The Abolition of Slavery in the North* (Chicago: University of Chicago Press, 1967), and Melish, *Disowning Slavery*, chapters 2 and 3. For a discussion of the need for legislation to deter slave owners from selling their slaves out of state in anticipation of the passage of abolition legislation or in response to its effects, see Zilversmit, *The First Emancipation*, 120, 151, 158, 161, 163, 201, and especially 208.

13. The National Park Service's "Network to Freedom" website is www .nps.gov/subjects/ugrr/education/index.htm. The National Underground Railroad Freedom Center's "Enabling Freedom" website is http://freedom center.org/enabling-freedom/history.

14. An excellent one-page biography of Prudence Crandall and a summary of the attack on her school is available on the website of the National Women's History Museum: http://www.nwhm.org/education-resources/biography /biographies/prudence-crandall/. "A Canterbury Tale: A Document Package for Connecticut's Prudence Crandall Affair" is available from the Gilder Lehrman Center: http://www.yale.edu/glc/crandall/index.htm.

15. *A Narrative of the Life and Adventures of Venture, a Native of Africa* . . . (1798), available online at http://docsouth.unc.edu/neh/venture/venture .html; Hosea Easton, *A Treatise on the Intellectual Character and Civil and Political Condition of the Colored People of the United States; and the Prejudice Exercised Toward Them*, in *To Heal the Scourge of Prejudice: The Life and Writings of Hosea Easton*, ed. George Price and James Brewer Stewart (Amherst: University of Massachusetts Press, 1999); Harriet E. Wilson, *Our Nig, or, Sketches from the Life of a Free Black: in a Two-Story White House, North* . . . (1859; reprint, New York: Random House, 1983).

Slave Resistance

KENNETH S. GREENBERG

Since the first modern historians began to write about slave resistance, the topic has generated much debate. Any student hoping to understand the nature and significance of resistance to slavery must first understand the nature and significance of these disagreements. At one extreme, some historians have contended that there was virtually no resistance from those who were enslaved. At the other extreme, some historians have argued that enslaved people resisted in every way all the time and that such resistance shaped every aspect of the institution. Nearly all contemporary historians have rejected these extreme positions; a more nuanced and complex view of resistance prevails today. But if teachers and students want to understand where we are today, they must first understand where we have been. This essay is divided into two sections. The first reviews the major themes in historical writing on slave resistance over the past century. The second focuses on how we can teach this complex subject to our students.

It is important to begin on a note of humility. In the area of what became the United States, slavery spanned three centuries as well as a vast geographic landscape characterized by significant regional variation. Moreover, slave resistance itself is not separable from all the larger questions about the nature of slavery. So, humility seems in order for the way teachers should approach this subject. At the heart of good teaching is the problem of selection. Teachers should begin discussion of this subject by noting its vast scope and announcing their intention to focus on a few themes characteristic of slave resistance in the southeastern portion of the United States during the nineteenth century.

What Historians Have Said about Slave Resistance

Modern scholarship on slavery began with the work of the historian Ulrich B. Phillips, who wrote during the early years of the twentieth century. To a current student, much of Phillip's writing seems dated and deeply rooted in racism. He casually assumed black inferiority and rejected the idea that enslaved people might have helped shape slavery. Like many planters of the antebellum period, masters, he believed, created their slaves, that "a negro was what a white man made him." Assuming a benevolent planter class intent on civilizing their inferiors, paying little attention to the voices of African Americans, Phillips gave academic respectability to the racist assumptions of his age and portrayed enslaved people as contented and passive in their subservient condition.[1]

The Phillips view of slave resistance dominated American historical writing through most of the first half of the twentieth century. But there were also important dissenting opinions. A group of African American historians under the leadership of Carter G. Woodson founded the Association for the Study of Negro History and Life in 1915 and began to pay attention to the voices of African Americans. They offered an image of enslaved people as actors who shaped slavery as much as they were shaped by it. Similarly, the Marxist scholars Herbert Aptheker and W.E.B. Du Bois wrote important books on the subject of slave resistance. In American Negro Slave Revolts, Aptheker presented a compendium of slave rebellions and conspiracies that had largely been ignored by Phillips.[2] When Phillips wrote about slave rebellions, he confined the discussion to a chapter on "slave crime," implying that such acts of resistance were no different from ordinary criminal activity found in any society. For Aptheker, slave rebellions evidenced a powerful American revolutionary tradition. The historian W.E.B. Du Bois carried this idea even further. In Black Reconstruction, he turned his attention to the moment of emancipation, and, in a chapter titled "The General Strike," he argued that slavery collapsed because of the actions of enslaved people.[3] This was quite a leap from the Phillips position that the "a negro was what a white man made him."

Ultimately, it was the historian Kenneth Stampp, in The Peculiar Institution, published in 1956, who developed an interpretation of slavery that completely rejected the Phillips world view. In one key chapter, "To Make Them Stand in Fear," Stampp dramatically replaced the Phillips image of benevolent masters patiently civilizing slaves with the image of masters intent on preserving their "peculiar institution" through force and coercion. In Stampp's view, enslaved people were held in their position by the whip and the gun and not by an appreciation of their gentle and kind owners.[4]

It is deeply ironic that Stampp's image of slavery did not have the effect of completely destroying the Phillips view of slave resistance. In fact, at least one core element of that view immediately re-emerged in Stanley M. Elkins's 1959 *Slavery: A Problem in American Institutional and Intellectual Life*. Elkins fully accepted the Stampp image of slavery as rooted in force and coercion, even adopting a more brutal view of slavery and likening it to Nazi concentration camps. However, in Elkin's hands, slavery was so violent and threatening that it deeply damaged enslaved people, who responded to their horrific circumstances through a series of psychological adaptive mechanisms by becoming "docile . . . irresponsible, loyal but lazy, humble but chronically given to lying and stealing . . . infantile."[5] Here we have all the racist stereotypes of the Phillips world view but reframed in a different context. In Phillips's hands, enslaved people became "docile" because of their racial inferiority and the kindness of their masters; in Elkins's hands, enslaved people became "docile" as a psychological defense against the extreme brutality of their masters.

How could it have been possible that two historians with such completely opposed views of slavery could come up with such remarkably similar ideas? Phillips and Elkins differed about many things, but they shared one key assumption. They both believed that slave rebellions and other significant acts of resistance were rare throughout the history of slavery. They had radically different ways of explaining that fact, but neither one rejected it. In many ways, it is possible to understand much historical writing about the nature of slave resistance during the past fifty years as ways of responding to this basic assumption that united Elkins and Phillips.

Consider the issue of slave rebellions. Both Elkins and Phillips agreed that there were few slave rebellions and conspiracies both before and after the creation of the United States. However, it seems quite clear now that there were many more such organized acts of resistance than either of these historians ever recognized. Herbert Aptheker's compendium of rebellions was written after Phillips had completed his book, but Elkins and most other American historians writing before the 1960s still largely ignored his work. Aptheker never held a position in an American university, and, to many, his historical writing seemed to stray from the facts because it appeared unduly influenced by his Marxist ideology. Yet, it seems clear now that, while the number and the nature of many of the conspiracies and rebellions noted by Aptheker were inflated, there were far more of these episodes than had previously been recognized. Knowledge about many of these acts of resistance had been repressed—in part because African American voices were ignored and in part because the antebellum white population feared that discussion about resistance might generate more resistance. By cleverly rereading the sources, recent scholars have discovered repeatedly the existence of conspiracies and rebellions that no one had ever recognized before. A classic example of this kind of work can be found in Winthrop Jordan's 1993 *Tumult and Silence at Second Creek*, in which he discovered a conspiracy in Mississippi in 1861 that led to the hanging of twenty-three people.[6]

No matter how many additional rebellions and conspiracies have been uncovered by modern historians, it still remains the case that by many measures both the size and the number of slave rebellions in the United States were relatively small. Some of the most famous slave "rebellions," such as one led by Gabriel Prosser in 1800 or one led by Denmark Vesey in 1822, never made it past the stage of conspiracy. Rebellions that actually occurred typically never moved beyond their immediate location, lasted more than a day or two, required the use of troops other than local militia, or involved the deaths of more than a few dozen whites. Overall, these were minor acts of resistance compared, for example, to the successful Haitian insurrection that took advantage of the French Revolution and created an independent black nation.

But modern historians agree that the absence of large-scale rebellions was not the result of some peculiar "docility" of the enslaved population in the United States. Several other factors played a role here. The American South had a larger white population than other New World slave societies, and it was well armed and organized and able to mobilize at the first hint of insurrection. Moreover, American plantations were generally smaller in size and more dispersed than plantations in other slave societies, so the black population could not hope to rise up all at once in sufficient numbers. The terrain was also a deterrent. The American South had relatively few inaccessible areas of the type that could hide a determined group of rebels. Hence slave rebellions in the United

States had little chance of success.[7] Enslaved people in America were not "docile"; they simply did not leap at the opportunity for nearly certain death.

Another significant theme in modern writing about slave resistance involves the expansion of the definition of resistance. A slave rebellion, in which a group of armed individuals rose up in collective action against their enslavers, is certainly recognized as the most extreme manifestation of resistance to slavery. But modern historians have become acutely aware that resistance could take many other forms. Enslaved people could physically confront their masters as individuals, or they could slow the pace of work, break tools, feign illness, engage in acts of thievery, run away, or learn to read.

Enslaved people also resisted by carving out areas of their lives that were independent of their masters. This is certainly the case with African American religion. Masters tried to get the people they enslaved to adopt a brand of Christianity that would make them subservient and pliable. But African Americans resisted by creating their own "invisible church," meeting outdoors in "hush arbors" outside the direct supervision of their masters, and creating their own distinctive forms of religious practice. Similarly, although slave marriage did not have the sanction of law, enslaved people created and preserved family structures that did not simply serve the interests or echo the practices of their white masters. While Phillips and Elkins assumed that African Americans were not active agents in the creation of their world, the central thrust of modern scholarship has been to recognize the existence of black agency in nearly every aspect of the lives of enslaved peoples.

By expanding the definition of resistance, modern historians have also better come to understand the important role that African American women played in resisting slavery. Under a framework in which armed rebellion was seen by historians as the primary measure of resistance, women played minor roles. Rebellions were largely the work of men. However, using a much broader definition of resistance, the historian Stephanie M. H. Camp has described the ways in which enslaved women challenged the spatial boundaries created by masters in order to control slaves. For example, masters sought to confine their slaves to cabins at night, yet women conspired with men to create a world of nocturnal movement and visitation that shattered those boundaries. Camp understood the subversive nature of the "illegal party" as a powerful form of resistance.[8] She and other historians have also described the ways in which women resisted sexual exploitation, a core feature of slavery that had largely been ignored by earlier historians.

Another key question that has shaped the work of modern historians is whether resistance mattered in any significant way. Overall, the consensus is that it mattered a great deal, but the exact ways in which it made a difference require specific discussion. Consider the issue of slave rebellion. It is true that rebellions in the United States were small and easily suppressed. But their impact was far greater than this fact alone would indicate. There were enough insurrections to seriously frighten the master class. Here is an area where the behavior of small groups of enslaved people significantly shaped the lives of masters. By engaging in acts of rebellion, however infrequently, it was African Americans who made white men "stand in fear." All over the South, every white community organized militias that stood ready to spring into action at the first signs of slave conspiracy or rebellion. Some masters came to oppose the foreign slave trade because they feared living in an area where the black population was so numerous that it might be tempted to insurrection. The threat of insurrection even caused some masters to question the wisdom of owning slaves at all. Similarly, although only a few thousand enslaved people ever successfully ran away to the North or to Canada (the vast majority of runaways remained in hiding locally for a short period of time), the possibility of a successful flight to the North had significant consequences.[9] It was this possibility that compelled the nation to develop federal fugitive slave laws requiring the return of fugitives from states that had abolished slavery. This was the kind of irritant that was central to the formation of the Republican Party, the party that eventually ended slavery. Republicans interpreted the pursuit of escaping slaves into free states as acts of southern aggression and threats to American liberty. When Anthony Burns was captured in Boston, in 1854, federal troops lined the streets to prevent angry mobs from liberating him. In the end, during the Civil War, acts of running away began to occur on a massive scale, and some modern historians have noted the key role played by this kind of flight in undermining the ability of the South to survive as an independent nation.

On the other hand, modern historians have also recognized that some acts of "resistance" may have paradoxically strengthened the power of masters. If the threat of slave rebellions required every local community to field its own militias, those same militias were easily mobilized to fight the North during the Civil War. Similarly, since most enslaved people who ran away did not head North, running away sometimes acted as a kind of safety valve, allowing an angry slave to hide in the woods for a few days and then return to the plantation and once again become a "productive" laborer. In the same vein, slowing the pace of work certainly lowered plantation productivity, but it also reinforced white racist attitudes that the people they enslaved were "lazy." Moreover, the partial autonomy of enslaved people in such areas as religious practices and family structures might have created just enough satisfaction with life under the plantation regime to prevent more serious attacks on the master class. Resistance should be understood as a double-edged sword, and students in this area must carefully evaluate what they are seeing.

Teaching about Resistance to Slavery

The best way to teach students about the themes noted in the first part of this essay is to have them focus on a few primary texts. One core useful edited volume is *The Confessions of Nat Turner and Related Documents*.[10] The central document in this volume is the "Confessions of Nat Turner," published in 1831, in the wake of the Virginia slave insurrection. But the book also contains a range of other materials, including newspaper accounts, excerpts from trial records, and selections from the diary of the governor of Virginia, as well as a contemporary summary of the Virginia legislature's discussion of the possibility of abolishing slavery.

One theme that can be addressed with these materials is the importance and the difficulty of listening carefully to African American voices. A teacher can begin this conversation by raising the question of where African American voices appear in this collection. Eventually, students should recognize that "unmediated" African American voices appear nowhere. *The Confessions* itself was structured and written by a white lawyer, Thomas R. Gray, assuming the voice of Nat Turner. Turner "confessed" to Gray while in his jail cell shortly before his execution, and Gray published his version of these confessions a few weeks later. Students who read this document should get the feeling that Nat Turner's voice is certainly contained within it, but they should also understand that it includes Thomas R. Gray's voice. Students need to ponder the question of how to distinguish the two voices. Similarly, the trial transcripts might seem at first to contain unmediated African American voices, but students should realize that is not the case. African Americans who testified in court in an insurrection trial spoke in a context of fear, and we cannot assume that they gave open voice to their real thoughts. Similarly, white reporters took down their words and summarized or excerpted them for preservation in the court records. The Nat Turner documents may come closer than any other set of slave rebellion documents to offering a glimpse of the world seen through the eyes of enslaved people, but they do not allow direct access. Students should think about the ways the documents available to us shape our interpretations, and they should recognize how difficult it is to avoid becoming trapped by their limitations.

The Confessions volume also allows students to learn about the way a small insurrection could generate major consequences. The Nat Turner rebellion was one of the largest American slave insurrections, and yet it involved no more than sixty to eighty active rebels, led to the deaths of fewer than sixty white people, was confined to a single Virginia county, and was suppressed by local militia in less than a day. But students should also read the newspaper accounts and the governor's diary to understand the great fear generated by this small group of rebels. Even after the rebellion had been repressed, whites continued to worry that it was an indication of widespread slave unrest or that it was part of a larger abolitionist attack from the North. They took extraordinary actions to protect themselves, and those actions shaped many aspects of their society and left them vulnerable to criticism for their repressive policies. The documents also include a description of the arguments made in the Virginia legislature about the possibility of abolition. Nat Turner and his small group of rebels nearly abolished slavery in this indirect way.

The Confessions can also be useful for making students aware of other forms of resistance. Nat Turner lived in a religious world outside the control of his master. He was a preacher who was inspired by signs from God to undertake the rebellion. We can also get a sense from *The Confessions* of a family and a community life that were distinctly African American. Turner's family and community seemed to believe he had been chosen from the moment of birth for some special purpose and that belief strengthened his resolve to resist. Moreover, before the rebellion, Turner had run away in a manner typical of other runaway enslaved people—remaining within the local area and returning after a short while. It should also be clear that the gathering of the conspirators the night before the rebellion, a gathering to which "Hark . . . brought a pig" and "Henry brandy," was just the kind of "illegal party" that had become a common form of slave resistance. Nat Turner certainly engaged in open rebellion, but his *Confessions* also indicate that during the course of his life he resisted slavery in many other ways.

Another excellent way to introduce students to the topic of slave resistance, especially focusing on women, is to have them read Harriet A. Jacobs's *Incidents in the Life of a Slave Girl*. While teachers should read the entire volume in the version edited by Jean Fagin Yellin, students could read excerpts or focus their attention on certain key chapters. Essential reading would include "The Trials of Girlhood," "A Perilous Passage in the Slave Girl's Life," "The Loophole of Retreat," "Competition in Cunning," and "Preparations for Escape." Here, students will see the sexual exploitation that was a core feature of enslavement, as well as the ways in which an enslaved woman could resist. Jacobs could physically resist or manipulate her location to avoid attack; she could ask for assistance from white friends; or she could call on the help of her powerful and respected free grandmother. In the end, it was her grandmother who hid her for protection in an attic for seven years until she could arrange an escape to the North.[11]

Students reading Jacobs should be asked to ponder the question of how successful were the various forms of resistance she employed. For example, how are we to understand Jacobs's description of choosing a sexual relationship with a powerful white man as a way of resisting her master? Few actions better illustrate the way in which an act of resistance simultaneously could be an act of submission.

Finally, another important document for teaching about slave resistance is chapter 10 of the 1845 edition of Frederick Douglass's autobiography. Here, Douglass describes his resistance to the "slave breaker" Mr. Covey. A teacher should use this excerpt to discuss the topic of resistance and emancipation. Over a period of several months, Covey repeatedly brutalized Douglass. Finally, Douglass could take it no more. Deciding he would no longer submit to whipping, he resisted Covey in a battle that lasted two hours. When the fight ended, Douglass described his feeling of elation: "It was a glorious resurrection, from the tomb of slavery to the heaven of freedom."[12] Of course, Douglass remained a slave after this confrontation, but, by openly confronting his master and by being willing to die in this confrontation, he achieved a sense that he had been liberated. There are many questions teachers can discuss with students about this episode. Why did Douglass feel liberated even though he remained a slave? Did Covey share Douglass's interpretation of this battle? What are the connections among Douglass's liberation in his battle with Covey, the liberation he experienced when he ran to the North, and the liberation he experienced when slavery finally ended as an institution in the United States?

Overall, by focusing on rich primary sources, students should come to recognize that masters and the people they enslaved together shaped the core features of slavery. They should also come to appreciate the many ways in which enslaved people resisted and the many different ways in which that resistance succeeded and failed, sometimes even succeeding and failing simultaneously.

NOTES

1. Ulrich B. Phillips, *American Negro Slavery* (New York and London: D. Appleton, 1918; reprint, Baton Rouge: Louisiana State University Press, 1966), 291.

2. Herbert Aptheker, *American Negro Slave Revolts* (New York: Columbia University Press, 1944).

3. W.E.B. Du Bois, *Black Reconstruction in America* (New York: Russell & Russell, 1935).

4. Kenneth M. Stampp, *The Peculiar Institution: Slavery in the Antebellum South* (New York: Knopf, 1956).

5. Stanley M. Elkins, *Slavery: A Problem in American Institutional and Intellectual Life* (Chicago: University of Chicago Press, 1959), 82.

6. Winthrop D. Jordan, *Tumult and Silence at Second Creek: An Inquiry into a Civil War Slave Conspiracy* (Baton Rouge: Louisiana State University Press, 1993).

7. Peter Kolchin, *American Slavery: 1619–1877* (New York: Hill & Wang, 1993), 155.

8. Stephanie M. H. Camp, *Closer to Freedom: Enslaved Women and Everyday Resistance in the Plantation South* (Chapel Hill: University of North Carolina Press, 2004).

9. John Hope Franklin and Loren Schweninger, *Runaway Slaves: Rebels on the Plantation* (New York: Oxford University Press, 1999), 97–123.

10. Kenneth S. Greenberg, *The Confessions of Nat Turner and Related Documents* (Boston and New York: Bedford Books of St. Martin's Press, 1996).

11. Harriet A. Jacobs, *Incidents in the Life of a Slave Girl, Written by Herself*, ed. Jean Fagan Yellin (Cambridge, MA: Harvard University Press, 1987).

12. Frederick Douglass, *Narrative of the Life of Frederick Douglass, an American Slave, Written by Himself*, ed. David W. Blight (Boston and New York: Bedford Books of St. Martin's Press, 1993), 79.

Slave Culture

BERNARD E. POWERS JR.

Much recent scholarship on slavery has focused on the two interrelated areas of slave agency and community formation. Unlike most of the pre-1960s scholarship, which privileged the master class, more recent scholarship places the slave at the center of the narrative to gain an interior view of the institution. Scholars have investigated slave initiatives taken in the areas of family life, expressive language, gender relations, resistance, spirituality, and even health care to penetrate the slave experience. We now have greater appreciation for the plantation as a site of community formation, where slaves created various networks through which they experienced and resisted their exploitation collectively. These approaches produced creative scholarship and challenged some of the most deeply entrenched, widespread misconceptions about slavery.[1]

The older conception of the slave as a mere extension of the master's will, the helpless, passive victim of Euro-American exploitation, offered little to stimulate scholarly or student interest. Conversely, the themes of agency and community formation projected wholly new representations of slaves as talented, aggressive, and creative people, who through dogged efforts created lives with a semblance of normalcy. This chapter focuses on slave ideas about spirituality and religion. These vital aspects of slave culture humanize slaves while exploring enslaved peoples' resilience, creativity, and quest for identity, separate from those who owned them.

In the seventeenth century, slaves' exposure to Christianity was rare. Many opposed proselytizing slaves, believing that conversion would require emancipation or make them insolent, indolent, or otherwise unfit for labor. About 1740, during the religious revivals known as the Great Awakening, the first mass conversions of enslaved people occurred. Slaves and free blacks found the evangelical style of the revival preachers appealing and attended the camp meetings in large numbers. The Baptist and Methodist denominations spread from 1790 and 1820 and had a special resonance with slaves, attracting large numbers to the Christian fold.[2] Finally, beginning in the 1830s, the reformist impulse sweeping the nation combined with the rise of abolitionism and the threat of slave insurrection gave new impetus to convert the slaves. The major denominations began concerted missionary work to counteract abolitionist critiques of slavery and to inculcate biblical lessons to prevent slave insurrections.[3] Even so, the opportunities for religious instruction varied considerably and were significantly affected by the receptivity of both masters and slaves.[4]

In embracing Christianity, Africans did not simply accept the belief system of the master class. They adopted those aspects of the faith and its practice that were most serviceable, while reinterpreting and adapting these to an African cultural framework.[5] What had been myriad cohesive African worldviews now fragmented under the pressures of the New World and the comparatively small number of Africans transferred to the Anglo-American mainland. Continuities with the African past continued to exist less as static retentions than, as the historian Charles Joyner observes, "in modes of expression that were the product of the slaves' creative response to a new environment." Africans lived in a sacred cosmos where every aspect of life was infused with spiritual significance. This orientation toward the world influenced their encounter with Christianity.[6] The result was a new synthetic Afro-Christianity with roots in both Euro-American and African traditions. We do not yet fully understand how the exact process of cultural fusion proceeded, but it is important to appreciate its magnitude. Two processes occurred simultaneously. The new Afro-Christianity was forged out of a "multiplicity of African rites and practices," just as New World Negroes, a group with a distinctive identity, became the composite of many melded African ethnic groups.[7]

Although traditional African religiosity differed substantially from Western beliefs and practices, there were important convergences between the two traditions. In these spiritual interstices Africans began to understand and reshape Christianity to meet their needs. Teachers can point to several different examples to demonstrate the syncretic nature of African spirituality and Christianity. The Christian Trinity and the

145

angels became the means to accommodate Africans' belief in multiple gods and lesser spirits. The Christian notion of resurrection was not completely foreign to Africans who believed in reincarnation. Africans had magical traditions similar to those found in the Bible. Finally, sometimes the two traditions shared religious objects, such as the BaKongo cosmogram, discussed later in this chapter, which although different in function were similar in form.[8] These points of commonality aided Africans in their transformation into Christians but also ensured they would place their unique stamp on the faith.

The slave preacher played a central role in creating and nurturing the Afro-Christian community. Frequently one of the few literate slaves on the plantation, the slave preacher was known for his powerful oratorical skills, creative imagination, and tremendous memory. Even when lacking formal literacy, these men were still effective; they believed the prerequisite for success was a personal connection to God and that book learning wasn't enough. As one preacher explained it: "wisdom in the heart is unlike wisdom in the mind." During the Civil War, Austa French, a northern missionary in Port Royal, South Carolina, confirmed this point. She observed that it was local, mainly illiterate slave preachers "of deep spiritual experience, sound sense, and capacity to state Scripture facts, narratives, and doctrines" who effectively ministered to the enslaved population over the years.[9] The man of God presided over highly emotional services characterized by enthusiastic singing, complex hand clapping, and foot stomping. Preachers began sermons in normal prose and gradually incorporated rhetorical flourishes, rhythmic cadences, and figurative speech, which elicited emotional responses from the audience. The sermon became a mutual performance in the African call-and-response tradition, which often culminated in worshippers shouting and experiencing religious ecstasy akin to spirit possession.[10]

Religious ecstasy, which established a special connection with the divine or spirits, was familiar to Africans and was fundamental to Afro-Christianity. The best example is the dance-like ceremony known as the ring shout, typically observed along the southeastern seaboard. Frequently held after a prayer service, the ring shout required worshippers to arrange themselves into a circle and to move rhythmically in a counter-clockwise direction, slowly at first but with increasing fervor and complexity, to the accompaniment of ecstatic clapping and singing. When the missionary teacher Laura Towne observed the ring shout in 1862, she said it was "certainly the remains of some old idol worship. The negroes sing a kind of chorus,—three standing apart to lead and clap,—and then all the others go shuffling round in a circle following one another with not much regularity, turning round occasionally and bending the knees, and stamping so that the whole floor swings. I never saw anything so savage."[11] The ring shout was an important manifestation of BaKongo culture in America. For the BaKongo, the cosmogram, a circle divided into four sections by a cross, was a powerful religious symbol. The circle represents the continuity of human life, and the vertical line of the cross connects God to man and the ancestors. The horizontal or kalunga line in the cross is the boundary between the land of the living above it and the land of the ancestors down below the surface of water. So when the BaKongo performed certain dances in a counter-clockwise fashion, they traced the cycle of life and were placed in contact with powerful ancestral spirits.[12] The ring shout might have begun as an African ritual that only gradually acquired Christian meaning and shaped Afro-Christianity's uniqueness.

The quest for religious conversion was the most important stage in enslaved peoples' spiritual life, and the process could reveal important African sensibilities. If slave owners refused to allow religious instruction or if the slaves simply found the authorized message unsatisfying, they took to the woods and convened secret meetings on their own "praying grounds." In Virginia, Elizabeth Sparks said "they called it stealin' the meetin." It was in these "hush arbors" that slaves gathered around pots that were turned down and propped up with sticks. They quietly sang and prayed, hoping their petitions would be heard by God but not by people.[13] In these meetings some "got religion," but these were mainly assemblies of the faithful. For others, religious conversion was achieved through the process known as "seekin'." The seeker first withdrew from worldly matters as much as possible in favor of religious study and prayer. Frequently the person was required to go out into the woods and pray and wait for a vision or word from God. After giving a successful report to church leaders or elders, the seeker was ready to be formally accepted into the community of saints through baptism.[14] Those who brought memories of Africa with them or were influenced by such sensibilities could understand seekin' in an African cultural framework. The historians Margaret Washington and Jason Young have both demonstrated the similarities between seekin' and the initiation rites of secret societies in West and Central Africa. In the latter, candidates temporarily removed themselves from society to wilderness areas, where they underwent a series of rituals that brought spiritual death followed by rebirth into a life of new power. Christian baptism could be understood in a similar vein. Here those with BaKongo and other African memories could recognize the spiritual death the candidate underwent as he or she was plunged under the surface of the water, known as the kalunga line, into the land of the ancestors. Yet that death was followed by the rebirth of a newly initiated and empowered Christian.[15] As processes, both conversion and baptism were probably understood as fully Christian only over time.

A proper funeral was particularly important for those slaves who lived in a world still fundamentally ordered by African cosmological ideas. Alice Sewell of Alabama said that on her plantation a deceased slave was buried as unceremoniously as cattle. She also recalled that an old woman, probably from a sense of duty, "done all de burying" of slaves and "said de funeral sayings by herself. She knew it by heart." In Georgia drums sometimes played important roles in the funeral ceremonies. "The drums of death" were played to announce the passing and the "settin-up" or wake. At the actual funeral, drums played the "dead march," which was long and slow, and the mourners marched around the grave site in a circle, shouting and praying. When drums weren't allowed, some deemed them so significant that they made hand motions mimicking the playing of drums.[16] The grave site was an important portal between the living and the dead, and the ring shout in this context must have prepared the way for the spirit of the newly departed to be received by the ancestors. To assist in the transition, objects important to that person were sometimes buried in the grave. Mourners had to properly mollify the spirit of the dead person, because, true to widespread African tradition, many slaves believed that ancestral spirits could affect people and events in the material world. Slaves ensured that grave-site surfaces were decorated with objects to placate and honor the departed spirit and to prevent it from becoming a "haunt," a wandering, malcontented ghost that tormented the living. Similarly, in South Carolina, the writer William Allen was told, when the head of a family passed away, after the family marched around the coffin in a circle, the adults passed the youngest child "over and then under the coffin." For further insight into slave burial traditions and how these related to their African counterparts, websites such as the one on New York City's eighteenth-century African Burial Ground are useful.[17]

The Africanized cosmos in which many enslaved people lived, especially those in Louisiana, Mississippi, South Carolina, and Georgia, was shared with a variety of spirits and cosmic forces. In addition to haunts, hags were "the disembodied spirits of witches" who, after shedding their skins, "rode" people who slept, giving them nightmares. There were also people with occult powers and malevolent intent who could cast spells to cause ill fortune, sickness, and even death. To navigate such an environment, even Christian slaves sometimes resorted to conjurers (also known as practitioners of hoodoo or root work) to heal or harm through "ritual harnessing of spiritual forces."[18] Many slaves believed that illness or other personal problems had a metaphysical basis and therefore resorted to the conjurer's occult powers to determine the problem's source, effect a remedy, and, if the problem was a spell, perhaps even turn it back on its author. Cornelia Bailey, of Sapelo Island, Georgia, explained that the old people resorted to conjure because God took his time to answer prayers but Dr. Buzzard (i.e., the conjurer) could bring results more quickly. When Frederick Douglass had a particularly brutal master, he resorted to an old and respected conjurer, who gave him a charm to prevent future whippings. Douglass was initially skeptical, even thinking such dealings were satanic, but he reconciled conjure and Christianity by asking: "How did I know but that the hand of the Lord was in it [?]"[19] Conjure could complement Christianity, and slaves used both to manipulate their environment to gain greater control over their lives.

Slave owners used Christianity to promote social control, justifying chattel slavery with biblical authority, but slaves rejected this "slaveholding priestcraft," as Frederick Douglass characterized it. He observed: "It was in vain that we had been taught . . . the duty of obedience to our masters—to recognize God as the author of our enslavement—to regard running away as an offense, alike against God and man . . . to consider our hard hands and dark color as God's displeasure." Douglass railed, "Nature laughed" such ideas "to scorn."[20]

While slaveholders used Christianity to undergird their mastery, in the hands of slaves lessons derived from the same faith condemned the very idea of human chattel. The historian Thomas Webber asserted that every time slaves had to sneak into the woods to worship God, it showed the master's hypocritical determination to keep "hidden the full, true message of Christianity." The Virginia slave Simon Brown recalled being taught that white masters were Christians and that "every white man was better than a black man, slave or free. We grinned in his face and said, 'Yes, sir, that's so, Master,' but behind his back we cursed him . . . deep down inside us slaves, hidden from the white men, our self-respect was always there."[21]

Slave culture, particularly slave religion, served as a defense mechanism shielding the enslaved from the most debilitating psychological abuses of slavery and also afforded them an offensive weapon. The scholar Jason Young observed that religion and culture were "salve for the wounds inflicted by slavery and functioned as a sword for battling the ideological framework upon which" it rested. John Brown, a Georgia fugitive, explained, "A slave is not a human being in the eye of the law, and the slaveholder looks upon him just as what the law makes him . . . and perhaps even [as] something less. But God made every man to stand upright before him, and if the slave law throws that man down; tramples upon him; robs him of his right, as a man . . . the law unmakes God's work," and no justification on earth "can make the thing right."[22]

In the Classroom

Religious songs are an excellent means of discerning slave psychology and values and can be used in the classroom to illustrate many of the aspects of slave religion and culture already discussed in this chapter. The best overall introduction to the subject remains Sterling Stuckey's "Through the Prism of Folklore: The Black Ethos in Slavery," which interrogates music and folklore as historical sources. Dena Epstein's *Sinful Tunes and Spirituals: Black Folk Music to the Civil War* is an excellent source for examining the social context and evolution of African American music and musical instruments. Lawrence Levine's *Black Culture and Black Consciousness* examines slave song as one aspect of African American culture.[23] This chapter has already explored the ways that slaves countered their masters' vision of religion as justification for slavery with a more reaffirming narrative of God's love. A related and important issue for discussion is whether Afro-Christians viewed their relationship to God in the same way whites did. Some evidence based on songs indicates that slaves saw their relationship to God as more familiar than whites did. For example, some lyrics from "Hold the Wind" are:

> When I get to heaven, gwine be at ease,
> Me and my *God gonna do as we please.*

> Gonna chatter with the Father, argue with the Son,
> *Tell um 'bout the world I just come from*

Another example is "Tell My Jesus 'Morning,'" the first line of which is "In de mornin' when I rise, Tell my Jesus huddy, oh." These examples suggests a less formal, even jocular connection to the spirit world that is more typical of West African religion than that of the white American South.[24]

William Allen's *Slave Songs of the United States* is an important anthology of antebellum and Civil War–era slave religious music, lyrics, and directions for singing. Here are songs that deepen our understanding of seekin' and the conversion process. "Go in the Wilderness" contains these lines:

> I wait upon de Lord, my God,
> Who take away de sin of the world
> If you want to find Jesus
> Go in de wilderness
> I wait upon de Lord[25]

Frequently candidates for conversion struggled in those lonely hours, as depicted in "Down in the Valley":

> You've heern talk of Jesus,
> Who set poor sinners free.
> De ligntnin' and de flashin', [thrice]
> Jesus set poor sinners free
> I can't stand de fire [thrice]
> Jesus set poor sinners free
> Way down in de valley

After "comin' through" (achieving salvation), worshippers sang joyous songs such as "Ain't I Glad I Got out of the Wilderness!"[26]

Another important point about the spirituals is the extent to which their expressions of liberty and freedom were otherworldly or reflected concerns about the slave's actual material world. The only certain answer is they reflected both spiritual and secular issues, but the emphasis probably varied depending on circumstances. William Wells Brown reported the following words sung by victims of the domestic slave trade:

> There's a better day a coming—
> Will you go along with me?
> There's a better day a coming,
> Go sound the jubilee!
> O, gracious Lord! When shall it be?
> That we poor souls shall all be free

This is a plaintive lament for secular emancipation, but what of the following words?

> O my Lord delivered Daniel
> O why not deliver me too?[27]

The meaning of the songs evolved, though. Booker T. Washington recalled, as the Civil War ended, that the slaves' sense of impending freedom was manifested in song. Now "there was more singing in the slave quarters than usual. It was bolder, had more ring, and lasted later into the night." Many of the songs referred to freedom, but the slaves "had been careful to explain that the 'freedom' in their songs referred to the next world. . . . Now they gradually threw off the mask" and admitted that they were singing about "freedom of the body in this world."[28] That was the assumption of whites in wartime Georgetown, South Carolina, where slaves were arrested for singing "We'll Soon Be Free." The song contains the lines:

> My brudder, how long,
> 'Fore we done sufferin' here?
> It won't be long [thrice]
> 'Fore de Lord will call us home[29]

Slave testimony is essential for depicting slave culture, and primary records are readily available. The multivolume *American Slave: A Composite Autobiography* contains wide-ranging interviews with former slaves. As Cynthia Lyerly discusses in this volume, these materials can also be used to discuss the challenges of using primary sources. "Born in Slavery: Slave Narratives from the Federal Writers' Project, 1936–1938" is available online in a digital version with photos. Relevant published documentary collections include Ira Berlin et al., *Remembering Slavery*, and Willie Lee Rose, *A Documentary History of American Slavery in North America.* Milton Sernett's *African American Religious History: Documentary Witness* focuses on religion.[30]

One area of special interest is how slave culture, particularly religion, influenced slave resistance. Nat Turner was a slave preacher who led the bloodiest slave insurrection in America; Kenneth Greenberg's *The Confessions of Nat Turner and Related Documents* depicts this episode and it is discussed in Greenberg's essay in this volume. Doug Egerton's *He Shall Go Out Free: The Lives of Denmark Vesey* shows how Christian and traditional African ideas gave power and structure to an important slave conspiracy. Finally, Mark Smith's anthology *Stono: Documenting and Interpreting a Southern Slave Revolt* shows how Christianity, first learned in Central Africa, shaped the most important slave revolt in eighteenth-century America.[31]

This essay has suggested how we might think of religion as a manifestation of slave culture. Slave religion counterbalances the image of the slave as passive victim, as we see the creative energies of a people employed to form an Afro-Christianity that was uniquely their own. In this area of life, slaves drew upon African traditions to construct their own ideas about God and to develop a vibrant musical life, which included spirituals and sacred dance traditions. These elements were part of a larger social fabric that enabled the enslaved to form a distinctive identity and to deflect some of the most oppressive psychological onslaughts of the slave system even while criticizing the master class. This subject changes our angle of vision, moving it from the "Big House" to the slave quarters, where there is still much to be learned.

NOTES

1. See Kenneth S. Greenberg, "Slave Resistance," in this volume for further information.

2. Albert Raboteau, "African Americans, Exodus, and the American Israel," in Paul Johnson, ed., *African American Christianity: Essays in History* (Berkeley: University of California Press, 1994), 2–6; Alan Gallay, *The Formation of a Planter Elite: Jonathan Bryan and the Southern Colonial Frontier* (Athens: University of Georgia Press, 2007), 38–39; Frank Klingberg, *Carolina Chronicle: The Papers of Commissary Gideon Johnston, 1707–1716* (Berkeley: University of California Press, 1946), 60.

3. Janet Cornelius, *Slave Missions and the Black Church in the Antebellum South* (Columbia: University of South Carolina Press), 28, 47; Albert Raboteau,

Slave Religion: The "Invisible Institution" in the Antebellum South (New York: Oxford University Press, 1978), 157–59, 161.

4. James W. Pennington, *The Fugitive Blacksmith* (London: Charles Gilpin, 1849), University of North Carolina–Chapel Hill electronic edition, 66. Many enslaved Muslims consciously rejected Christianity and continued to practice their faith as best they could. One example is Bilali Muhammad and some of his relatives on Sapelo Island, Georgia, and another is Ayuba Sulieman Diallo (Job ben Solomon), who was enslaved in Maryland. For more on these men see Sylviane A. Diouf, *Servants of Allah: African Muslims Enslaved in the Americas* (New York: New York University Press, 1998), and Philip Curtin, *Africa Remembered: Narratives by West Africans from the Era of the Slave Trade* (Madison: University of Wisconsin Press, 1967).

5. Raboteau, *Slave Religion*, 213.

6. Raboteau, *Slave Religion*, 92; Charles Joyner, *Down by the Riverside: A South Carolina Slave Community* (Urbana-Champaign: University of Illinois Press, 1984), 142–43, 159–60.

7. On the transformation from African ethnicity to a consciousness of race in the New World see Michael Gomez, *Exchanging Our Country Marks: The Transformation of African Identities in the Colonial and Antebellum South* (Chapel Hill: University of North Carolina Press, 1998); Joyner, *Down by the Riverside*, 141.

8. John Blassingame, *The Slave Community: Plantation Life in the Antebellum South* (New York: Oxford University Press, 1979), 21; Raboteau, *Slave Religion*, chapter 1; Robert Farris Thompson, *Flash of the Spirit: African and Afro-American Art and Philosophy* (New York: Random House, 1983), 108.

9. Blassingame, *Slave Community*, 131; George Rawick, ed., *American Slave: A Composite Autobiography*, 20 vols. (Westport, CT: Greenwood, 1972), 19:12; A. M. French, *Slavery in South Carolina and the Ex-Slaves* (New York: Winchell French, 1862), University of North Carolina–Chapel Hill electronic edition, 131.

10. Joyner, *Down by the Riverside*, 162; Raboteau, *Slave Religion*, 236–37.

11. Sterling Stuckey, *Slave Culture: Nationalist Theory and the Foundations of Black America* (New York: Oxford University Press, 1987), 11–14; John Mbiti, *African Religions and Philosophy* (Garden City, NY: Anchor, 1969), 224–31; Rupert S. Holland, ed., *Letters and Diary of Laura Towne* (Cambridge: Cambridge University Press, 1912), Google Books edition, 22–23.

12. Philip Curtin, *The Atlantic Slave Trade: A Census* (Madison: University of Wisconsin Press, 1969), 157. Curtin's study indicates that substantial numbers of Central Africans (including BaKongo) came to the United States at the height of the Atlantic slave trade; Thompson, *Flashes of the Spirit*, 108–9.

13. "Born in Slavery: Slave Narratives from the Federal Writers Project, 1936–38," Florida Narratives, 3:159, North Carolina Narratives, 2:133, http://memory.loc.gov/ammem/snhtml; Norman Yetman, *Life under the Peculiar Institution* (New York: Holt, Rinehart & Winston), 299.

14. Cornelia W. Bailey, *God, Dr. Buzzard, and the Bolito Man* (New York: Anchor, 2000), 162–63; *The Nation*, December 14, 1865, 745.

15. Jason Young, *Rituals of Resistance: African Atlantic Religion in Kongo and the Lowcountry South in the Era of Slavery* (Baton Rouge: Louisiana State University Press, 2007), 79–81; Margaret Washington, *A Peculiar People: Slave Religion and Community-Culture among the Gullahs* (New York: New York University Press, 1988), 47–50, 285–94.

16. Yetman, *Life under the Peculiar Institution*, 262; Georgia Writer's Project, *Drums and Shadows: Survival Studies among the Georgia Coastal Negroes* (Athens: University of Georgia Press, 1940), 67, 106–7.

17. Mbiti, *African Religions*, 195, 203; Charles Ball, *Fifty Years a Slave* (Indianapolis: H. Dayton, 1859), University of North Carolina–Chapel Hill electronic edition, 198; Reverend Irving E. Lowery, *Life on the Old Plantation in Ante-Bellum Days* (Columbia: The State Co., 1911), University of North Carolina–Chapel Hill electronic edition, 85–86; William F. Allen, *Slave Songs of the United States* (1867; reprint, New York: Peter Smith, 1951), 101. To explore New York's African Burial Ground visit http://www.coas.howard.edu/newyorkafricanburial ground/. An example of South Carolina slave burial traditions can be found at http://www.sciway.net/hist/chicora/gravematters-1.html.

18. On the traditional African cosmos see, for example, Victor C. Uchendu, *The Igbo of Southeast Nigeria* (Chicago: Holt, Rinehart & Winston, 1965), 11–15, 94–100, and Mbiti, *African Religions*, chapter 15; Joyner, *Down by the Riverside*, 146, 150; Sharla Fett, *Working Cures: Healing, Health and Power on Southern Slave Plantations* (Chapel Hill: University of North Carolina Press, 2002), 85.

19. Fett, *Working Cures*, 100–101; Bailey, *God, Dr. Buzzard, and the Bolito Man*, 189; Frederick Douglass, *The Life and Times of Frederick Douglass* (New York: Collier, 1962), 137–38.

20. Douglass, *Life and Times*, 157; "Born in Slavery: Slave Narratives from the Federal Writers' Project, 1936–1938," Georgia Narratives, 4:129.

21. Thomas Webber, *Deep Like the Rivers: Education in the Slave Quarter Community, 1831–1865* (New York: W. W. Norton, 1978), 205; William J. Faulkner, *The Days When the Animals Talked* (Chicago: Follett, 1977), 18–19.

22. Young, *Rituals of Resistance*, 12; L. A. Chamerovzow, ed., *Slave Life in Georgia: A Narrative of the Life, Sufferings, and Escape of John Brown* (London: n.p., 1855), University of North Carolina–Chapel Hill, electronic edition, 202–3.

23. Sterling Stuckey, "Through the Prism of Folklore: The Black Ethos in Slavery," *Massachusetts Review* 9 (Summer 1968); Dena J. Epstein, *Sinful Tunes and Spirituals: Black Folk Music to the Civil War* (Urbana: University of Illinois Press, 1977); Lawrence Levine, *Black Culture and Black Consciousness* (New York: Oxford University Press, 1977).

24. "Huddy" was equivalent to the expression "howdy." Allen, *Slave Songs*, 15; Stuckey, "Through the Prism of Folklore," 421.

25. Allen, *Slave Songs*, 14.

26. Thomas W. Higginson, "Negro Spirituals," *Atlantic Monthly* (June 1867), 685–94; Allen, *Slave Songs*, 14.

27. Blassingame, *Slave Community*, 140–43; William Wells Brown, *Narrative of William W. Brown, a Fugitive Slave* (Boston: Antislavery Office), Internet Archive, https://archive.org/details/narrativeofwillioobrow, 51.

28. *Three Negro Classics* (New York: Avon, 1965), 39.

29. Higginson, "Negro Spirituals."

30. Rawick, *American Slave: A Composite Autobiography*; Ira Berlin et al., *Remembering Slavery* (New York: New Press, 1998); Willie Lee Rose, *A Documentary History of Slavery in North America* (Athens: University of Georgia Press, 1999); "Born in Slavery: Slave Narratives from the Federal Writers' Project, 1936–1938"; Milton Sernett, ed., *African American Religious History: Documentary Witness* (Durham, NC: Duke University Press, 1999).

31. Kenneth S. Greenberg, *The Confessions of Nat Turner and Related Documents* (Boston and New York: Bedford Books of St. Martin's Press, 1996); Douglas Egerton, *He Shall Go Out Free: The Lives of Denmark Vesey* (Lanham, MD: Rowman and Littlefield, 2004); Mark Smith, *Stono: Documenting and Interpreting a Southern Slave Revolt* (Columbia: University of South Carolina, 2005).

The Diverse Experiences
of the Enslaved

DEIRDRE COOPER OWENS

Although scholars have written about the diverse experiences of the enslaved across time and space since the 1970s, very few students, whether elementary, secondary, or college level, fully grasp the import of this subject. Understanding the complexity of slavery undergirds much of the work that historians of slavery do, and yet, students, like most other Americans, are woefully uninformed about American slavery. One of the most enduring false narratives of slavery is that all enslaved people picked cotton while singing happily in fields that framed grand neoclassical antebellum plantation homes.

Many of these narratives and the images that accompany them originate from popular culture, such as Margaret Mitchell's culturally significant and popular novel *Gone with the Wind* and the majestic film based on her book. In these productions, black women were depicted as comically sassy mammies who possessed a fierce devotion to the white families they served. Black men were rendered subservient and lived in a state of arrested development as perennial children. Unfortunately, at least for historians of American slavery, these films have taught more Americans about slavery than my colleagues and I have. So why is there such a gap between what specialists and students know? How do and should we, as educators, transmit what we know about American slavery to our students and, more broadly, to all Americans?

Unlike other fields that are viewed as less controversial and allegedly more value neutral, such as economics and science, the history of slavery conjures feelings of racial guilt, anger, and embarrassment. These emotional responses often accompany deep shame and anger over the antiblack racism that has defined much of the United States' treatment of African Americans. Further, the mention of slavery harkens back to a historical moment that many Americans wish to leave behind, especially in light of the claim that the country has entered a postracial phase in the new millennium. Some teachers share similar concerns and are often wary of entering into what they consider a historical minefield that could very easily, and without warning, blow up in their faces. A March 2011 event evidences how challenging teaching slavery can be for educators who have not been trained in the politics of race and racism. A fifth-grade teacher in Gahanna, Ohio, had her students reenact a slave auction as a social studies project. The students were made to act as either "masters" or "slaves." The teacher instructed her white students to physically examine their classmate, a ten-year-old African American boy, as he pretended to be a slave on an auction block.[1] Had that elementary teacher been taught to emphasize, with sensitivity to her students' needs, how slave sales separated families and the growing impact slave markets had on the nineteenth-century economy and had she used the words and stories of the formerly enslaved about their experiences at slave markets and on auction blocks, perhaps this sort of ineffectual historical reenactment would not have occurred.

So how can teachers teach American slavery to their students while demonstrating sensitivity? I tend to rely on three approaches. Initially, I introduce the concept of race to my students. Second, I examine the ways that attention to gender colors our understanding of the institution. Last, I follow a chronological and region-based approach that demonstrates how slavery developed in different parts of the country and how the crops that slaves produced shaped their experience of slavery. Throughout these discussions, I emphasize how utterly "American" the institution of slavery was. By the late eighteenth century slavery was becoming largely a southern affair because of the cash crops produced in the region, including tobacco, rice, indigo, and, later, cotton. By the mid-nineteenth century, however, northern industries profited greatly from southern slavery, especially textile mills that relied heavily on cotton grown in the Deep South. American slavery—its existence, growth, and maintenance—was not unique to the South, and the institution affected all parts of the country.

Eric Kimball's essay in this volume demonstrates that as more European nations entered into what we now term the trans-Atlantic slave trade, they worked out an evolving definition of a single blackness even though they were intimately aware of how diverse African ethnic groups were. Kimball has noted several ways to teach this complicated history to students. Discussions of race and labor also can start with one of the most common figures of both American and world history: Christopher Columbus. Columbus is usually discussed as the explorer linked to the "founding" of the Americas and as the architect of Indian genocide. As contentious as Christopher Columbus has become, he is also a good exemplar to use in the study of American slavery. As a young man, Christopher Columbus was trained in the Madeira sugar trade. On behalf of the Spanish Crown, he brought this experience working on Portuguese sugar plantations to the islands he called the West Indies. During his second voyage to the New World, in 1493, Columbus introduced sugar cane to the Caribbean. Indigenous people were not good laborers on sugar plantations for many reasons, particularly because so many got sick and died as a result of disease and violence. The Spanish, in turn, began primarily to use African slaves, much as the Portuguese had done in Madeira.[2] Columbus, therefore, is central to discussions of American slavery because he introduced chattel slavery to the New World and established on behalf of a European nation the first successful cash crop that used native people and African-born slaves. As Laird Bergad's essay in this volume also demonstrates, by the turn of the sixteenth century West Africans had become more important to New World slavery than indigenous people. Many Africans were skilled in sugar cane cultivation, and as New World slavery developed, the labor system became increasingly associated with blackness.

As the North American colonies grew and thousands of West and Central Africans were brought in primarily as slaves, the English began to codify the labor and preservation of slavery on the basis of race and gender. Teachers can ask students to examine parts of Robert Beverly's early writings on Virginia to understand the ways in which the system of slavery influenced American notions of race and gender. In 1705 Robert Beverley Jr., a legislator and the son of a prominent Virginia plantation owner, authored *The History and Present State of Virginia*, to document the colony's then current state of affairs. Also, Beverley's book was meant to attract more English men and women to immigrate to the British colony. The early historian needed to assure settlers that they would not enter Virginia as slaves, and he distinguished between the labor of slaves and that of indentured servants. Beverley was direct.

He wrote that "Because I have heard how strangely cruel and severe the Service of this Country is represented in some parts of England, I can't forbear affirming that the work of their Servants and Slaves is no other than what every common Freeman does." In terms of the work that black slaves and English servants were to perform, the legislator stated, "The Male-Servants and Slaves of both Sexes are employed together in Tilling and Manuring the Ground, in Sowing and Planting Tobacco, Corn, &c. [etc.]" The legislator also noted that slaves "were Negroes" who would inherit "the condition of the Mother."[3]

Once students have dissected the meaning of Beverley's writing for race and gender in the Americas, teachers can explain the ways in which this dictum on labor, race, and gender reverberated across colonial America, determining how enslaved men and women would be treated on plantations and smaller farms. First, black women were perceived as physically stronger than white women and would perform the same strenuous agricultural labor as both black and white men. Further, white male legislators altered the legal status of white men with regard to their offspring. Recognizing the importance and economic value of enslaved women's reproductive labor, white men determined that bondwomen's children would inherit their mother's status, a statute that did not exist in England. As a result, "Negro" became synonymous with slavery. While white women became a protected class not meant to perform harsh agricultural labor in the Virginia tobacco fields, black women were considered akin to black men in terms of the agricultural labor they did. As slavery became a permanent fixture in Virginia and, more broadly, within colonial British America and later the United States, these assumptions about race, gender, and slavery followed the institution.

While Virginia's early slavery statute codified the institution on the basis of the physical characteristics of the enslaved, slavery was a labor system dependent not only on black bodies but also on the valuable labor those captive bodies produced. As was evident in Beverley's writing, the labor of enslaved men and women was interchangeable. Teachers may ask students to analyze Mary Ella Grandberry's Works Progress Administration narrative to see how both men and women were engaged in the same kind of agricultural work on large southern plantations and on smaller slave farms. In the 1930s, Mary Ella Grandberry, a formerly enslaved laborer, recounted her experiences working as a slave in an oral interview conducted by a government worker for the WPA. Asked to compare the living conditions of free African Americans in the twentieth century with the conditions endured by those who lived in bondage, Grandberry derided younger people for their complaints about life's hardships. She quipped, "dey is livin' just like kings and queens." Grandberry continued to provide specific details about life for field slaves who lived on her former plantation. She stated, "Dey don't have to get up before day when it's so dark you can just see your hands before your eyes. Dey don't know what it's like to have to keep up with de leader. . . . Iffen you didn't keep up with de leader you got a good thrashin'."[4]

This quotation tells modern students much about slave labor. It elucidates how ordered the system of work was for enslaved black men and women but also intimates to contemporary Americans how the specter of violence infiltrated every aspect of enslaved people's lives. Also, Grandberry's narrative reveals how overseers and masters meted out violence equally to men and women. After carefully considering its appropriateness for a given class, teachers may use the 2013 movie *12 Years a Slave* to further demonstrate this point. The film is based on the slave narrative of Solomon Northup, a free man who was illegally sold into slavery and later freed. The character Patsy demonstrates the malleability of gender categories and the importance of violence. As one of the strongest cotton pickers, Patsy was the field leader on the Eppses' Louisiana cotton plantation. In a moving but jarring scene, she is brutally whipped. Mary Ella Grandberry's words are haunting: "Iffen you didn't keep up with de leader you got a good thrashin'."

While both Grandberry's and Patsy's examples demonstrate labor in the fields, as cash crops began to flourish in the eighteenth century slave owners began to demand "house servants and craftsmen" as an addition to the slave population on their plantations and large slave farms.[5] Wealthy white men who owned large numbers of black men and women, usually upwards of thirty or more, demanded that slaves perform more specialized work and domestic chores. Because of this demand, more of the enslaved engaged in increasingly diverse and non-agricultural labor, especially in regions such as South Carolina's Low Country and Georgia. Enslaved men performed "skilled labor" such as driving, carpentry, and smith work, and their abilities to do so greatly increased their economic value among white slave owners and traders.[6]

Like most enslaved men, bondwomen were mainly confined to fieldwork in the late eighteenth century; however, there were a few skilled domestic workers, slave nurses, and midwives who began to appear on slave lists.[7] Using gender as a lens through which to view women slaves' experiences helps students to dislodge views that are narrow and restrictive when it comes to understanding how men and women were "supposed" to live and work according to early American gender conventions. In particular, teachers can discuss with their students how notions of gender were critical to the resistance of enslaved women. For example, Anna Baker, who lived in Aberdeen, Mississippi, recounted how she transmitted news from the enslaved to her master for treats but would also lay bare the master's private conversations to members of the slave community. Anna recalled, "Marster would tell me, 'Loosanna (his pet name for me), if you keep yo' ears open an' tell me what de darkies talk 'bout, dey'll be somp'n' good in it for you.' I'd stay 'roun' de folks an' make lak I was a-playing. All de time I'd be a-listenin'. Den I'd go an' tell Marster what I hear'd. But all de time I mus' a-had a right smart mind, 'cause I'd play 'roun' de white folks an' hear what dey'd say," and she told members of her enslaved community.[8]

Although nursing was tedious labor for enslaved women, who continued to work in fields and homes and also took care of their families, their healing work allowed them to garner respect from the members of their slave communities and, if they were sent to assist the local white community, to earn money for their owners. Slave nurses and midwives relied on a West African "relational vision of health" in their practice, which viewed healing as an integration of the secular and the sacred worlds.[9] Black women's adherence to this ideology placed them at odds with white owners and male medical doctors, who derided their "folk" practices as voodoo and ineffective. For slave owners and doctors, the African roots of voodoo and slave folk medicine proved problematic because their continuing popularity was evidence that enslaved people held onto the remnants of West African belief systems. Thus, enslaved women's reliance on the African healing arts they privileged and controlled signaled one of the myriad ways black women in bondage resisted their enslavement differently from bondmen. Out of the view of prying white men's eyes, black women could utilize some of the very crops they planted to aid in healing sick slaves in their communities.

The importance of "place" in understanding the diverse experiences of the enslaved also cannot be overstated. Studying "place" in American slavery often is tied to the study of slave labor, as the unskilled fieldwork that occupied many slaves was based on cash crops that varied by region. The task labor system was an earlier system of labor created to meet planters' "need to have slaves support themselves while the plantation economy developed." Under the task system, slaves were given a certain amount of labor to complete in one day. Enslaved men and women could work at their own pace and were done for the day when the given job was complete. The task system was not as physically taxing for the enslaved as the later gang labor system because once tasks were completed, enslaved workers could exercise some autonomy and control their personal time. There is some controversy about how the task system originated, but it seemed to characterize work on rice plantations and involved more women than men.[10]

Most students will be more familiar with the gang labor system, associated with cotton slavery. Cotton plantations, and the labor system that fueled them, emerged on a large scale after Eli Whitney's invention of the cotton gin, in 1793. Until this time, cotton had been an insignificant crop in North America, largely because of the difficulty of separating the cotton seeds from the fibers that could be woven into fabric. Before the invention of the cotton gin, it would take a single slave an entire day to clean the seeds from one pound of cotton. After Whitney's invention, the same slave could clean fifty pounds of cotton in a given day.

The enslaved feared cotton slavery because they knew the strenuous nature and brutality of the gang labor system that surrounded it. The gang system was a much more efficient system for plantation owners than the task labor system because the work pace was continuous throughout the day. The enslaved worked all day at a given job. A driver or overseer monitored the slaves' pace to make sure that they worked swiftly. Slave drivers were often drawn from the ranks of the enslaved, while overseers were white men who had been hired by the plantation master. Three groups constituted the gang labor system. The first gang, called the "great gang," was given the most laborious work, meant for the fittest slaves. The second gang was composed of less able slaves such as teenagers, older slaves, and workers who were not well. The third gang, assigned the easiest work, might include young children, the handicapped, pregnant women, the elderly, and the infirm. Because of the sunup-to-sundown work schedule and the backbreaking labor cotton cultivation required, it was a brutal labor system.

The labor of the enslaved men and women on gangs across the South was at the heart of the cotton boom that followed the invention of the cotton gin. Teachers can use the case of Mississippi to demonstrate the scope of this cotton boom and the importance of gang labor. As Mississippi became a US territory, in the 1790s, cotton became its major cash crop. Enslaved men and women worked two hundred days each year growing and harvesting cotton, largely on plantations there. Bond-women had additional duties that were domestic in nature, including growing their own gardens, birthing and tending to their children, and serving as nurses for family members and friends. In 1790, 3,000 bales of cotton were produced; twenty years later, in 1810, 178,000 bales were produced. By 1817, the year Mississippi became a state, its booming cotton-based economy had changed the lives of black Mississippians because of the nearly universal adoption of the gang labor system. At the start of the Civil War, in 1861, more than four million bales of cotton were produced in Mississippi. Mississippi was both the "blackest" state and the richest state in the Union by 1861. The state held that distinction because of the massive amounts of cotton it produced.

Although Congress outlawed the international slave trade in 1807, a domestic slave trade replaced it and flourished because American slavery was a lucrative big business. The domestic slave trade in America moved more men and women of African descent "down South" than the international slave trade had during its entire existence. Virginia Bell, a former slave, shared the story of her parents, Della and Jim Blair, and their migration in her oral history narrative: "Both of them was from Virginny, but from diff'rent places, and was brought to Louisiana by nigger traders."[11] Like Virginia Bell's parents, approximately one million enslaved people were transported from the Upper South to the Lower South between 1790 and 1860. As the enslaved were shipped from Maryland, Virginia, and the Carolinas, they were transplanted to Kentucky, Tennessee, Georgia, Alabama, Mississippi, Louisiana, and Texas. As Peter Kolchin notes, "Every decade between 1810 and 1860 saw more than 100,000 slave migrants."[12] The phenomenal growth of cotton in the Lower South and a sluggish economy in the Upper South contributed to the increase in what has now become known as the "Second Middle Passage." As southern planters made more money because of the global demand for cotton and northern industrialists needed the crop to keep their textile mills successful, the market for black bodies boomed.

Enslaved people responded to these changes that devastated their communities and lives in a number of ways. Enslaved men and women composed folk songs that addressed the pangs of despair they felt as family members were sold "down South" from the Upper South. In an oral history interview, a former bondwoman, Emma Howard, shared the lyrics of a popular song enslaved men and women sang on her Alabama plantation. She called out, "Mammy, is ol' Massa gwin'er sell us tomorrow? Yes, my chile. Whar he gwin'er sell us? Way down South in Georgia." The former bondwoman later recounted, "That was one of de saddest songs we sung endurin' slavery days. It always did make me cry."[13] Thus black migration was transformed from international oceanic-based travel to domestic mainland migration. Ultimately, the Civil War represented the final phase of black migration as the enslaved escaped to Union lines by the thousands and forced the federal government to create refugee camps to accommodate black people who were considered contraband. Bethany Jay's essay in this volume provides a more detailed discussion of this practice.

Focusing on race, labor, gender, and place as organizational concepts allows teachers to emphasize for their students how varied the experiences of the enslaved were over three centuries. Enslaved men and women worked in a range of occupations that this essay has not had an opportunity to address: in husbandry, in naval stores, as cultivators of hemp and corn, and even in southern industry. Teachers can introduce interviews from the 1930s Works Progress Administration to stress the diverse experiences of the enslaved and the various kinds of labor they performed. As contested as these primary sources are, they have allowed my students to humanize and personalize "slaves." Cynthia Lyerly's essay in this volume discusses these sources.

Overall, teaching American slavery does not have to be a task fraught with difficulty. It is one of the subfields of US history that has flourished. With the plethora of primary and secondary sources available, teachers can employ a variety of pedagogical approaches that evidence how the enslaved lived through and responded to their bondage over time. Through an examination of race, labor, gender, and place, students are able to move past the one-note generalizations that describe the enslaved. They can grapple with the realization that slavery was not solely a southern phenomenon but began as a colonial American institution, with tentacles that reached across the Atlantic world. As such, slavery informed how the United States would ultimately treat people of African descent who lived within its borders, even after the labor system was abolished. For history teachers, the reward in teaching these kinds of lessons about American slavery is that a new generation of Americans can appreciate how all members of society contribute to the building of a nation, even those considered the most oppressed.

NOTES

1. "Chapelfield Elementary School Sorry for Making Black Student 'Slave,'" http://www.huffingtonpost.com/2011/03/04/chapelfield-elementary-sc_n_831318.html.

2. For more information on the origins of the Atlantic World sugar industry and slave trade, readers may consult Cesar J. Ayala, *American Sugar Kingdom: The Plantation Economy of the Spanish Caribbean, 1898-1934* (Chapel Hill: University of North Carolina Press, 1999), and Richard Dunn, *Sugar and Slaves: The Rise of the Planter Class in the English West Indies, 1624-1713* (Chapel Hill: University of North Carolina Press, 2000).

3. Robert Beverley Jr., *The History and Present State of Virginia* (1705 and 1722), http://nationalhumanitiescenter.org/pds/becomingamer/growth /text1/virginiabeverley.pdf.

4. Norman R. Yetman, *Voices from Slavery: 100 Authentic Slave Narratives* (Mineola, NY: Dover, [1970] 2000), 145.

5. Peter Kolchin, *American Slavery, 1619-1877* (New York: Hill & Wang, 2003), 51.

6. For a classroom resource, see http://www.thehistoryblog.com/wp-content/uploads/2013/05/Joshua-Grimball-1758-estate-inventory.jpg. The carpenter, Sam, is listed as the most valuable slave.

7. A planter's listing of enslaved women and their occupations and value can be found at http://www.pbs.org/wgbh/aia/part3/3h503b.html.

8. Anna Baker, Aberdeen, Mississippi, Works Progress Administration, 1936-38, http://www.gutenberg.org/files/12055/12055-h/12055-h.htm#Baker Anna.

9. Sharla Fett, *Working Cures: Healing, Health, and Power on Southern Slave Plantations* (Chapel Hill: University of North Carolina Press, 2000), 34.

10. Daniel C. Littlefield, "The Varieties of Slave Labor," *Freedom's Story: Teaching African American History and Literature* (National Humanities Center), http://nationalhumanitiescenter.org/tserve/freedom/1609-1865/essays /slavelabor.htm. For a more comprehensive study of slavery and labor see David R. Roediger and Elizabeth D. Esch, *The Production of Difference: Race and the Management of Labor in U.S. History* (Oxford: Oxford University Press, 2012).

11. Yetman, *Voices from Slavery*, 26.

12. Kolchin, *American Slavery*, 96.

13. Emma Howard, Alabama, Works Progress Administrations, 1936-38, http://nationalhumanitiescenter.org/pds/maai/community/text2/plantation communitywpa.pdf.

Slavery and the Civil War

BETHANY JAY

Few historical topics are as emotionally charged as the role of slavery in causing the Civil War. While historians have conclusively linked these two subjects, portions of the larger public remain unconvinced. This fact was starkly evident in 1998, when the National Park Service decided to start discussing slavery as a cause of the war in Civil War battlefield parks. Following this decision, Dwight Pitcaithley, chief historian of the National Park Service, recalled, "The National Park Service was inundated with approximately 2,400 cards and letters from the Sons of Confederate Veterans, members of Civil War Roundtables, and the general public."[1] Pitcaithley noted that many of the letters charged the Park Service with "'demonizing and slandering' the South with its 'new' interpretation of the war" and using the battlefields as "South-bashing, hate-generating propaganda centers." Another letter characterized the addition of slavery as "some momentarily fashionable, politically correct, sensitive etc., ideology."[2] For these letter writers, the Park Service's link between slavery and the Civil War distorted their region's history, their ancestors' history, and the history of the nation.[3]

For teachers, charged topics such as the connections between slavery and the Civil War present both opportunities for useful classroom discussions and potential minefields. Teachers, even those in the regions where the link between slavery and the Civil War is expected, can mitigate the potential pitfalls of this discussion and foster genuine content knowledge and understanding among their students by guiding student analysis and discussion of several key topics. This essay discusses teaching the role of slavery in the Civil War by examining resources in two separate subject areas: slavery as a cause of the Civil War and the role of slaves and the end of slavery in the progress of the Civil War.

167

The angry letter writers who rallied against a discussion of slavery in Civil War battlefield parks surely pointed to states' rights as the true cause of the war. Teachers will likely encounter this preconception from students across the country, even those who are not emotionally attached to the subject. A quick Internet search will provide teachers with documents that demonstrate the persistence of this narrative. As the historian Charles Dew discusses in his informative and accessible book *Apostles of Disunion*, the clearest articulation of states' rights as an issue separate from slavery came after the Civil War when former Confederates such as Jefferson Davis pointed to "constitutional govern-ment," "the supremacy of law," and "natural rights of man" as the chief causes of the war.[4] These are likely the kind of generalizations that students will have heard before reaching the classroom. Of course, the tension between state and federal authority predates the immediate antebellum era, having roots as far back as the country itself. This larger topic is outside the scope of this essay. Teachers can complicate student understanding of the connections between the issue of states' rights and slavery in the immediate antebellum era, however, by examining several key issues with students.

In the 1850s, the issue of state versus federal authority was at the forefront of the nation's mind as northern and southern states clashed over the enforcement of federal laws relating to slavery. The Constitution protected slave property in Article IV, Section 2, which described slaves vaguely as persons "held to Service or Labour in one State" to ensure that slaves who fled to free states would be able to be returned to slavery.[5] Much of the power of this Constitutional protection for slavery, how-ever, was undercut by northern states' "personal liberty laws" that prevented the return of slaves hiding in the North.[6] In response to these statutes, southern lawmakers argued for increased federal attention to the issue of returning escaped slaves. These slaveholders got what they wanted when Congress passed the 1850 Fugitive Slave Act, which added significant federal enforcement power to existing federal codes, as part of the Compromise of 1850. The specific provisions of the Fugitive Slave Act raised the ire of northerners. First, it created commissioners who, instead of judges, issued warrants for the capture and return of suspected fugitive slaves. A commissioner would earn $10 if he returned a fugitive to slavery and $5 if he found in favor of the fugitive.[7] In addi-tion, the 1850 act allowed an affidavit from a slaveholder to be used as sufficient proof of ownership; suspected slaves were not allowed to testify during the proceedings. Last, the law allowed commissioners to deputize any citizen to help enforce the law. Those citizens who refused faced harsh punishments, including fines and imprisonment.[8]

Predictably, this beefed-up law caused significant reaction in both the South and the North. Southerners reacted by increasing their efforts to recapture fugitive slaves. White northerners bristled at the idea of being compelled to enforce the law, vowing civil disobedience if needed. Black northerners, on the other hand, worried about their personal freedom as the number of kidnappers and fraudulent claims increased. Many fugitives, even those who had been living in the North for decades, fled to Canada or went into hiding.[9]

The 1854 case of Anthony Burns provides an example of the way southern slaveholders used the federal government's Fugitive Slave Law in the years before the Civil War. Further, it illustrates the depth of sectional tension over this law. Enslaved in Virginia, Burns escaped to Boston, a city with both a significant free black population and a powerful abolitionist movement. In May 1854, Burns was arrested and jailed in Boston's federal courthouse. Boston's abolitionists mobilized in response to Burns's arrest, and separate meetings of white and black abolitionists eventually convened on the courthouse in an attempt to free Burns. In the ensuing chaos, a police officer was fatally wounded, but Burns remained in jail. Despite this opposition, federal authorities were determined to make an example out of Anthony Burns and declared him to be a fugitive slave. Upon Burns's conviction, fifty thousand Bostonians lined the streets to watch as he was marched in shackles to a waiting vessel. Reaction to Burns's arrest and return to slavery was profound. One Massachusetts native, Amos A. Lawrence, wrote, "We went to bed one night old fashioned, conservative, Compromise Union Whigs & waked up stark mad Abolitionists."[10]

The 2013 PBS documentary *The Abolitionists* offers a nice overview of the Anthony Burns case.[11] In discussing the Fugitive Slave Law and Anthony Burns, teachers should ask students questions such as, "What did the southern slaveholders want?," "Did they have the authority to go into Massachusetts and capture Burns? What gave them that power?," and "Why do you think northerners resisted? How might northerners feel being forced to search for a fugitive slave?" This discussion should lead students to the conclusion that these examples represent instances in which southern politicians firmly stood in favor of federal law superseding state law to protect southern slave property. Students should also recognize that by making northerners complicit in the capture of fugitive slaves, the law galvanized northern public opinion in opposition to the slaveholding South.

In the months surrounding the immediate secession crisis, southern politicians articulated the "immediate causes" of secession in numerous documents and speeches. In many of these public pronouncements, the failure of the federal government to protect the interests of slaveholders coexisted alongside impassioned defenses of the sovereignty of the states within the Union. These documents demonstrate that southern lawmakers firmly stood in favor of using the power of the federal government to uphold or strengthen their interests in slave property. In cases where federal statutes were seen as threatening slavery, these same lawmakers rallied behind the sovereignty of the state. In these documents, the example of the Fugitive Slave Act and the existence of personal liberty laws in northern states loomed large. For example, South Carolina's "Declaration of the Immediate Causes Which Induce and Justify the Secession of South Carolina from the Federal Union," the first document of its kind, passionately denounced both the abolitionist movement and attempts to aid runaways:

> Those [nonslaveholding] States have assumed the right of deciding upon the propriety of our domestic institutions, and have denied the rights of property established in fifteen of the States and recognized by the Constitution; they have denounced as sinful the institution of Slavery; they have permitted the open establishment among them of societies, whose avowed object is to disturb the peace of and eloin [seize] the property of the citizens of other States. They have encouraged and assisted thousands of our slaves to leave their homes.[12]

These same themes recurred in speeches that secession commissioners from Mississippi, Alabama, South Carolina, and Georgia made in an attempt to induce other slaveholding states to secede from the Union. For example, Mississippi's W. L. Harris addressed the Georgia Assembly on December 17, 1860, to advocate for Georgia's secession. Northern reaction to the Fugitive Slave Act was prominent among his arguments for secession:

> Our Constitution, in unmistakable language, guarantees the return of our fugitive slaves. Congress has recognized her duty in this respect, by enacting proper laws for the enforcement of this right.

And yet these laws have been continually nullified, and the solemn pledge of the Compromise of 1850, by which the North came under renewed obligations to enforce them, has been faithlessly disregarded, and the government and its officers set at defiance.[13]

Ask students to put these arguments in their own words. Again, the use of federal authority to protect slavery is clearly articulated in these documents, thus complicating the simplistic "states' rights" narrative of the coming of the Civil War.

Southern politicians also unabashedly declared that secession was necessary to protect the institution of slavery. Students can analyze and put a variety of documents into their own words to understand the ways in which southern politicians connected the preservation of slavery to secession. For example, South Carolina's "Immediate Causes" document declared that with Lincoln's election, northerners conspired to elect "a man to the high office of President of the United States whose opinions and purposes are hostile to Slavery." In light of Lincoln's election, southerners declared "that the public mind must rest in the belief that Slavery is in the course of ultimate extinction."[14] Georgia's secession commissioner W. L. Harris argued:

Our fathers made this a government for the white man, rejecting the negro, as an ignorant, inferior, barbarian race, incapable of self-government, and not, therefore, entitled to be associated with the white man upon terms of civil, political, or social equality.

This new administration comes into power, under the solemn pledge to overturn and strike down this great feature of our Union, without which it would never have been formed, and to substitute in its stead their new theory of the universal equality of the white and black races.[15]

Mississippi's "A Declaration of the Immediate Causes which Induce and Justify the Secession of the State of Mississippi from the Federal Union" asserted:

Our position is thoroughly identified with the institution of slavery—the greatest material interest of the world. Its labor supplies the product which constitutes by far the largest and most important portions of commerce of the earth. These products are peculiar to the climate verging on the tropical regions, and by an imperious law of nature, none but the black race can bear exposure to the tropical sun. These products have become necessities of the world, and a blow at slavery is a blow at commerce and civilization. That blow has been long aimed at the institution, and was at the point of reaching its consummation. There was no choice left us but submission to the mandates of abolition, or a dissolution of the Union, whose principles had been subverted to work out our ruin.[16]

Confederate vice president Alexander H. Stephens famously declared of the Confederacy, "its cornerstone rests, upon the great truth that the negro is not equal to the white man; that slavery, subordination to the superior race, is his natural and moral condition. This, our new Government, is the first, in the history of the world, based upon this great physical, philosophical, and moral truth."[17]

Not only was slavery the cause of the Civil War but its presence in the southern and border states also greatly affected the prosecution of the war. Union policy regarding slaves in the South and the wartime use of African Americans in the military evolved slowly, however. The first instance of Union forces using enslaved people as wartime resources occurred in 1861, when Brigadier General Benjamin Butler declared that three slave men who had escaped to Union lines were "contraband of war and therefore subject to confiscation."[18] Butler's spontaneous actions later became codified by the First Confiscation Act, which was itself strengthened by the 1862 Second Confiscation Act, which freed all slaves of rebel masters who made it to Union lines. The historian Joseph Glatthaar argues that these early policies were important to the Union war effort in two main ways. First, they "set the Lincoln administration on the rocky trail toward emancipation." In addition, because the confiscation policy called for escaped slaves to be employed in support of the Union army as laborers, it freed Union soldiers for duty on the front lines as it simultaneously robbed the Confederacy of valuable manpower.[19]

Few black Americans were content with serving only as laborers for the Union army. While as many as ten thousand African Americans served as part of the navy, African Americans initially were not allowed to enlist in the army. From the onset of the conflict, however, free blacks in the North clamored for a chance to serve as soldiers in the Union army. Frederick Douglass, whose sons would eventually serve as Union soldiers, was prominent among these voices. As Glatthaar notes,

Douglass criticized Union policy, which forbade the enlistment of black soldiers, observing, "This is no time to fight with one hand, when both are needed; that this is no time to fight only with your white hand, and allow your black hand to remain tied."[20]

As Douglass knew, the outcome of the Civil War could affect the future of both free blacks and enslaved people: "Once let the black man get upon his person the brass letters, U.S., let him get an eagle on his button, and a musket on his shoulder and bullets in his pocket, and there is no power on earth which can deny that he has earned the right to citizenship in the United States." Even Confederate politicians recognized the implications of black military service. Georgia governor Joseph E. Brown famously stated, "Whenever we establish the fact that they are a military race, we destroy our whole theory that they are unfit to be free."[21]

A variety of factors, including northern prejudice and the need to keep the border states in the Union, combined to delay any changes in military policy regarding African Americans until 1862. By 1862, however, Lincoln moved forward on a dual path of emancipation and enlistment. Responding to the need to increase enlistment and to ensure that Britain would withhold support from the Confederacy, Congress passed the Militia Act of July 17, 1862, which authorized Lincoln to use blacks in the military. In September of that same year, Lincoln issued the preliminary Emancipation Proclamation, which promised freedom to slaves in states still in rebellion as of January 1, 1863. Black soldiers were quick to respond to the opportunity to fight for the Union, and many white soldiers were quick to acknowledge their bravery. By the end of the war, nearly 180,000 black soldiers had fought as soldiers in the Union army. Of these soldiers, 98,500 had been slaves who fled from the Confederacy. Recognizing the strategic importance of these southern recruits, H. W. Halleck, the Union general in chief, asserted, "So long as the rebels retain and employ their slaves in producing grains &c., they can employ all the whites in the field. Every slave withdrawn from the enemy is equivalent to a white man put *hors de combat* [out of combat]."[22] After a particularly valiant effort by African American soldiers, one white soldier wrote, "I have been one of those men, who never had much confidence in colored troops fighting, but these doubts are now all removed, for they fought as bravely as any troops."[23] In 1864 Abraham Lincoln commented on the importance of black soldiers to the Union army:

> Any different policy in regard to the colored man, deprives us of his help, and this is more than we can bear. We can not spare the hundred and forty or fifty thousand now serving us as soldiers, seamen, and laborers. This is not a question of sentiment or taste, but one of physical force which may be measured and estimated as horse-power and Steam-power are measured and estimated. Keep it and you can save the Union. Throw it away, and the Union goes with it.[24]

As Glatthaar asserts, "Blacks alone did not win the war, but timely and extensive support from them contributed significantly and may have made the difference between a Union victory and stalemate or defeat."[25]

Black participation in the army is an important way to understand and teach issues surrounding slavery and the Civil War. It is also important, however, for teachers to acknowledge the actions of the millions of enslaved people who did not serve as soldiers but who, in the process of ensuring their own freedom, affected the war effort. The historian Stephanie McCurry notes in her important book *Confederate Reckoning: Power and Politics in the Civil War South* that slaves immediately recognized the significance of the war to their personal freedom. Just a few months into the war, some planters were forced to acknowledge that the Union troops were not their only enemies. On John Berkley Grimball's family plantations on the mainland in South Carolina, carefully orchestrated mass exoduses of up to eighty slaves at a time occurred. These escapes did not just include men who were running to join the army but also encompassed male and female slaves of all ages.[26] This pattern repeated itself as Union troops moved further into the interior of the Confederacy and slaves risked their lives to make it to the federal lines. As McCurry and others note, these mass departures greatly affected the Confederate war effort. First, by removing valuable laborers from the fields, it diminished the Confederacy's ability to supply its army and feed those on the home front. Perhaps equally as important, however, was the effect that this exodus had on Confederate morale. As those who southerners had considered trusted servants and virtual members of the family continually left southern farms and plantations, the Confederates, especially the women who were left on the home front, became increasingly demoralized. Teachers can use the candid recollections of Confederates on the home front to examine these issues with students. For example, in her journal, Gertrude Thomas described the emotional impact of fleeing slaves on her plantation. Ask your students how Thomas portrays her relationship with her slaves before the war. How has that relationship changed? What, specifically, are the slaves doing? How does Thomas react? Students will be able to recognize the sense of betrayal, surprise, and increasing bitterness that existed alongside her matter of fact rendition of events:

> *Monday, May 29, 1865.* . . . . Susan, Kate's nurse, Ma's most trusty servant, her advisor, right hand woman and best liked house servant has left her. I am under too many obligations to Susan to have harsh feelings toward her. During six confinements Susan has been with me, the best of servants, rendering the most efficient help. To Ma she has always been invaluable and in case of sickness there was no one like Susan. Her husband Anthony was one of the first to leave the Cumming Plantation and incited others to do the same. . . . Aunt Vilet the cook a very excellent one at that left Sunday night. She was a plantation servant during her young days and another favorite of Ma's. Palmer the driver left the same morning with Susan, remained longer than anyone expected that he would.
>
> *Belmont, Monday June 12, 1865.* I must confess to you my journal that I do most heartily despise Yankees, Negroes, and everything connected with them. . . . Everything is entirely reversed. I feel no interest in them whatever and hope I never will—[27]

Of course, not all slaves could make it to Union lines. Teachers should note that many of those who were forced to stay behind, however, also contributed to the Union war effort. Slaves proved invaluable to Union troops operating within the South, risking their own lives to provide valuable intelligence about Confederate troop positions and fortifications.[28] Confederate president Jefferson Davis's own slaves engaged in open rebellion while remaining on the plantation. The Davis slaves acted well before the Union army arrived. Taking their cue from Davis's brother's flight from the plantation with the household slaves, those remaining took control of two Davis plantations, helping themselves to the plantations' valuables and refusing to work. These slaves maintained tenuous control over the Davis plantations even after federal troops arrived in the area.[29]

Stephanie McCurry notes that the actions of slaves who conspired against the Confederacy on the home front often put planters at odds with Confederate military officials. For example, in November 1862

Confederate forces near the Ashepoo River in South Carolina confirmed that several slaves were openly sabotaging the Confederate war effort by giving Union soldiers "all the information an enemy could desire in regard to the position and strength of [Confederate] pickets." Despite concrete intelligence regarding this slave conduct, however, local planters refused to relocate those slaves who were aiding the enemy, preferring to wrest whatever labor they could out of the slaves on the farms. This pattern repeated itself across the South. Thus, military commanders were forced to divert precious troops from the official war front to guard against and squash these internal rebellions. As McCurry notes, "The slaves' determined war against their masters and their masters' state opened an internal front in the Confederate war and demanded the diversion of military resources to fight it."[30]

Students must understand that these acts of open rebellion, whether fleeing to Union lines or sabotaging the Confederate war effort, point to the numerous ways in which enslaved people contributed to their own emancipation. Proving themselves to be willing and able military tools, slaves gave credence to Abraham Lincoln's decision to accept former slaves and free blacks "into the armed service of the United States" as a "fit and necessary war measure for suppressing said rebellion."[31] Confederates regretfully acknowledged this fact. As Kirby Smith exclaimed from Shreveport, Louisiana, "Our plantations are made his recruiting stations."[32]

The 1863 Emancipation Proclamation officially turned the Union army into an army of liberation, aggressively recruiting slaves as it moved through the Confederacy. Just as slaves' decisions to flee to Union lines made the policy of emancipation attractive and possible before Lincoln issued his proclamation, slave actions after the Emancipation Proclamation demonstrated their determination to mold the policy to their ends. While in some areas slaves on large plantations could flee en masse to Union lines, slaves on smaller farms or in those areas where territory rapidly changed hands embarked on a more complicated process to free themselves and their loved ones. In many instances, male slaves fled to Union lines and then used the power of the Union army and the Emancipation Proclamation to free their families. In Virginia, for example, Yankee soldiers returned to a farm with orders from the commanding general to liberate the family of a man who had fled the week before. When the plantation owners told the soldier that the general had no authority over slaves who "do not belong to him," the Yankee soldier demonstrated the power of the Emancipation Proclamation, stating "O, they do not belong to any one, the government has fixed that."[33]

Teachers may conclude their classroom discussion of slavery and the Civil War with Abraham Lincoln's eloquent Second Inaugural Address, delivered just weeks before the war's end. Acknowledging that everyone knew that slavery was "somehow" the cause of the war, Lincoln admitted that few believed the institution would end even before the conflict. Lincoln continued to posit that the war's terrible human cost may have been God's way of forcing the United States to serve penance for the sin of slavery: "Yet if God wills that it continue until all the wealth piled by the bondsman's two hundred and fifty years of unrequited toil shall be sunk, and until every drop of blood drawn with the lash shall be paid by another drawn with the sword, as was said three thousand years ago, so still it must be said 'the judgments of the Lord are true and righteous altogether.'" However eloquent, Lincoln's ambiguous "somehow" in describing slavery as a cause of the war and his attribution of divine will in determining the end of slavery leave historians and our students unsatisfied. By highlighting extant sources surrounding the Fugitive Slave Act and documents related to secession in individual states, teachers can help students to flesh out the ways in which slavery was at the heart of the secession crisis and the complications that come with using "states' rights" as an alternative explanation for the conflict.[34] By examining the ways in which slaves seized the opportunities that came with the chaos of war to free themselves and to proclaim their loyalty to the Union cause, teachers also can complicate the narrative of slaves being given their freedom and instead help students to understand the ways that slaves helped to bring about and mold their own emancipation.

NOTES

1. Dwight T. Pitcaithley, "Public Education and the National Park Service: Interpreting the Civil War," *Perspectives* [online journal] (November 2007), http://www.historians.org/perspectives/issues/2007/0711/0711pro2.cfm. See also Dwight T. Pitcaithley, "'A Cosmic Threat': The National Park Service Addresses the Causes of the American Civil War," in James Oliver Horton and Lois E. Horton, eds., *Slavery and Public History: The Tough Stuff of American Memory* (New York: New Press, 2006).

2. Correspondence to Representative Frank Wolfe, January 17, 2000, Front Royal, Virginia, in "Civil War General-2" file, Park History Subject Files, National Park Service, Washington, DC, quoted in Pitcaithley, "Public Education."

3. A version of this discussion appears in Bethany Jay, "The Representation of Slavery in Historic House Museums: 1853–2000," PhD dissertation, Boston College, 2009, 154. Proquest (AAT 304832028).

4. Jefferson Davis, *The Rise and Fall of the Confederate Government*, 2 vols. (reprint, New York: T. Yoseloff, 1958), 1:xix, 78–80, 83, 2:763, quoted in Charles Dew, *Apostles of Disunion: Southern Secession Commissioners and the Causes of the Civil War* (Charlottesville: University of Virginia Press, 2001), 17.

5. See Paul Finkelman's essay, "Slavery in the New Nation," in this volume for further explanation of the legal interpretation of the Constitution and slavery.

6. The constitutionality of personal liberty laws was murky. An 1842 Supreme Court decision in *Prigg v. Pennsylvania* declared unconstitutional Pennsylvania's anti-kidnapping statute, which prevented slave owners from forcibly retrieving their slaves and returning them to bondage, but upheld the state's law forbidding state officers from assisting in the enforcement of fugitive slave laws. This decision led to a wave of northern laws that prevented state law enforcement officials from enforcing federal fugitive slave laws. See James M. McPherson and James K. Hogue, *Ordeal by Fire: The Civil War and Reconstruction*, 4th ed. (New York: McGraw-Hill, 2010), 84, for more information.

7. According to the Westegg Inflation Calendar, $5 in 1850 was the equivalent of roughly $137 in 2013 dollars, and $10 in 1850 was the equivalent of roughly $275 in 2013. See www.westegg.com/inflation.

8. McPherson and Hogue, *Ordeal by Fire*, 85–86.

9. Ibid., 87.

10. Jane H. Pease and William H. Pease, eds., *The Fugitive Slave Law and Anthony Burns* (Philadelphia: Lippincott, 1975), 51, in McPherson and Hogue, *Ordeal by Fire*, 88.

11. See *The Abolitionists* (DVD), end of part two (approximately 43:00) and beginning of part three, directed by Rob Rapley (Boston: PBS, 2013).

12. "Declaration of the Immediate Causes Which Induce and Justify the Secession of South Carolina from the Federal Union," in Michael Perman and Amy Murrell Taylor, *Major Problems in the Civil War and Reconstruction*, 3rd ed. (Boston: Wadsworth, 2011), 105. This document is widely available online.

13. Quoted in Dew, *Apostles of Disunion*, 86. Dew nicely articulates the ways in which slavery was at the heart of these commissioners' arguments.

14. "Declaration of the Immediate Causes Which Induce and Justify the Secession of South Carolina from the Federal Union," quoted in Perman and Taylor, *Major Problems*, 106.

15. Quoted in Dew, *Apostles of Disunion*, 29.

16. "A Declaration of the Immediate Causes which Induce and Justify the Secession of the State of Mississippi from the Federal Union," http://sunsite.utk.edu/civil-war/reasons.html#South%20Carolina.

17. Alexander H. Stephens, "Cornerstone Speech," March 1861, in Frank Moore, ed., *The Rebellion Record*, vol. 1 (New York: G. P. Putnam, 1861), 45, in Perman and Taylor, *Major Problems*, 108.

18. Joseph Glatthaar, "Black Glory: The African-American Role in Union Victory," in Gabor S. Boritt, ed., *Why the Confederacy Lost* (New York: Oxford University Press, 1992, 1993), reprinted in Perman and Taylor, *Major Problems*, 311.

19. Ibid.

20. Ibid., 314.

21. Ibid., 314, 310.

22. Stephanie McCurry, *Confederate Reckoning: Power and Politics in the Civil War South* (Cambridge, MA: Harvard University Press, 2010), 319. Glatthaar also quotes this; see "Black Glory," 313.

23. Glatthaar, "Black Glory," 319.

24. Ibid., 309.

25. Ibid.

26. McCurry, *Confederate Reckoning*, 243–46.

27. Ella Gertrude Clanton Thomas, *A Secret Eye: The Journal of Ella Gertrude Clanton Thomas*, ed. Virginia Ingraham Burr (Chapel Hill: University of North Carolina Press, 1990), in Perman and Taylor, *Major Problems*, 297–98. Glatthaar makes a similar argument in "Black Glory," 313, as does Stephanie McCurry in *Confederate Reckoning*.

28. McCurry, *Confederate Reckoning*, 296.

29. Ibid., 255.

30. Ibid., 295–97.

31. Emancipation Proclamation; Abraham Lincoln, interview of August 19, 1864, quoted in Robert F. Durden, *The Grey and the Black* (Baton Rouge: Louisiana State University Press, 1972), 23–24, cited in McCurry, *Confederate Reckoning*, 318.

32. Lieutenant General Kirby Smith to Major General Price, September 4, 1863, and Lorenzo Thomas, all in Ira Berlin et al., *Destruction of Slavery*, series 1, vol. 1 (Cambridge: Cambridge University Press, 1986), 772–73, 309, quoted in McCurry, *Confederate Reckoning*, 320.

33. Sigismunda Stribling Kimball Journal, February 24, 1863, University of Virginia, in McCurry, *Confederate Reckoning*, 250.

34. Many of the documents discussed in this essay are also available in James W. Loewen, *The Confederate and Neo-Confederate Reader: The Great Truth about the Lost Cause* (Jackson: University Press of Mississippi, 2010).

Comparative Slavery

LAIRD W. BERGAD

Slavery in the Americas developed as part of a global
system that enslaved millions of Africans from the
sixteenth century through much of the nineteenth century, yet even the
most stalwart students of slavery have only a partial understanding of
the institution outside of its US context. This essay gives attention to
the development and patterns of slavery in Latin America and the Caribbean to provide teachers with a deeper understanding of the international context of slavery in the United States. While placing slavery in
the United States into its international context is necessary to understand the institution, few high school or college instructors have the
time to devote to such comparative analysis. Because of this, statistical
information provides a compact and useful way to examine the characteristics of US slavery, particularly its timing and demographics in
different regions.

The Development and Impact of the Slave Trade
across the Americas

The development of slavery in the Americas was condi-
tioned by the volume, timing, and destinations of the trans-Atlantic
slave trade, which lasted from roughly 1525 until 1866. The first major
point that must be understood is that Latin American and Caribbean
societies received approximately 96 percent of all slaves who survived
the Atlantic crossing.[1] It is estimated that about 10.7 million slaves arrived in the Americas from the early sixteenth century until the final end
of the trade to Cuba in 1866 and that only about 390,000, or 3.6 percent
of all slaves, disembarked in the British colonies that would become the

United States. This is in stark contrast to the massive trade to Brazil, which amounted to some 4.8 million slaves, some 46 percent of all slaves forced into the trans-Atlantic slave trade. About 2.3 million slaves arrived in the British West Indies (22 percent of the total trade) and 1.1 million slaves in the French Caribbean (11 percent of all slaves); the Spanish colonies absorbed 1.3 million slaves (12 percent of the total).

When talking about the evolution of slavery, teachers need to appreciate the chronology of the slave trade to the various regions in the Americas in order to understand the development of slavery in each area. The ebb and flow of the slave trade was related to economic cycles as well as to politics.[2] Prior to 1650, just after British colonization had begun in North America and Barbados during the 1620s and before the 1655 occupation of Jamaica, the slave trade was directed almost entirely to the Spanish colonies and to Portuguese Brazil. About 725,000 Africans arrived in all of the Americas between 1525 and 1650. Mexico, Peru, and other contiguous Spanish colonial possessions imported fully 48 percent of these slaves. Another 48 percent disembarked in Brazil. Slaves were an important component of diversified labor systems in these Central and South American colonies. The lucrative silver-mining economies of Mesoamerica and the Andes created extraordinary demands for labor in the mines themselves and in a variety of urban and rural supporting industries as well. In Brazil, the sugar plantation economy of Bahia, Pernambuco, and some regions in the southeast of the Portuguese colony was the driving factor behind the colony's demand for slaves.[3] In fact, the first sugar/slave complexes in the Americas were established in Brazil after failed experiments with Indian slavery. African slaves also worked in a wide variety of other occupations, urban and rural. While slavery rarely enters the curriculum for early Spanish colonization, the institution of slavery in the mid-seventeenth century Americas was emphatically neither Caribbean nor North American, where there was only a marginal African presence. From the perspective of 1650, nearly 150 years after the onset of European colonization, slavery and African culture in the Americas were centered in Brazil, Mexico, and Peru.

During the second half of the seventeenth century, the slave trade entered a period of transformation, although there were some elements of continuity. Teachers may find it useful to highlight the ways in which patterns of slave importations were directly tied to the demand for

PART TWO: TEACHING SPECIFIC CONTENT

labor in different regions. First, the trade to the Spanish colonies declined precipitously. Traders had imported about 350,000 slaves to Mexico and Peru prior to 1650. Between 1650 and 1700 only 46,000 slaves arrived in these regions. This decline can be traced to the increase in the availability of local labor, namely the growing Indigenous and mestizo populations that survived the demographic holocaust unleashed by the sixteenth-century Spanish conquests. This meant that colonists needed less slave labor. Second, the development of sugar/slave economies in Barbados and Jamaica and the absence of a local workforce meant that planters needed to import labor. British colonists initially utilized indentured servants in Barbados but ultimately turned to African slavery as the British emulated the Brazilian model of slave-based plantation development. More than 150,000 slaves were imported to Barbados and more than 90,000 disembarked in Jamaica between 1651 and 1700. This presaged the massive importation of slaves that would occur during the eighteenth century. Before 1700 British North America was still a negligible importer of Africans, although the Chesapeake region began to emerge as a small-scale destination of the slave trade. British colonists in the Chesapeake imported about twelve thousand slaves during the second half of the seventeenth century, largely because of the growth in tobacco production. Many of these slaves came from the Caribbean rather than directly from Africa. Despite these changes, Brazil maintained its position as the principal destination of the international slave trade, importing 460,000 Africans between 1650 and 1700. This number represented 47 percent of all slaves arriving in the Americas.

The geographical and quantitative parameters of slavery in the Americas were transformed by two factors: the British and French occupation of specific Caribbean islands and the establishment of slavery as a major labor system in the southern colonies of the future United States. More than 1.8 million slaves were imported into the British Caribbean colonial possessions between 1701 and 1800, with Jamaica (850,000) and Barbados (304,000) the leading slave importers. But smaller possessions such as Antigua, St. Kitts, Grenada, and Dominica each imported more than 100,000 slaves during the eighteenth century. Additionally, the future United States received nearly 300,000 Africans, with most of these imported into the Chesapeake region and into the Carolinas and Georgia, where rice and cotton cultivation emerged as lucrative activities. Nearly one million slaves were brought to French Caribbean colonies with St. Domingue, the future Haiti, leading the way with 767,000

182

imports. Martinique was another major destination, with about 160,000 slaves imported into this relatively small island. In total, about 5.6 million slaves were imported into the Americas during the eighteenth century, and this represented more than half of all slaves disembarking over the entire tragic history of the trans-Atlantic trade. The Caribbean had been sparsely populated after the decimation of Indigenous societies as a result of the Spanish conquest. By 1800 it, along with Brazil, was one of the epicenters of slavery and African culture in the Americas. The older regions that had been central to slavery's development prior to 1650, Mexico and Peru, no longer imported many slaves, and the African component of their populations receded as Indigenous and mixed-race populations increased steadily.

Teachers can explain these demographic changes by discussing the need for labor across the New World colonies. The driving factor behind the slave trade was colonial demand for labor to produce tropical staple products, which were highly profitable because of consumer demand in Europe's constantly expanding markets. Thus, the development of plantation agriculture drove the slave trade to much of the Americas after 1650. While African slave labor produced coffee, tobacco, indigo, and rice, close to 80 percent of all slaves exported from Africa were destined for sugar-producing regions. Unlike the Spanish colonies, where Indigenous populations were able to meet the labor demand in the eighteenth century, in the sparsely populated Caribbean islands, for example, there was no adequate local labor supply. Colonists needed to import workers to fuel the economy. Planters could produce sugar profitably only on fairly extensive plantations, which required a reliable, disciplined, and large-scale labor force. There may have been other options for Caribbean sugar planters, but the readily available and inexpensive supply of slaves in West African slave markets, which were mostly controlled by African slave traders, was decisive.[4] In many ways the British and French emulated the Brazilian model of production and labor procurement. Eighteenth-century planters also benefitted from well-developed credit and transportation systems to finance and move slaves across the Atlantic. These systems, which had been operative and refined since the sixteenth century, were critical in colonists' decisions to resolve labor demands with African slaves.

When teaching about slavery, teachers should highlight several slave rebellions and the rise of abolitionism in England and, to a lesser extent, the United States during the second half of the eighteenth century. These movements led to dramatic transformations as slavery entered its last century in the New World.[5] The slave uprising in French St. Domingue in the early 1790s and the French Revolution itself led to the virtual end of the slave trade to the French colonial possessions by the early nineteenth century. The United States and Great Britain abolished the slave trade through a formal treaty in 1808, and Great Britain abolished slavery in its empire in 1833. The British also exerted pressures on Spain, Brazil, and Portugal to end slaving. These efforts were largely unsuccessful. Between 1801 and 1850, more than 3 million African slaves crossed the Atlantic, a volume that nearly matched the 3.4 million slaves imported between 1751 and 1800, the most intense period of British and French slaving to the Caribbean. The volume of slave trading to Brazil, which was driven by the rise of slave-based coffee production, also highlighted the ineffectiveness of efforts to suppress the slave trade. In the first half of the nineteenth century, more than 2 million slaves disembarked in the newly emerging nation, which became formally independent in 1822. These imports into Brazil represented nearly two-thirds of all slaves forced into the Atlantic crossing between 1801 and 1850.

Additionally, Cuba emerged as a new destination for large-scale slaving, despite its illegality after the British imposed an antislave trade treaty on Spain in 1820 and again in 1835.[6] Slavery as a largely urban institution had been established in Cuba since the sixteenth century. But, beginning in the second half of the eighteenth century, Cuba turned to the intensive cultivation of sugar and coffee, in many ways emulating the success of the British and French Caribbean colonies. Market conditions in Europe and the United States after 1790 favored the expansion of these slave-based plantation crops; supplies of these products from the French and British colonies plummeted because of the Haitian slave revolt and the end of slavery in Jamaica and the other British possessions in the 1830s. Cuba had imported about sixty-eight thousand slaves prior to 1800, most arriving after 1750. Between 1801 and 1866 the Spanish colony was the destination of more than 700,000 slaves, and it was Cuba that became the last major destination of the slave trade. Once the British finally put an end to slaving to Brazil by occupying the port of Rio de Janeiro in the early 1850s, Cuba remained the only major importer of slaves into the Americas. Because of all this, Cuba was converted into another great center of African culture in the Caribbean and the last slave society to develop in the Americas.

A Comparative Look at Slavery

Teachers can discuss the timing and destinations of the slave trade to facilitate an understanding of when slavery developed in the different regions in the Americas. These statistics, however, tell us very little about how the institution functioned in each area and nothing about the lives of slaves. These numbers also tell us very little about an institution that, although universally brutal, was extraordinarily diverse and constantly transforming.

Historians who have studied slavery in the Americas have long recognized the uniqueness of slavery's development in the United States.[7] It was the only large-scale slave system in which slaves reproduced naturally in impressive numbers, thus reducing reliance on the slave trade to increase slave labor supplies. Every other society in the Americas that relied on slavery to mine or produce staple crops relied on the slave trade to meet labor demands. The quantitative data stand out. It was noted previously that before the slave trade was abolished, in 1808, the British colonies that became the independent United States accounted for a relatively small percentage of the overall slave trade, about 390,000 total slaves or 3.6 percent of all Africans disembarking in the Americas. Just prior to the beginning of the Civil War, the 1860 US census showed about 4 million slaves in the South, despite the fact that there had been no legal imports after 1808. In contrast, Brazil, the largest importer of slaves, had only 1.5 million slaves in its national census of 1872, despite having imported more than 4.8 million slaves. Cubans imported nearly 800,000 slaves, most in the nineteenth century. Nonetheless, the 1862 census revealed that the Spanish colony's slave population stood at about 370,000. This general decline in slave populations was also found in the British, French, and Dutch Caribbean.

The explanation for these divergent demographic patterns is complex. In general terms, without free or forced immigration, any population, slave or free, may increase naturally only when births outpace deaths. The slave trade to the United States ended in 1808. In 1810 the census revealed that the nation had about 1.1 million slaves. The increase to nearly 4 million slaves in 1860 was almost entirely due to natural reproduction. This also means that by the Civil War, nearly all slaves in the United States were born there, not in Africa. Thus, the slave population of the United States by 1860 had no direct experience or recollection of freedom other than through the accounts of their ancestors who passed down their history and culture through oral traditions. All other large-scale slave societies in the Americas were dominated by slaves who were born in Africa and thus had once been free.

Teachers should consider with their students why there were such high birth rates among slaves in the United States in comparative perspective. There is no simple answer to this question. There had to be a level of general health for women of childbearing age to conceive and successfully give birth to infants who would survive beyond the critical first year of life. The achievement of this level of health was related to diet. Slaves in the United States had better access to a variety of food products than slaves elsewhere. This led to better nutrition, higher birth rates, and lower infant mortality rates. Slaves in the United States also had longer life expectancies and grew to taller heights and heavier weights.[8] As in all sweeping generalizations, this was not always the case; there were regional and temporal variations, to be sure.

Climate and occupation also contributed to the relatively low death rates among slaves in the United States. Most of them labored in temperate and semitropical zones. Slaves in the Caribbean and Brazil generally worked in tropical climates more conducive to the spread of diseases and high mortality rates, especially when accompanied by poor diets. Additionally, slaves laboring in sugar-producing economies suffered comparatively higher death rates than those working elsewhere.[9] Overwork, poor treatment, and general abuse also contributed to higher death rates in these plantation zones.

Teachers must exercise care in interpreting this US demographic slave exceptionalism in comparative perspective. Better diet and natural reproduction did not mitigate the cruelty, barbarity, and suffering that were endemic to slavery everywhere and may not be used to justify interpretations of slavery as more humane in one place than in another.

Another factor that may have contributed to declining slave populations in the Hispanic colonies and in Brazil was manumission rates. Prior to the conquest of the Americas, Spanish and Portuguese slaveholders in the Iberian Peninsula continued a tradition that originated in Roman juridical codes, permitting slaves to own property, earn cash, and purchase their own freedom.[10] The process of self-purchase was of extraordinary importance to slaves themselves, and it was commonly found throughout the Spanish colonies, although scholars cannot quantify the number of slaves who were able to self-purchase. This opportunity simply did not exist in the United States or in any of the British, French, or Dutch colonies in the Caribbean.

Additionally, owners in Spanish and Portuguese America voluntarily freed their slaves at a much greater rate than owners elsewhere. Planters freed slaves from all age, sex, and origin categories and not just, as once thought, old, infirm, and unproductive slaves. Still, some patterns exist. Planters were more likely to free female slaves and domestic workers than males or field slaves. There were higher rates of manumission for urban than for rural slaves. Sick or dying owners also bestowed grants of freedom in last wills and testaments.

Another factor that may have had some significance for the declining slave populations in the Iberian colonies was the comparatively greater number of slaves fleeing captivity. Slaves commonly escaped to rural areas in Brazil, with its vast and sometimes impenetrable frontier. Slaves in Spanish colonies could also find freedom in large free black and mulatto communities. Slaves ran away in the United States, as well, and in every other American slave society. As in the case of manumissions, however, there are no accurate data on the numbers of successful runaways that would enable us to calculate the long-term demographic impact on overall slave populations or to determine how important this factor was in the decline of slave populations outside the United States. Although manumissions, whether by masters or through self-purchase, and the higher volume of runaways may have contributed to diminishing slave populations, it is clear that higher death rates were the principal causes of the decline in the slave populations in the major slave societies in the Americas.

Although the United States had the largest slave population in the Western Hemisphere by the mid-nineteenth century, it was also the only major slave society in which African slaves were a fairly small percentage of the overall population.[11] The 1790 census of the newly independent United States revealed that slaves were about 18 percent of the total population and that free people of color were another 1.5 percent. By 1860, despite the meteoric rise in the number of slaves through natural reproduction, their percentage of the overall population had declined to 13 percent, while the percentage of free blacks and mulattos had held steady at 1.5 percent of all inhabitants of the United States. The white free population, through reproduction and immigration, had expanded at a faster rate than the population of slaves. Yet, these data do not capture regional differences. On the eve of the Civil War, slavery existed only in the southern states, and about one-third of the total population was enslaved. In comparative perspective, slaves constituted about 27 percent of Cuba's total population in 1862; in Brazil, although slaves had made up around 30 percent of the total population in 1820, they accounted for 15 percent in 1872. Each of these slave societies may be contrasted with the British and French Caribbean colonies, where slaves constituted about 80 to 90 percent of populations before the abolition of slavery in the 1830s and 1840s.

What was most significant about the United States, Cuba, and Brazil—the three remaining large-scale slave societies by the mid-nineteenth century—was the difference in the numbers and percentages of free people of color. In the United States and in the British and French Caribbean, there were relatively small populations of free blacks and mulattos, while in Cuba and Brazil, for example, there were more free people of color than slaves by the nineteenth century. The very small percentage of free blacks and mulattos in the United States was heavily concentrated in urban areas, most in the nonslave states. To be a person of African descent in the United States almost always meant to be a slave, and this was the way free people, mostly of European racial origins, conceived of people of color. Prior to abolition, this also was the case in the British and French colonies. However, in the Spanish colonies from the sixteenth century on and in Brazil there were relatively large free populations of people with African heritage. In Mexico City, Vera Cruz, Lima, Salvador, Rio de Janeiro, São Paulo, and Havana it would have been as common to encounter free blacks and mulattos as to encounter slaves, and often the differences could not readily be determined by physical observation. This was the case in most cities and towns and in the countryside as well, with the exception of the sugar plantation zones. Additionally, if the slave and free colored population were combined statistically, they composed a very large sector of the population and sometimes the majority, as was the case in Brazil. The data tell the story. In the Cuban case, in 1792, 31 percent of the population was enslaved and 20 percent was made up of free blacks and mulattos, a total of 51 percent. By 1862, 27 percent of the population was enslaved and 17 percent was composed of free people of color. In the Brazilian case there are no national-level data on free blacks and mulattos until 1872, but in 1819 it was known that about 31 percent of the overall population was enslaved. In 1872 this figure had fallen to 15 percent, and this relative decline was paralleled by a soaring free colored population, which accounted for 43 percent of all people in the same year. Thus, in the Brazilian case some 58 percent of the population was composed of people of African descent, most of them free.

Teachers can consider the ways in which these demographic characteristics influenced the experience of slavery and concepts of race in different regions. African slaves in the United States lived within the confines of a predominantly white society and had few contacts and interactions with free peoples of African descent. In the case of the Spanish colonies and Portuguese Brazil, to be black was emphatically not necessarily to be a slave, and there were constant interactions between Africans who were enslaved and peoples of color who were not. This was especially common in urban areas and even in the countryside, where planters often employed free peoples of color alongside their slaves in a variety of occupations.

These communities of free people of color, some born in the Americas and others in Africa, were important to slave populations in many ways. The emergence of ethnic-based African social, cultural, and religious organizations—*cabildos de nación* in the Spanish possessions and *confradías*, or brotherhoods, in Brazil—suggests extensive connections between slaves and free blacks and mulattos in Spanish colonial America and in Brazil. Slaves often were members of these formal organizations, which were based on African ethnicity and which were legally recognized by colonial authorities.[12] These groups functioned as burial societies, organized officially sanctioned cultural and social events, and served to bring together peoples of common African ethnic backgrounds, free or slave. What may have been most important to slave populations, however, was the example of ex-slaves and other blacks and mulattos living in freedom, even if there was segregation and discrimination. There is little question that for slaves the hope and aspiration of eventual freedom was an integral part of their lives, even if the probability of achieving freedom was small in most cases.

Having established some of these general chronological and demographic contours of slavery in the Americas, teachers should take care to use these trends to combat the stereotypical images of slaves, which describe only certain communities of slaves. These generalizations include gang laborers on sugar plantations, the cotton-picking slaves of the US South, and perhaps "house" slaves or domestic servants. While these may be accurate for particular places in specific time periods, they are only partially indicative of the slave experience in the Americas. This is because of the extraordinary diversity of what it meant to be a slave in different epochs and regions. The patterns of daily life for a slave laboring on the Texas cotton frontier in the 1840s were dramatically different from those for a slave working in the eighteenth-century Chesapeake region or for a slave living in urban Richmond, Virginia, Havana, Cuba, or Rio de Janeiro. Other than the horrifying and degrading reality of being treated and regarded as property, a powerful commonality no doubt, it is important to recognize that slavery was a complex institution with enormous variations as it developed and evolved regionally in the Americas from the early sixteenth century until its final abolition in Brazil in 1888.

Despite the variety of slave experiences, teachers can highlight a few generalizations about slavery that may be useful to generate classroom discussions. While the image of the plantation is a paradigm for rural slavery, large numbers of slaves lived on relatively small-scale farms in "lots" of fewer than five slaves. Even the British and French Caribbean colonies were dominated by small farms prior to the development of slave-based sugar economies during the eighteenth century for which the plantation-slave imagery is, in fact, accurate. Even in Brazil, where the slave-based plantation was pioneered in the Americas during the seventeenth century, many slaves lived and labored on much smaller farms. In the gold-mining economy of Minas Gerais, Brazil, which developed between 1690 and 1750, this was also the case.

The Spanish colonies and Brazil also had large numbers of urban slaves who held diverse occupations. This diverse urban slavery was much more pronounced than in the monoculture economies of the southern United States or in the British and French Caribbean colonies. In fact, slaves labored in every occupation in cities and towns, often alongside free people, who could be white, black, or mulatto. Teachers can note that slaves were stevedores, carpenters, goldsmiths, drivers, prostitutes, and itinerant peddlers. Slaves ran open-air markets for their owners and otherwise labored in every occupation imaginable. Many had access to cash, something that was a priority for slaves not only because it allowed them to improve their material lives but also because of the institution of self-purchase. Earning small amounts of money could mean a down payment toward emancipation for themselves or their children, and the aspiration for freedom was always front and center to the slave experience. This possibility highlights the fact that slaves were individuals who struggled to assert themselves at every turn and to try to control their own destinies as much as possible within the context of this horrific institution. The ability of slaves in Spanish colonies to buy their freedom, however, should not be glamorized, nor should this possibility be applied universally.

Too often slaves have been faceless to historians and to those reading about slavery, and they have been conceived of as a mass of humanity that was victimized and exploited in conditions that were, in fact, unimaginable in their barbarity. Slaves may have been regarded by their masters as property, but they were human beings with all of the idiosyncrasies, motivations, and abilities to cooperate or not with their masters' grand schemes for making money and turning profits. They could feign illness, slow down work rhythms individually or collectively, sabotage equipment, lose valuable tools, or "discover" fires in various fields or broken carts and other transportation vehicles. Slaves could seriously disrupt the functioning of any economic enterprise large or small, urban or rural. Of course, a slave needed a great deal of cleverness and caution to exert pressures by disrupting or subtly threatening to disrupt production, since masters could unleash terribly harsh punishments if sabotage or outright disobedience was suspected. But masters knew very well that while they regarded their slaves as chattel, they were indeed human beings and had to be negotiated with at many different levels in order for economic enterprises to run smoothly. Too often the image of master/slave relations invokes an absolute power that indeed existed at the ultimate level but that also was mitigated to varying degrees by slaves through their ingenuity, intelligence, and insistence upon certain prerogatives as human beings. Again, this element of the slave experience—acting as their own "agents"—ought not to be exaggerated, for in the end the master class held a monopoly on power over the slaves they owned. A slave who pushed too far in seeking to assert more control over his or her life could be sold off at a moment's notice, the worst possible fate if the slave had close family members nearby. Thus, the ability of slaves to negotiate the terms of their lives existed within particular parameters and required much skill, diplomacy, finesse, and a carefully calculated knowledge of the limitations available for negotiation in any given circumstance. For more information on slave resistance, see Kenneth Greenberg's chapter in this volume.

Although approximately 60 percent of slaves imported were males, there were enough slave women that legal marriage and consensual cohabitation were found in all slave societies. In most regions this was encouraged and recognized by authorities and masters to create stability and maintain control, a pervasive preoccupation for elites, who were always fearful of resistance and rebellion. Many masters believed that if slaves were bound by wives, husbands, and children, they would be less likely to run away or be disruptive to masters in different ways. Slave owners were wary of marriages or informal relations particularly between slaves living at significant distances from one another, since this would encourage too much physical mobility, authorized or not. Nevertheless, the formation and maintenance of slave families, regardless of attitudes by slave owners, were of extraordinary importance to slave populations. Creating families affirmed individual and collective identities, optimism, and spirit and fostered hope that slave children would lead better lives and perhaps become free in the future. Students should not romanticize or misinterpret the possibilities of forming family structures, nuclear or extended, as an attempt to portray slavery as humane in any way. Rather, they are testimony to the intelligence and resilience of Africans in the New World, who created their own lives, institutions, traditions, communities, and subcultures within the framework of the most degrading and brutal of all human conditions.

Slaves in urban areas enjoyed a fairly equitable distribution of men and women, which allowed for greater possibilities to create slave families and kinship networks. Indeed, in early colonial Mexico and Peru, there were large concentrations of urban slaves, especially in colonial and provincial capitals. Urban slavery in Brazil also was widespread despite the prevalence of plantation agriculture from the seventeenth century through abolition in 1888. This was the case in Cuba even during the nineteenth century, when the slave/sugar complex became dominant. In rural areas, however, the possibility of creating a slave family was determined by a variety of factors. The ratio of men to women, which was often determined by the type of rural labor the slaves provided, was critical. In many areas, slaves lived and worked on a variety of small-scale farms, in mines, as muleteers, and in nearly every other rural activity. Even in these rural areas, however, slaves forged family and kinship networks.

The ability of slaves to form families was critical for them over the long and tragic history of slavery in the Americas. Teachers should stress, however, the arbitrary power of masters to destroy these families and extended kinship networks. The dreadful interregional slave trade in the United States, where slaves were transferred in mass from the traditional areas of slavery in the eastern states such as Virginia, the Carolinas, and Georgia to the expanding cotton frontier in the western southern states, especially Texas during the 1830s, was devastating to slave families. The same phenomenon took place in Brazil after the end of the slave trade in the early 1850s. Planters transported slaves, via ship, from the northeastern regions of the nation to the coffee-growing south, especially to the state of São Paulo during the 1850s and after. These internal slave trades inevitably destroyed family structures, thus underscoring the ultimate powerlessness of slaves despite their valiant efforts to control as much of their lives as possible.

Teaching Comparative Slavery

As a classroom tool, the statistics and descriptions presented in this chapter can be used to facilitate a lively and analytical discussion of slavery. Teachers can use a simple methodology to stimulate these kinds of meaningful discussions. This methodology begins with simply presenting students with a relevant set of data and asking them, "What do you see?" Students should not provide analysis at this point but should simply spend time recognizing and identifying relevant data points. Once students have highlighted much of the useful information, instructors can begin to ask students contextualizing questions that draw on prior knowledge. These questions will help students to make meaning of the statistical information.

In an example from the text, instructors might ask students what happened in the early nineteenth century that led to the dramatic decline in slave importations to the United States and British Caribbean. This would lead to a conversation about the end of the legal international slave trade in the United States and Britain. Teachers can then highlight the contrasting information from Brazil and ask students about the circumstances in Spanish and Portuguese colonies. Any statistical analysis should conclude with analytical questions that link a particular data set to a larger issue. In this example, an instructor might ask what the data on the international slave trade tells us about public opinion about the trade in individual colonies. Or, teachers might ask what effect the end of the international trade may have had on domestic slavery. Using this strategy will ensure that students actively engage with the data in a way that promotes a deeper understanding of its import.

In the end, it is important for teachers to remember that it is difficult to present a generalized portrait of African slavery in the Americas. The data and discussions in this chapter will help classroom discussions be mindful of the regional diversity of this barbaric institution, as well as the changes that occurred over time in different places from the sixteenth through the nineteenth century.

NOTES

1. It has been estimated that about 12.5 million slaves disembarked from Africa and that the mortality rate during the crossing was about 15 percent. For the most complete and accessible data on every quantitative aspect of the African slave trade see the website the Trans-Atlantic Slave Trade Database at http://slavevoyages.org/tast/index.faces.

2. For a general discussion see Laird W. Bergad, *The Comparative Histories of Slavery in Brazil, Cuba, and the United States* (Cambridge and New York: Cambridge University Press, 2007).

3. For the best survey of Brazilian slavery see Herbert S. Klein and Francisco Vidal Luna, *Slavery in Brazil* (Cambridge and New York: Cambridge University Press, 2010).

4. See John Thornton, *Africa and Africans in the Making of the Atlantic World, 1400–1680* (Cambridge and New York: Cambridge University Press, 1992).

5. For the best synopsis see Seymour Drescher, *Abolition: A History of Slavery and Antislavery* (Cambridge and New York: Cambridge University Press, 2009).

6. David J. Murray, *Odious Commerce: Britain, Spain and the Abolition of the Cuban Slave Trade* (Cambridge and New York: Cambridge University Press, 1980).

7. See Robert William Fogel, *Without Consent or Contract: The Rise and Fall of American Slavery* (New York: W. W. Norton, 1989).

8. See Robert William Fogel and Stanley L. Engerman, *Time on the Cross: The Economics of American Negro Slavery* (Boston: Little, Brown, 1974), 109–17, which argues that US slaves were well fed. There is by no means complete agreement among scholars on the quantitative or qualitative aspects of slave diets. For a view that contradicts that of Fogel and Engerman see Richard Sutch, "The Care and Feeding of Slaves," in Paul A. David, Herbert G. Gutman, Richard Sutch, Peter Temin, and Gavin Wright, *Reckoning with Slavery: A Critical Study in the Quantitative History of American Negro Slavery* (New York: Oxford University Press, 1976), 231–301. For diets of Caribbean slaves see Kenneth F. Kiple, *The Caribbean Slave: A Biological History* (New York: Cambridge University Press, 1984), especially "Plantation Nutrition" and "Malnutrition: Morbidity and Mortality," 76–103. Also see Kenneth F. Kiple, "The Nutritional Link with

Slave Infant and Child Mortality in Brazil," *Hispanic American Historical Review* 69, no. 4 (1989): 677–90.

9. See Michael Tadman, "The Demographic Cost of Sugar: Debates on Slave Societies and Natural Increase in the Americas," *American Historical Review* 105, no. 5 (December 2000): 1534–75.

10. This institution of self-purchase was called *coartación*. For a discussion of these legal codes see Herbert S. Klein, *Slavery in the Americas: A Comparative Study of Cuba and Virginia* (London: Oxford University Press, 1967), Part 2, "The Legal Structure," 37–85.

11. This was also the situation in early colonial Mexico and Peru, but African slavery in these Spanish colonies never developed on the same scale as in the United States, Brazil, and the British and French Caribbean during the eighteenth century or in Cuba in the nineteenth century.

12. See Philip A. Howard, *Changing History: Afro-Cuban Cabildos and Societies of Color in the Nineteenth Century* (Baton Rouge: Louisiana State University Press, 1998).

The Challenge of Slavery since Emancipation

From 1865 to the Twenty-First Century

JAMES BREWER STEWART

One of the abolitionist movement's most perceptive thinkers, Wendell Phillips, offered this disturbing comment just after Congress formally ended slavery in 1865 by passing the Thirteenth Amendment: "We have abolished the slave," he observed darkly, "but the master remains." As Phillips saw it, this epoch-making constitutional amendment was as full of danger as it was of promise.

Teachers may begin a discussion of slavery after emancipation by asking their students to consider to what danger Phillips was referring. After all, emancipation meant that four million African Americans had thrown off their shackles and were vigorously exercising their freedom. Emancipation also marked the destruction of what once had been the national economy's second-largest capital asset, slaves, who were second in value only to the land itself. Emancipation represented the largest forcible governmental appropriation of private property prior to the Russian Revolution. Moreover, emancipation confirmed the demise of what before the Civil War had been the nation's most powerful political interest group—the South's "planter aristocracy." Finally, the Fourteenth Amendment to the Constitution (1868) as well as the Fifteenth (1870) guaranteed African Americans full citizenship and universal manhood suffrage. What could Phillips have possibly been worrying about? The answer, supported by incontestable historical documentation, provides teachers with an entrée into one the most important subjects for any US history class—the fact that once emancipated African Americans began asserting their rights as citizens, their former owners began re-enslaving as many of them as possible.

Most students will be surprised to learn that the enslavement of African Americans persisted long past 1865. Moreover, many contemporary activists claim that the postemancipation slavery begun in the nineteenth century continues to this day. They locate it in what is so commonly referred to as "the prison/industrial complex," that sprawling system of highly lucrative privatized prisons scattered all over the United States in which 80 percent of the inmates are people of color. Educators may ask students to decide whether or not the following facts might be considered as evidence of race-based enslavement:

- Whites make up 72 percent of the nation's illegal drug users. Whites are eight times more numerous in the US population than blacks. Yet blacks incarcerated for drug violations outnumber whites 4:1. White drug users usually receive probation. Black and Latino drug users are almost always imprisoned.
- Over the past two decades incarceration rates have skyrocketed as crime rates have fallen.
- The two largest private prison corporations, Correction Corporation of America and Wackenhut Inc., post combined profits of close to $5 billion annually.
- Prison labor has supplanted free workers in the production of hundreds of types of goods and services. Victoria's Secret, Chevron, Boeing, IBM, Motorola, Honda, Toys R Us, Compaq, Dell, Texas Instruments, Honeywell, Hewlett-Packard, Microsoft, Nordstrom's, Revlon, Macy's, Pierre Cardin, Target Stores, and AT&T constitute only the beginning of a list of companies that are using or have used prison labor. Inmates in federal prisons manufacture practically all the clothing and small-scale equipment items necessary to outfit our entire armed forces. Prison "workers" are paid an average of twenty-five cents per hour.

However you and your students might evaluate these shocking facts, they urge us to inquire about the origins and nature of the slavery that followed emancipation. Douglas Blackmon's book *Slavery by Another Name* is a good resource for teachers who want to learn more about this topic. The PBS documentary by the same name provides an accessible, if brutal, overview of the same topic. In short, answers emerged during the collapse of the Confederacy, in 1865, just when Phillips was issuing his warning. Even as the war was concluding, former slaveholders began developing clear precursors to the "prison/industrial complex." They incarcerated dark-skinned people by the tens of thousands on petty or trumped-up charges, shackled them, abused them grievously, transported them by rail in cages, and leased them out to cotton plantations, iron manufacturers, and construction companies. They also turned former plantations into high-yield profit centers by making them into prisons that wrung the fullest value out of inmates shackled in chain gangs overseen by rifle-toting guards on horseback. And finally, they adopted debt peonage, a practice that involved individual landowners enmeshing poor black cotton farmers in outrageous debts and then coercing "payment" through forced labor while denying those victimized their right to walk away. Some planters extracted compliance paternalistically, but far too frequently they used guns, whips, and manacles to reduce entire families to lifetimes of enslavement. Though blatantly illegal, debt peonage spread rapidly across the Deep South during the late nineteenth century and continued until at least the 1960s. Phillips's warning has proved all too true. The United States undeniably "abolished the slave." Nevertheless, "the master remains."

Of course, educators need to take care when discussing the issue of slavery after emancipation. Historians agree that slave emancipation in 1865 constituted an epoch-defining moment in our history. It transformed dramatically the lives of those set free. It likewise revolutionized our national understandings of how we define American citizenship (for good and ill) and how citizens of differing skin colors treat one another. In these respects the United States post-1865 and the United States pre-1865 could hardly have been more different. Nevertheless, slavery did not disappear, and southern whites knew just what they were doing when continuing it. Understanding the full context of slavery in the United States leads us to confront the problem of global slavery. If transported back a century and a half, the criminals and corporate exploiters who today are enslaving millions all over the globe would recognize exactly what these slaveholders were up to—and would be eager to join them.

Today's global slavery exploits between twenty-four and thirty-five million people and assumes a bewildering variety of forms, all of them illegal. Just as in the postemancipation United States, every nation (North Korea, China, and Sudan among them) has put laws on the books that are stringently antislavery. And in striking similarity to the post-emancipation South, slavery has flourished in all these nations, ours wholly included, by turning itself into criminal enterprises that are winked at by corrupt politicians and law enforcement officials. Roughly 30 percent of today's enslaved are sexually exploited women and children. The forced labor of the remaining 70 percent is embedded in the shoes and clothing we wear; the cosmetics and oils we apply to our bodies; the fruits, vegetables, seafood, meat, and chocolate we consume; the tea and coffee that addict us; the computers and smartphones we rely on; the vehicles we drive; and the furniture and carpeting that grace our homes.

For all its enormous size and horrific nature, most Americans, including our students, pay scant attention to the problem of modern slavery. They fail to recognize that slavery infects their nation, blights their local communities, and makes them deeply complicit in exploiting enslaved labor as a consequence of what they consume. In dramatic contrast to the decades before the Civil War, there is today no serious, sustained American abolitionist movement. Hand wringing? Yes. Specialized nongovernmental organizations that combat slavery far outside the United States? Yes. Mass moral outrage, sustained mobilization, and constant headline-grabbing agitation here at home? Not so you'd notice.

To drive this point home, educators may ask students to create a list of causes that have generated significant interest among Americans over the past two decades. Students will likely name movements to uphold the rights of fetuses and embryos, to undermine capital punishment, to advocate for the environment and for the ethical treatment of animals, or to press the humanitarian case for gay and lesbian rights. In my experience, most students exclude the modern antislavery movement. When asked to name prominent organizations that advocate for important issues, students will likely name the Sierra Club, the National Organization for Women, the Tea Party, and the National Rifle Association, among others. Almost all students will be unaware of the Polaris Project, an exceptionally effective nongovernmental organization that combats slavery today across the globe.

What can we, as educators, do to change the situation? How might we ignite a new, grassroots abolitionist movement in the United States?

The answer to this question is rooted in our role as educators. Instructors can teach students standard historical content and educate them about modern slavery by asking them to apply historical analysis to the problem of contemporary slavery. Students can begin this project by accessing the website for any of the leading antislavery nongovernmental organizations, such as Free the Slaves, the Polaris Project, Not for Sale, the International Justice Mission, and End Slavery Now, and looking for historical perspectives. Students will quickly realize that they *cannot find any*. The focus is exclusively fastened on today.

Educators and students should consider the impact of this focus on the present. All of these sources present slavery so ahistorically that ordinary Americans have very little reason to connect the problem today to their understanding of slavery in the past and how their nation has developed over time. Also, by ignoring the history of slavery, antislavery activists employ the term "slavery" without acknowledging that it has a radically different meaning for ordinary Americans than it has for them. For Americans, slavery is profoundly about "then" and about the current implications of "then." It is purely not about "now." Of course, people of the United States (also those of the Caribbean, Latin America, and the continent of Africa, incidentally) know in their bones that the legacies of "old" slavery continue to shape their world—the forced removal of nine million Africans and their brutal dispersal throughout the Western Hemisphere and subjection to race-based enslavement. Still, if you ask US citizens, whatever their skin color, about slavery, their answers will be rooted in the past, full of conflicting moral content and inextricably tied to "blackness" and "race." It's simply not possible to create a movement to attack slavery today when Americans' minds are instinctively turning to thoughts of cotton, sugar, and Abraham Lincoln. It is little wonder that modern slavery remains so invisible for the vast majority of Americans.

Fortunately, there is a powerful remedy close at hand. It involves deploying American history to make today's slavery vividly come alive in the minds of our students. Educators can illuminate the plight of the enslaved today while discussing antebellum slavery, when the institution dominated the South and the nation's political economy. After examining antebellum American slavery and introducing students to the concept of modern slavery, teachers can ask students to use the websites for the organizations mentioned earlier to explore the obvious differences between slavery "then" and slavery "now. This analysis will not only hone critical thinking skills but also inform students' understanding of today's problem of slavery at home and abroad. After this examination, students should identify several of the main points:

- Back then, slavery was not only legal, it was deemed by most to be quite respectable. In the South, owning slaves elevated your status. Slavery was therefore easy to see close up. Though most whites living in the North lived distant from the institution, its opponents were able to criticize it at close range. Today's slavery is all but universally outlawed and judged to be morally indefensible. Nobody defends slavery as the planter class once did, so there's no one for abolitionists to argue against. Without controversy, abolitionist movements die as soon as they are born.

- Back then, slaveholders dominated national politics and ascended to the Republic's highest offices. Their cash investments in human beings were open to public criticism. Today, slaveholders hide in the shadows, bribe corrupt officials, and smuggle their captives across international borders. It seems almost impossible to confront them directly. Governments everywhere meantime cynically insist that they stand for abolition.

- Back then, enslaved people constituted our nation's second-largest capital investment, next to land. A "prime" slave in the 1850s was worth the equivalent today of as much as $40,000. Everyone had a stake in disagreeing about its morality. Today, slaves have no obvious impact on our formal economy, and their bodies can be purchased for as little as $50—this despite the fact that any ambitious pimp can net well over $200,000 annually by "running a stable" of prostituted women. In today's economic terms, who cares?

- Back then, slaves troubled the white nation by rebelling, fleeing, and turning themselves into formidable abolitionists. Today's slaves seem quiescent. They are quite often isolated, invisible to one another. There is no contemporary slave rebel like Nat Turner to rouse our anxieties, no Frederick Douglass or Sojourner Truth to embody the problem in a compelling way.

- Back then, slavery divided the nation. It was easy for antislavery northerners to oppose their geographically defined antagonists. Today's slavery, like the international drug trade, does not respect boundaries. Traffickers in humans remain well out of sight. So do the people they buy and sell.

Classes should consider the meaning of these differences, which can be summed up by visibility versus invisibility. More than anything, this difference explains why Americans today do not consider the world's enslaved as "our problem." Simply put, because we cannot identify today's slaves easily, Americans still associate slavery with antebellum America and "black" skin color. These associations make it easy to conclude from history that since all the enslaved were "black," that since all their owners were "white," slavery ended almost 150 years ago. It is all but impossible for Americans who conflate bondage with "black" to comprehend that far-flung systems of enslavement are ensnaring people of every imaginable pigmentation—"white" sex slaves from Chechnya as well as "yellow" sex slaves in Bangkok, "red" woodcutters in Manaos, Brazil, "brown" carpet weavers in Bangalore, "black" diamond miners in Angola, or people with any of these skin tones enslaved in Chicago.

After researching modern slavery on the websites suggested earlier, teachers and students can discuss the ways that slavery today mirrors slavery throughout American history. The example of post–Civil War America demonstrates some of the connections that teachers and students can make. Debt peonage is strikingly similar to what traffickers all over the world today demand after smuggling unsuspecting immigrants across national borders; smugglers demand the victim's documentation (if any) and the repayment of an impossible sum for services rendered while victims are unable to pay but are powerless without their identification, thus creating the pretext for enslavement. In much the same fashion, unscrupulous governments enslave "guest workers" after luring them across borders with promises of jobs. Post–Civil War prisons and chain gangs likewise anticipated perfectly how slave labor is currently deployed on Indonesian palm oil plantations and in Indian brick yard production and Brazilian charcoal manufacturing facilities. And finally, the worldwide sexual exploitation of enslaved women today reminds us of whites all over the postemancipation South who took it as their undisputed right to "have their way" with African American women. In all of these instances, modern slavery has replicated the American experience.

By engaging in this historical analysis, our students will begin to "see." Thanks to historical perspective, students can begin to understand why the enslaved today have remained so hard to relate to. Students can begin to comprehend their situations, to extend empathy, and to ask that most disturbing question—"What's causing this?" Formerly "invisible" people start to materialize. Students can begin imagining their experiences and thus find themselves motivated to work on their behalf. "Slavery" will no longer be a word that engenders guilt, shame, avoidance, and weariness. Instead, historical perspective based on African American experience becomes a provocation to "see" with great clarity the challenges of slavery today. In like manner, this same historical perspective challenges and empowers us to confront the legacies of American slavery that bear so heavily on American people of color today.

In short, and in conclusion, historical perspective empowers us to begin acting like abolitionists. Ann Terry Greene Phillips, the formidable Bostonian abolitionist and wife of Wendell Phillips, sharply enjoined her famous husband: "Wendell! Don't Shilly Shally!" Historians and their students should not be "shilly shallying" either. Informed by a sense of history that speaks directly to the present, we equip ourselves and our students to face down the most terrifying evil of our time.

SUGGESTIONS FOR FURTHER READING

Alexander, Michelle. *The New Jim Crow: Mass Incarceration in the Age of Color-blindness.* Washington, DC: New Press, 2012.

Bales, Kevin. *Disposable People: New Slavery in the Global Economy.* Oakland: University of California Press, 2000.

Blackmon, Douglas A. *Slavery by Another Name: The Re-Enslavement of Black Americans from the Civil War to World War II.* Norwell, MA: Anchor Press, 2008.

Foner, Eric. *Reconstruction: America's Unfinished Revolution 1863–1877.* New York: Harper Perennial, 1989.

Shelley, Louise. *Human Trafficking: A Global Perspective.* Cambridge: Cambridge University Press, 2010.

Skinner, E. Benjamin. *A Crime So Monstrous: Face to Face with Modern Day Slavery.* Washington, DC: Free Press, 2008.

PART THREE

Sources and Strategies for Teaching Slavery

Using the WPA Slave Narratives in the Classroom

CYNTHIA LYNN LYERLY

Thanks to the Library of Congress's American Memory website, more than two thousand interviews of former slaves, interviews conducted by the Federal Writer's Project of the Works Progress Administration (WPA), are online and accessible for our classroom use.[1] But what will our students make of a narrative like that of Henrietta McCullers? McCullers, whose interview was titled by the WPA worker "A Good Mistress," reported that "miss Betsy's" slaves ate the same food and slept in the same kind of beds that she did. When the "wuck was pushin' we wucked from sunup till dark and Mis' Betsy wucked too." McCullers claimed that "I loves [Miss Betsy] better dan I does my own chilluns now" and described lavish Christmas parties that lasted a whole week. Miss Betsey made such an impression on McCullers that she reported, "All my life when I done a bad thing I think 'bout Mis' Betsey's teachin's an' I repents." McCullers's interview ends with the most surprising statement of all: "[Black people] ort ter be back in slavery now, dey'd be better an' happier dan dey is."[2] There are many such narratives in the collection, narratives in which masters kept whipping to a minimum or even banned it altogether, where slaves ate well and were clothed well, and even where the former slaves reported fond memories of their former master or mistress.

It is because of such problems and not in spite of them that the WPA narratives make wonderful classroom resources. They teach students to think critically about sources, to look for biases, to do close readings, and to balance their research in primary sources with readings in the scholarly literature. We have to lay the groundwork, of course, for the students' understanding of these problematic sources. I have used the WPA narratives in a variety of different kinds of classes, to excellent effect.

There are several important things about these sources that every educator needs to know before using them in the classroom. First, the word "nigger" is common in the narratives. At this distance, and knowing what we know about the problems of the narratives, it is impossible to tell if the WPA worker substituted the offensive epithet when the former slave actually said "Negroes" or whether the former slaves used the word because they believed the white interviewers expected it. Another problem is the use of supposedly authentic "Negro dialect" in these interviews. White WPA workers, because of a mix of racism, paternalism, and folkloric efforts to preserve local vernacular, rendered the majority of the WPA narratives into a dialect that resembles that of the minstrel stage. While students might easily understand that "mornin'" was a short form of "morning," some of the narratives are quite racist in their use of "dialect." Cecilia Chappel's interviewer, to cite one of the worst examples, not only used "ax" for "ask" but also used "kum" for "come," "sum" for "some," "nit" for "knit," and "weav" for "weave." Since these last four renderings are pronounced exactly the same as their standard English counterparts, the "dialect" substitutions can only be viewed as egregiously racist means of demeaning Chappel and her speech.[3]

In a small class that focuses mainly on the WPA narratives, students can quickly become well informed about the WPA narratives and their problems. In my writing seminar, I had students read many of the articles about the WPA narratives as sources. I had students read scholars who praised the WPA narratives as sources as well as scholars, like John Blassingame, who privileged the nineteenth-century autobiographies of former slaves over the narratives. At first it vexes the students to see that prominent historians disagree. But it eventually emboldens them; they see that there is no one right answer and they get to use their judgment and decide for themselves. The Library of Congress American Memory website has a very nice introduction (written by Norman Yetman) to the narratives and the problems they present as sources.[4]

In some courses where I have used the narratives, reading all (or even enough of) the articles appraising the narratives as sources is not possible. In those courses I summarize the problems with the narratives in a lecture or presentation. The skeleton of that presentation is simple to recount.

First, the narratives were not transcriptions of verbatim interviews but were WPA interviewers' renditions, mostly after the fact, of what they thought the former slave had said in the interview. Some of the interviews were heavily edited to fit the agenda of the WPA workers or supervisors.

Second, the majority of the interviewers were white, often white women. In the 1930s South, Jim Crow ruled, and there were things it just was not safe to say to a strange white lady representing the federal government. A significant number of the interviewees knew the interviewer, and some were even enslaved by relatives of the interviewer. Nelson Cameron actually tried to capitalize on the prior relationship he had with his interviewer. Cameron asked if the interviewer remembered "when my pappy made you a pair of boots for $10.00 and when you pay him, him knock off one dollar and you pay him nine dollars? You does? Well dat is fine, for I sure need dat dollar dis very day."[5] Some of the freedmen and freedwomen interviewed believed that the WPA interviewer had some connection to the agency that granted pensions and relief checks. Alec Pope asked his interviewer if she was "one of dem pension ladies" and was disappointed when she said no.[6] Certainly these interviewees were careful to say what they thought a white interviewer wanted to hear. These conditions obviously shaped what the former slaves could say.

Third, the kinds of questions asked heavily shaped the narratives. The interviewers were interested in some things about slavery and not in others. Some WPA offices controlled the list of questions asked, while others left it up to the interviewer. Moreover, the interviewers often asked leading questions. You can see this in the responses of the former slaves. In Henrietta McCullers's interview, with which I opened, the second paragraph begins, "Yo' ax me iffen Mis' Betsy wus good ter us?" This sort of loaded question is very common, and the narratives have a lot of evidence to this effect. Most interesting are the occasions when former slaves resisted the positive interpretations the WPA interviewers were trying to evoke. Delia Garlic's interviewer did not include her question in the text, but it is obvious, from the context, that Margaret Fowler, the WPA worker, asked about good times. "No'm, dey warn't no good times at his house," Garlic replied. Garlic went on to describe two horrific incidents of violence perpetrated by slaveholding women against her when she was a child.[7]

Fourth, the ex-slaves were very old in the 1930s. This fact has several implications—one of which is that these ex-slaves were often young children when enslaved. Young children did not usually suffer the worst violence, hunger, and deprivations of slavery, in large part because their parents and other enslaved adults tried to protect and shield them. Historians also have debated the reliability of memories of the elderly interviewees. Because the interviews took place during the Depression, a time when former slaves were suffering from hunger and want at catastrophic levels, their distant memories of having enough good food to eat during childhood were undoubtedly affected. Besides these major problems with the sources themselves, the students need to have a basic understanding of antebellum slavery—at a minimum, labor routines, plantation management, slave family structure, and material conditions should be addressed.

Before I send my students to the narratives, I do several final bits of preparation. I print out a short narrative and go over it with them, highlighting how the interviewer asked leading questions and suggesting that what the 1930s interviewers asked was not what we were most interested in as historians. I also warn them about some things that are common in the narratives that they should watch for, things that will help them be better interpreters of these sources. I have them watch for deliberate silences and elisions in the narratives. Millie Barber, for example, said, "My mammy name, Nicie. Her b'long to de Weir family; de head of de family die durin' de war of freedom. I's not supposed to know all he done, so I'll pass over dat." Barber's interview includes a description of a horrible whipping her father received by patrollers, who "stripped him right befo' mammy and give him thirty-nine lashes, wid her cryin' and hollerin' louder than he did." What was worse, so much worse than this that it couldn't be spoken of? Was Barber afraid to speak of sexual abuse and rape? Was Master Weir cruel and sadistic?[8]

I have them watch for contradictions. Often, when directly asked, the former slaves would say yes, their master was good to his slaves. But the same narratives also contained evidence of overwork, the separation of enslaved families, meager rations, and cruelty. Henrietta McCullers, who belonged to the saintly Miss Betsy, described the slaves walking behind the carriage each Sunday as Miss Betsy rode. She used language that demarcated Miss Betsy's control over the slaves' lives: "She'd *let us have* a co'n shuckin' onct a year" and "*she let us have* candy pullins and such." Miss Betsy did not, however, allow her slaves to dance because of her own evangelical Christian beliefs, an admission that on its surface allegedly highlights what a "good Christian" Miss Betsy was but that also glaringly illustrates how Miss Betsy's slaves could not exercise their own ideas about right and wrong. Most notably, McCullers remarked about church services: "We can't read de hymns eben iffen we had a book 'cause we ain't 'lowed ter have no books."[9] Aunt Adeline supposedly told her interviewer twice that "My master's folks always treated me well," but she also bitterly noted that "we colored folks" were not allowed to read and write and described, at the age of five, being separated from her family when she was given as a wedding present to her master's daughter. At the end of Aunt Adeline's interview, the WPA worker noted that the freedwoman was dependent on her former master's family for support. Her narrative then, pays the requisite lip service to the white family she belonged to while also revealing some telling moments of slavery's cruelty.[10]

I have them look for qualifications, and here too they have to learn to read carefully and analyze their sources. Millie Barber added the not uncommon "such as it was" when asked about material conditions of slavery. She recalled that she had "plenty coverin' and plenty to eat, sich as it was." Then she added, "Us never git butter or sweet milk or coffee. Dat was for de white folks."[11] Savilla Burrell also noted that "Dere was plenty to eat sich as it was" but added that "in the summer time . . . de flies would be all over de food and some was swimmin' in de gravy and milk pots."[12] Marriah Hines reported: "We always had plenty of food, never knowed what it was to want food bad enough to have to steal it like a whole lot of 'em. Master would always give us plenty when he give us our rations." So far, a positive enough report, although we should note that Hines slid in the information that "a whole lot" of slaves had to steal because of hunger. But Hines complicated her story further with the following caveats: "Of course we slaves were given food and clothing and *just enough to keep us going good.* Why master would buy cloth by the loads and heaps, shoes by the big box full; den he'd call us to the house and give each [one of us] our share. Plenty to keep us comfortable, *course it warn't silk nor satin, no ways the best there was,* but 'twas plenty good 'nough for us."[13] Butter, sweet milk, coffee, silk, and satin were for white people, not for slaves.

I have them look for loaded questions. In some cases, the interviewers included their questions in the transcripts. Ferebe Rogers was asked how she met her husband and who married them; more tellingly, the interviewer asked, "Aunt Ferebe, are these better times or do you think slavery times were happier?" Judging by the way many narratives end, this seems to have been a very common question. Ferebe Rogers's safest bet was to tell her interviewer, Ruth Chitty, what Chitty wanted to hear. But Rogers did not: "Well now, you ax me for de truth, didn't you?—and I'm goin' to tell yo' de truth. I don't tell no lies." Note here how Rogers has framed her response—she is a woman who is so upright she has to tell the truth, even if that means saying negative things about white folks. Rogers replied: "Yes, mam, dese has been better times to me. I think hit's better to work for yourself and have what you make dan to work for somebody else and don't get nuttin' out [of] it. Slav'ey days was mighty hard. My marster was good to us (I mean he didn't beat us much and he give us plenty plain food) but some slaves suffered awful."[14]

With that preparation, I distribute a handout with some particularly problematic or interesting excerpts from the narratives that we read out loud and discuss together. For homework, I have students read at least a dozen interviews at random and answer questions I give them beforehand, such as what subjects were commonly covered and what subjects were never covered, how the interviewers tried to shape the responses, and how the former slaves attempted to shape the interview. But the assignment I think is most valuable is this—I have them print out two interviews of at least three pages in length. They have to reconstruct the interview by imagining the questions asked on the basis of the answers given. They have to be alert to changes in subject—the paragraphing of the narratives is not a helpful indicator of a change in subject.

This exercise in reconstructing the interview helps them to see the precise interventions the WPA interviewers made. The interviewers sometimes tried to divert the former slaves from talking about horrific experiences. Savilla Burrell's interview transcript, to show a case in point, reads: "Dey sell one of mother's chillun once, and when she take on and cry 'bout it, Marse say, 'stop dat sniffin' dere if you don't want to git a whippin'.' She grieve and cry at night 'bout it. Clothes? Yes Sir, us half naked all de time. Grown boys went 'round bare footed and in dey shirt tail all de summer." All of this is in the same paragraph in the typescript. Clearly, the WPA interviewer interrupted Burrell's dismal tale of her heartsick mother grieving after a sold-away child to ask Burrell about clothes. We can only cheer on Burrell when we see that she continued to speak the awful truth about slavery, only now by describing clothing rations.

Students learn to be good historians, to challenge sources, to discard some interviews as too biased, to read between the lines, to understand context, and to interpret by using the WPA narratives. They also learn a great deal about slavery. Some of what they learn is possible only after in-depth study of these sources, their creation, and the historiography. Another interesting and useful assignment is to have the students compare what the WPA narratives reveal about a subject with what the autobiographies written by former (often escaped) slaves do.[15] Having used these sources for many years in my classroom (even before they were available on the Web!), my students and I have discovered some things that help us understand how former slaves tried to get the truth of slavery out despite the context of race relations in the Jim Crow South.

We discovered that ex-slaves were routinely asked their opinions of Abraham Lincoln and Jefferson Davis (and sometimes of Franklin D. Roosevelt, Robert E. Lee, and Booker T. Washington). And in their answer to this question, the ex-slaves could accomplish a great deal. There are many interviews that proceed without criticism and sometimes with praise of masters, but when the interviewees were asked about Lincoln, the former slaves treated Lincoln as reverently as if he were heaven sent and praised Lincoln for emancipation in such a way as to make perfectly clear what their opinion of slavery was.

Another convention my students and I have noted is former slaves' practice of claiming that their master was good and kind and generous but that the master next door was the meanest, cruelest, or stingiest man in the South. Annie Price remembered that slaves on her plantation "always had plenty of clothes . . . while those on the plantation next to ours never had enough."[16] Price described the bounty on the slaves' tables at her plantation and the scarcity of provisions at the next one. This very common trope in the narratives provided former slaves with a way of critiquing the system of slavery without critiquing the specific white people who had owned them.

What is striking when you study these sources enough is not how many former slaves were reluctant to discuss slavery's cruelty but how many were brave enough to openly confront its brutality and how it affected the men and women under its yoke. It is fitting to close with the words of Martin Jackson, who serves as a useful counterbalance to Henrietta McCullers and her tale of the saintly Miss Betsy. Jackson told his interviewer that "Lots of old slaves closes the door before they tell the truth about their days of slavery. When the door is open, they tell how kind their masters was and how rosy it all was. You can't blame them . . . because they had plenty of early discipline, making them cautious about saying anything uncomplimentary about their masters."[17] Jackson was adamant that "the life of the average slave was not rosy" but was full of "plenty of cruel suffering." Although he himself had good treatment in slavery, Jackson confessed to his WPA interview that "I spent most of my time planning and thinking of running away."

NOTES

1. The Library of Congress's American Memory website is http://memory .loc.gov/ammem/snhtml/ and will hereafter be cited as LOC-WPA. The entire collection is also in print: George P. Rawick, ed., *The American Slave: A Composite Autobiography* (Westport, CT: Greenwood Press, 1972–79).

2. Henrietta McCullers interview, LOC-WPA.

3. Cecelia Chappel interview, LOC-WPA. For more on the use of dialect, see Sharon Ann Musher, "Contesting 'The Way the Almighty Wants It': Crafting Memories of Ex-Slaves in the Slave Narrative Collection," *American Quarterly* 53, no. 1 (March 2001): 1–31.

4. Paul D. Escott, "The Art and Science of Reading WPA Narratives," in Charles T. Davis and Henry Louis Gates Jr., eds., *The Slave's Narrative* (New York: Oxford University Press, 1985); Musher, "Contesting 'The Way the Almighty Wants It'"; Stephanie Shaw, "Using the WPA Ex-Slave Narratives to Study the Impact of the Great Depression," *Journal of Southern History* 69, no. 3 (August 2003): 623–58; Donna J. Spindel, "Assessing Memory: Twentieth-Century Slave Narratives Reconsidered," *Journal of Interdisciplinary History* 27 (Autumn 1996): 247–61; C. Vann Woodward, "History from Slave Sources," *American Historical Review* 79, no. 2 (April 1974): 470–81; David Thomas Bailey, "A Divided Prism: Two Sources of Black Testimony on Slavery," *Journal of Southern History* 46 (August 1980): 381–404; John Blassingame, "Using the Testimony of Ex-Slaves: Approaches and Problems," *Journal of Southern History* 41, no. 4 (November 1975): 473–92; Lydia M. Hill, "Ex-Slave Narratives: The WPA Federal Writers' Project Reappraised," *Oral History* 26, no. 1 (Spring 1998): 64–72; Norman R. Yetman, "The Background of the Slave Narrative Collection," *American Quarterly* 19, no. 3 (Fall 1967): 534–53; Yetman, "Ex-Slave Interviews and the Historiography of Slavery," *American Quarterly* 36, no. 2 (Summer 1984): 181–210.

5. Nelson Cameron interview, LOC-WPA.
6. Alec Pope interview, LOC-WPA.
7. Delia Garlic interview, LOC-WPA.
8. Millie Barber interview, LOC-WPA.
9. Henrietta McCullers interview.
10. "Aunt Adeline" interview, LOC-WPA.
11. Millie Barber interview.
12. Savilla Burrell interview, LOC-WPA.
13. Marriah Hines interview, LOC-WPA. For another of the interviewees who used "such as it was," see Lucinda Miller interview, LOC-WPA.
14. Ferrebe Rogers interview, LOC-WPA.
15. Fortunately, the University of North Carolina's Documenting the American South website has online versions of every published slave narrative: http://docsouth.unc.edu/neh.
16. Annie Price interview, LOC-WPA.
17. Martin Jackson interview, LOC-WPA.

Teaching the History of Slavery through Film

RON BRILEY

Teachers seeking to incorporate cinematic images of American slavery, from both documentaries and feature films, into the history classroom would do well to approach this methodology with some trepidation. Slavery is a painful reminder of a racial past that many Americans would prefer to ignore. But it is the crucible in which modern America was forged, and it is our duty to expose our children and students to this troubling past. Nevertheless, controversial issues such as social stereotyping, victimization, agency, and "presentism" are only exacerbated by their depiction on film. In addition to dealing with the emotional impact of celluloid depictions of slavery, teachers in the schools are still subjected to accusations that the use of film is a waste of valuable class time that could be better employed preparing for high-stakes testing. Teachers at all levels, of course, must make judicious use of limited time; however, a survey of how historians and teachers are increasingly relying upon cinematic history, especially depictions of slavery discussed in this chapter, suggests that film is too valuable a tool to be ignored in the history classroom.

The persistent and negative stereotypes of film in the classroom center around absent or lazy teachers who mindlessly use film as a substitute for teaching, without adequately preparing or debriefing students regarding the images to which they are exposed.[1] In 2011, for example, a substitute teacher in a fourth-grade Chicago suburban classroom played excerpts from the HBO-produced film *The Middle Passage* (2000) that depicted graphic images of brutality, suicide, and child rape. The screening provoked outrage among some parents, resulting in a more restrictive school-district media policy and the dismissal of the substitute teacher.[2] The point here is not whether it is appropriate to censor depictions of a brutal institution such as slavery for younger children. Rather, it is essential that, as teachers, we prepare our students for the images they are about to see on the screen and provide them with some historical and cultural context. Carefully introducing film into the history classroom requires additional work on the part of teachers, but, as numerous scholars suggest, the benefits of employing film are well worth the effort.[3]

Some of the challenges of incorporating film into the classroom include the fact that filmmakers must fit complex historical stories into the two-hour format of the feature film. Accordingly, it is often necessary for the filmmakers to compress stories that take place over a longer period of time and to employ composite characters so that viewers do not become confused by a plethora of characters on the screen. Despite the potential limitations of film as an historical source, most Americans obtain their history through film rather than from the printed page or the history classroom. Thus, any history teacher considering the incorporation of film into the curriculum, especially on a topic as controversial as slavery, would do well to consult *Past Imperfect: History According to the Movies* edited by Mark C. Carnes. In *Past Imperfect*, historians examine fifty international historical films, including at least five feature films—*Young Mr. Lincoln* (1939), *Abe Lincoln in Illinois* (1940), *Glory* (1989), *Gone with the Wind* (1939), and *The Birth of a Nation* (1915)—that could be incorporated into a film unit on slavery. Carnes concludes that historians ignore film at their own peril because cinema displays a "unique capacity for stimulating dialogue about the past."[4]

Several pedagogical resources can help history teachers as they bring film into the history curriculum. For example, in his text *Screening America*, James J. Lorence insists that feature films "may be studied as primary sources from which students may derive important knowledge and frame conclusions about the historical period in which the film first appeared. Studied in combination with print sources, films can open a door that enables us to better understand the people and problems of the past."[5] In a special issue of the *Organization of American Historians (OAH) Magazine of History* on teaching with film, Ron Briley and Robert Brent Toplin argue, "The historical engagement of film texts should encourage students to pursue more background reading and research into the topics depicted on movie and video screens."[6] Writing in the same issue of the *Magazine of History*, John O'Connor, the founder of the academic journal *Film and History*, provides a framework for the analysis of film and television sources. O'Connor maintains, "Each visual document should be analyzed in terms of its content—what is pictured and what is said; its production—how it came to portray what it does; and its reception—what sense people made of it when it was first produced and how it may have influenced attitudes or events over time."[7] These scholars all agree that films are rich sources that should be critically analyzed, not transparent versions of the past they depict. Thus, *Gone with the Wind* is most profitably screened as a source about Civil War memory and race relations in the late 1930s, when the film was produced.

Film certainly offers ample opportunities to enhance student understanding of American slavery. Ideally, it would be advantageous to offer an elective course on slavery and screen a number of films in their entirety.[8] While this may be possible in a college class, the reality of the high school curriculum's emphasis upon breadth over depth renders this approach unlikely. Accordingly, the study of slavery is usually part of the American history survey course, and there is little time to screen an entire film. Teachers can compensate for these time limitations by screening key ten- to fifteen-minute film clips that convey the meaning of the larger cinematic texts. For this approach to work, however, teachers must carefully select the appropriate scenes and provide students with context for the characters and images that they will witness. This means, of course, that history teachers will need to be as familiar with the film sources as they are with primary-source print documents. Teaching film requires considerable advance planning on the part of the teacher.

But what are the most appropriate films to use in the history curriculum on slavery? Many teachers might be more comfortable with documentaries. One must recognize, however, that documentary filmmakers can be as subjective as directors of feature films. In addition, the lack of visual material through which to document slavery may render the documentary avenue less likely to evoke the student empathy film usually provides.

Nevertheless, perhaps the best place to begin a discussion of slavery in the history classroom is the acclaimed 1990 PBS documentary *The Civil War*, directed by Ken Burns.[9] *The Civil War* first aired on PBS for five consecutive evenings, from September 23 to September 27, 1990. Burns includes a "chorus of voices" reading from primary documents such as personal papers, diaries, and letters in addition to commentary from scholars. Rather than attempting to reenact historical events, Burns relies upon the images of old photographs, drawings, and paintings as well as modern photographs of artifacts, cemeteries, and now peaceful battlefields, accompanied by period music.

Burns's approach tends to undermine the collective actions of enslaved people and has sparked a debate about the documentary's true message regarding slavery. The first episode of the series, titled "The Cause," firmly establishes slavery as the major cause of the Civil War. Most historians concur with this conclusion, though many Americans continue to disavow slavery as the root cause of the conflict.[10] This is the historiographical argument made by Burns, yet, as the historian James M. Lundberg asserts, Burns tends to undermine his own argument through romantic images of the war. Writing in *Slate*, Lundberg insists that Burns's film presents "an unapologetic patriotism and an appealing version of war as a source of honor, high ideals, and unity of purpose—precisely what had been lost in Vietnam and its aftermath." Lundberg also takes exception to the folksy narrative of the Civil War historian Shelby Foote, who emerged as the media star of the film. Reading Foote as prominently injecting southern notions of states' rights and the Lost Cause into the Civil War, Lundberg concludes, "As much as we want to remember the Civil War as a war for freedom, emancipation, and the full realization of American ideals, there is Foote calling us back into the mythical world of the Confederacy and the Old South in spite of all they stand for."[11] On the other hand, Bruce Chadwick, in *The Reel Civil War*, insists that Burns deserves considerable credit for not ignoring the subject of slavery. Observing that Burns included stark photographic evidence of slaves with deep scars on their backs from beatings, Chadwick argues that the filmmaker "was intent on portraying powerful Southerners as men fighting a war that killed many thousands of people to defend what Burns saw as the indefensible slave system."[12] This argument highlights the interpretive nature of documentaries, which are not transparent representations of the truth.

Classroom teachers who want to engage students in how we should perceive the legacy of slavery would do well to incorporate Burns's *The Civil War*, especially the first episode, which deals with slavery, into the curriculum. They should also introduce the diverse perspectives of scholars such as Lundberg and Chadwick, thus stimulating critical thinking upon documentary filmmaking, slavery, and the Civil War.

As a teaching activity after screening the film, it is interesting to have students briefly write their thoughts on the Old South and slavery. After discussing students' ideas, the perspectives of Lundberg and Chadwick could be introduced to the class, giving students an opportunity to reassess their original statements. As one teacher, Kevin M. Levin, concludes, Burns's *The Civil War* "supplemented with various primary and secondary sources, places students in a position where they can better appreciate the strengths and weaknesses of documentary history as well as the challenges involved in interpreting the past."[13]

Teachers can also use the 2005 PBS documentary *Slavery and the Making of America* to great effect in the history classroom. The black filmmaker Dante Josef James, who produced *Slavery and the Making of America*, asserted, "One of the primary purposes of the series was to deconstruct myths about the lives of the enslaved. In the past, they were often portrayed as passive victims. However, the new scholarship redefines enslaved Africans and African-Americans as the proactive freedom fighters they were."[14] The four-part series documents the history of American slavery from its origins in the British colonies through the premature end of Reconstruction and the emergence of Jim Crow in the American South during the 1880s. The film makes it quite apparent that slavery was an integral part of the emerging American economy and social life. Episode 1, titled "The Downward Spiral," is especially worth screening in the classroom as it describes the complex story of how indentured servitude in the colonies evolved into racial slavery. By the early eighteenth century, the African slave trade was expanding to provide a labor supply for southern plantations. Following the 1676 Bacon's Rebellion in Virginia and the 1731 Stono Rebellion in South Carolina—which is reenacted in the film—many of the colonies adopted "black codes" that institutionalized legal racial oppression and slavery. Episode 3, "Seeds of Destruction," is also extremely useful in the classroom. In a one-hour episode it traces the westward expansion of cotton culture and slavery, while in the North an abolitionist movement, led by figures such as Frederick Douglass and Sojourner Truth, challenged slavery. National events in this episode are viewed through the perspectives of Harriet Jacobs and Louis Hughes, who escaped from slavery and produced narratives exposing its brutality. Teachers could further pursue the significance of black abolitionists by introducing the writings of Douglass or Jacobs into the classroom.

Slavery and the Making of America is a valuable learning tool in the history classroom. It draws upon the distinctive voice of the ubiquitous actor Morgan Freeman for its narration. The documentary also employs historical reenactments, which give it somewhat the feel of a feature film. Teachers who use the series in the classroom will also find the companion volume by James Oliver Horton and Lois E. Horton helpful, and the series website includes lesson plans and primary documents based upon slave narratives. In particular, the website feature "Slave Memories" allows a student to hear the voices of African Americans, recorded by the New Deal's Works Progress Administration, regarding their experiences during slavery and Reconstruction. The narratives include accounts of slave auctions and everyday work life. The account of Laura Smalley talks about slaves who ran away to avoid beatings. She observes that her father was not beaten but was sometimes fed only one ear of corn per day if he did not adhere to the expectations of his owner. On the other hand, George Johnson claimed to have once been a slave owned by Jefferson Davis, president of the Confederacy, and Johnson extolled Davis as a benevolent master. Perhaps telling his white interviewer what Johnson assumed he wanted to hear, the former slave remarked that if one gave the white masters "a little honor," they would "help you do what you want to do." *Slavery and the Making of America* received positive reviews from scholars and the media, which praised the series for emphasizing the complexity of African American responses to slavery.[15]

Although the ratings for the series were above average for PBS, *Slavery and the Making of America* did not enjoy the cultural impact of Burns's *The Civil War*. Teachers should ask students why this stellar production did not resonate as well with audiences. The history of slavery, which contradicts the founding principles of the nation contained in the Declaration of Independence, is a subject with which many Americans are uncomfortable. Does a largely white audience prefer the story of romantic Civil War battles to narratives of black rebellion against the white people who oppressed blacks for the sake of money and power? This is a troubling question that deserves to be addressed in history classrooms.

While documentaries such as *The Civil War* and *Slavery and the Making of America* provide excellent strategies for tackling the difficult topic of slavery in the classroom, feature films focusing upon slavery, the Civil

War, and Reconstruction offer the appeal of character-driven narratives. In addition, the Hollywood feature film allows students to consider how the movie reflects the racial attitudes of the time period in which it was made. Accordingly, teachers who want to examine how Hollywood has both reflected and influenced perceptions of race and slavery should tackle D. W. Griffith's controversial *The Birth of a Nation* (1915), in which emancipated black males are driven by their lust for white women until the Ku Klux Klan is forced to restore sexual and racial order.[16] Studying *The Birth of a Nation*, which was based upon the racist novel *The Clansman* (1905) by Thomas Dixon Jr., allows teachers and students an opportunity to investigate the racial assumptions of the Progressive era. The film reflects the state of American historiography in 1915, which depicted Reconstruction as the rape of white southern civilization by northern carpetbaggers, traitorous southern scalawags, and the lecherous freedmen.[17]

Students, however, need to be carefully prepared before being exposed to images from Griffith's films. Many students will be appalled by the romantic and heroic rendering of a terrorist organization such as the Klan, while blacks, portrayed by whites in blackface, are reduced to racist caricatures. In addition to offering depictions of lecherous black men, Griffith presents blacks as incompetent and unable to handle the responsibilities of emancipation. Freedmen elected to the Reconstruction era South Carolina state legislature are portrayed as gambling, enjoying cock fights, and eating watermelons. In fact, most students will struggle with this silent film, which is almost two and one-half hours in length. Rather than screen this entire epic, which covers both the Civil War and Reconstruction, teachers might use the last twenty minutes of the film to document how Griffith presents the Klan rescuing white women and restoring white rule by denying blacks the right to vote guaranteed by the Fifteenth Amendment.

The racial caricatures in *The Birth of a Nation* are so exaggerated that students may be tempted to laugh at the images. It is, therefore, advisable that students research the film's Progressive-era reception, including the response by the NAACP, and recognize that *The Birth of a Nation* contributed to an increased wave of lynching in the United States that was based on alleged sexual attacks by black men upon white women. Although difficult to discuss in the classroom, these elements of sexual racism, which were used to justify lynching and segregation, must be addressed. Protecting white females from the predatory advances of blacks during the Great Migration of the 1920s provided the excuse for racial violence such as the 1924 Tulsa race riot and the rise of the Klan on to the national stage.[18] It is appropriate to give the cultural historian Leon Litwack the final word on *The Birth of a Nation*. Writing in *Past Imperfect*, Litwack asserted, "For much of the twentieth century, *The Birth of a Nation* molded and reinforced racial stereotypes, distorting the physical appearance of black men and women, making a mockery of their lives and aspirations, and fixing in the public mind the image of a race of inferiors—sometimes amusing and comical, sometimes brutal and subhuman, but in either case less than white men and women."[19]

The Lost Cause was still alive and well in 1939 when Hollywood filmed the epic *Gone with the Wind*, based upon the 1936 best-selling novel by Margaret Mitchell. Both the film and the novel depict an idyllic southern civilization complete with a paternalistic system of slavery that was destroyed by the ravages of the Civil War. The heroine Scarlett O'Hara is the symbol of a resilient southern way of life that survives the loss of the plantation system.

Teachers, who cannot devote four hours of class time to this lavish costume epic, might do well to screen a fifteen-minute segment that suggests the continuing influence of Griffith. Early in the second half of the film, which deals with Reconstruction, Scarlett is attacked outside a shantytown by poor whites and freedmen. Before she can be violated, however, Scarlett is rescued by Big Sam, a former slave who remains loyal to the O'Hara family. Her husband, Frank Kennedy, then leads a raid on the shantytown in revenge for this assault upon southern womanhood and civilization. Yankee troops, however, are waiting in ambush, and Mr. Kennedy is killed before Rhett Butler is able to warn him. This scene represents the image of black men as sexual predators, while Mr. Kennedy and the other southern white men seeking to avenge Scarlett represent the gallant Klan defending southern women and values. Racial stereotypes are also perpetuated in the female slaves Mammy and Prissy. For example, early in the film, when Mammy is dressing Scarlett for the barbeque at the Twelve Oaks plantation, the loyal and rotund Mammy in her kerchief bosses around the white family as if they were her own relatives, even mentioning how she raised Scarlett's mother. For her portrayal of Mammy, Hattie McDaniel won the Academy Award for Best Supporting Actress, becoming the first black performer to win an Academy Award. During class discussions of the film, teachers might ask students whether McDaniel's assumption of a stereotypical role made her performance more palatable to white audiences in 1939.[20]

The emergence of the post–World War II civil rights movement finally brought a challenge to Hollywood's depiction of contented slaves with the 1977 premiere of the television miniseries *Roots*.[21] Although the book by Alex Haley, upon which the series was based, has flaws, *Roots* still deserves a place in the history curriculum. Other television productions dealing with slavery and its legacy, such as *The Autobiography of Miss Jane Pittman* (1974) and *A Woman Called Moses* (1978), which dramatizes the life of Harriet Tubman, are told from the perspective of a white narrator. *Roots* is the story of slavery from a black perspective. *Roots* chronicles the life of Kunta Kinte (LaVar Burton), of the Mandinka nation, who is captured by slavers when he is fifteen. The film portrays the brutal Middle Passage as Kunta Kinte is transported to colonial America in 1750 and sold into slavery. *Roots* focuses on the struggle of Kunta Kinte and his ancestors to resist slavery and to maintain some allegiance to their African heritage. The series concludes during Reconstruction, when Chicken George Moore (Ben Vereen) is able to purchase land in Tennessee for the freed family.

The series originally aired on ABC television for eight consecutive evenings in 1977. Although the network was apprehensive about the ratings, *Roots* proved to be a great success, drawing an estimated audience of 140 million viewers with a 66 percent share of homes with televisions. The series is a powerful teaching tool in the classroom. For example, the scene where Kunta Kinte is placed on the auction block for the first time in Virginia highlights the depravity of treating humans as property by showing how slave dealers packaged slaves for sale in 1750. In addition, the scene demonstrates how integrated slavery was into colonial life. Teachers might also want to screen the story of Kunta Kinte's daughter, Kizzy Reynolds, from the 1790s to the late 1840s, which is told in parts 3, 4, and 5 of the re-edited series. This story highlights the perspective of female slaves, who had to fight off the sexual assaults of white masters while struggling to raise and protect children who might be sold by the master. This perspective is all too often ignored by feature films on slavery. Teachers can pair Kizzy's story with Harriet Jacobs's *Incidents in the Life of a Slave Girl* to explore the impact of female slavery.[22]

The film historian Bruce Chadwick praises *Roots* for providing its black audience with a sense of pride in the perseverance of their ancestors. Chadwick argues, however, that the major impact of the series was on the larger white group of viewers, who "could never look at blacks the same way again after watching in the comfort of their own living room—soda on the lamp table, bags of chips on their laps, their own kids leaning against a chair, watching over them—what had happened to black people."[23] Class discussions regarding contemporary issues of race in America, focusing upon economic inequality and disparities in the criminal justice system, could raise some questions as to just how revolutionary *Roots* really was in American race relations.

The series, however, was not free from controversy. Some white viewers believed that the show overly emphasized the cruelty of white masters and ignored the fact that some owners were benevolent toward their slaves. On the other hand, the producers, realizing that the target audience was largely nonblack, featured well-known white television performers such as Lorne Green, Robert Reed, and Ralph Waite. Nevertheless, the historian William L. Van Deburg asserts, "Despite its 'whitening,' *Roots* was a veritable Black Power manifesto compared to the 1980 made-for-TV movie *Beulah Land*." This production focused primarily upon the sex lives of the planter class, while reducing the enslaved population of the plantations to mere backdrops.[24]

PBS produced a more interesting film on slave resistance that featured the historian Robert Toplin as a consultant. *Solomon Northup's Odyssey* (1984) tells the story of a free man of color who was sold into bondage. Northup labored for twelve years in the cotton fields before he was able to secure his release through a sympathetic Canadian agent. *Solomon Northup's Odyssey* has been somewhat eclipsed by the filmmaker Steve McQueen's Academy Award–winning film *12 Years a Slave* (2013), which is based upon Northup's classic slave narrative. An excellent scene from McQueen's film that could be incorporated into the classroom shows how Northrup, a free man of color living in the North, was kidnapped and sold into slavery, demonstrating the vulnerability of all blacks living in the United States during the antebellum era. This critically acclaimed film by McQueen, however, may encounter difficulty finding its way into some school curriculums for it includes graphic scenes of beatings and sexual violence embedded into the experience of American slavery. Yet, brutality and sexual exploitation

were crucial aspects of the racial slave system, and the story of the in-
dignities suffered by the enslaved Patsey (Lupita Nyong'o) at the hands
of her master, Edwin Epps (Michael Fassbender), are painful but illu-
minating. Nevertheless, *Solomon Northup's Odyssey* may be a more appropriate choice for younger students, although it lacks the visual
power of *12 Years a Slave*.[25]

Glory (1989) addresses issues of black agency. This film tells the
story of the 54th Massachusetts Volunteer Infantry—composed of free
men of color and former slaves—from its formation in the winter of
1862–63 to the regiment's assault upon the well-defended Confederate
Fort Wagner, at the entrance to Charleston harbor. While the attack
proved unsuccessful, with more than half of the regiment perishing
along with its white commander, Colonel Robert Gould Shaw, the battle
demonstrated that black troops were prepared to fight valiantly for
their freedom. The Civil War historian James McPherson credits the
Academy Award–winning film, directed by Edward Zwick, with getting
the larger truth straight. Writing in *Past Imperfect*, McPherson concludes,
"*Glory*'s point is made symbolically in one of its most surreal and, at
first glance, irrelevant scenes. During a training exercise, Shaw gallops
his horse along a path flanked by stakes, each holding a watermelon.
Shaw slashes right and left with his sword, slicing and smashing every
watermelon. The point becomes clear when we recall the identification
of watermelons with the 'darky' stereotype. If the image of smashed
watermelons in *Glory* can replace the use of moonlight and magnolias
in *Gone with the Wind* as America's cinematic version of the Civil War, it
will be a great gain for truth."[26]

Daniel Nathan addresses the popularity of *Glory* with students in a
lesson plan for the *OAH Magazine of History*, concluding that the film
"vividly animates the past and does so with integrity." Nathan also
credits *Glory* with exposing northern racist opposition to and discomfort
with arming black troops—a perspective with which many of his students proved unfamiliar. At the film's core, Nathan and his college
students find that the specter of slavery is powerfully demonstrated in
the scene where Silas Trip (Denzel Washington), with scars from previous lashings on his back, is ordered to be whipped for disobeying orders.
This scene occurs about halfway through the film as Shaw attempts to
foster a degree of discipline in his untrained black soldiers. However,
rather than deserting the regiment, it turns out that Trip was looking
for shoes, which had not been supplied to the black recruits. Trip's

scarred back and defiance are essential to the narrative, and Nathan concludes, "In subtle and not-so-subtle ways, *Glory* suggests that slavery was a scourge, a principal cause of the war, and a nasty, deep scar."[27] Zwick's film, however, is not without its critics. Class discussions should consider the fact that the leading black figures are composite characters, while the story is told essentially from the perspective of the white commander, Shaw (Matthew Broderick), with a primary source for the film being the letters from Shaw to his New England parents. Thus, cultural historian Robert Burgoyne laments that the film fails to present a social movement or national ideology cutting across racial identity, concluding that in the final analysis the film emphasizes "the fear and hatred of the other as the constant feature of the national experience."[28]

Questions of racial agency also play a key role in the analysis of Steven Spielberg's 1997 film *Amistad*, which has found a place in many history classrooms. *Amistad* chronicles an 1839 slave revolt aboard the Spanish slave ship *La Amistad* by enslaved Mende people from West Africa. After the ship was intercepted by a US revenue cutter, the Africans were incarcerated, and the Spanish crown sued for the return of its cargo. After a series of trials, the *Amistad* case reached the Supreme Court. Former president John Quincy Adams argued before the court that the Africans, led by Cinque, should be set free. The court agreed and called for Cinque and his compatriots to be freed and returned to Africa. Howard Jones, the author of the historical account upon which the film is based, acknowledges some factual errors in the production, but he believes that Spielberg accurately portrayed the larger truths of the *Amistad* story. Jones credits Spielberg with not losing sight of the essential story of enslaved Africans battling for their freedom and maintaining their dignity in a cultural milieu where human and property values clashed. In addition, Jones praises the film director for showing that the African slave trade was a "brutal business and constituted a Black Holocaust."[29] Spielberg's film includes a powerful flashback depicting the slave trade and the Middle Passage before the revolt. This crucial scene occurs after the legal team defending the *Amistad* mutineers is able to find a black sailor who understands the Mende language, so that Cinque is at last able to tell his story and explain that the enslaved people of the *Amistad* were not Spanish slaves but rather free African people who were captured by slavers. Presenting a visualization of the brutality associated with the Middle Passage should provide an avenue for teachers to address the dehumanization of the international slave trade, which was based upon demeaning calculations of profit.

Amistad, however, also raises controversial questions about the nature of film and history that teachers should incorporate into discussions and writing assignments on the film. Natalie Zemon Davis believes that *Amistad* deserves a place in the history curriculum, but she thinks that the film strays too far from the truth when it seeks to establish a personal relationship between Adams (Anthony Hopkins) and Cinque (Djimon Hounsou). She concludes, "The historical strength of *Amistad* is in its portrayal of the Africans, and most strikingly, in its representation of the seizure of Cinque, the Middle Passage, and the revolt."[30]

Yet, many critics of the film assert that by concentrating the majority of *Amistad*'s screen time on the court case, whites are privileged at the expense of the enslaved, who lack agency and become dependent upon whites for their deliverance. Critics like to point out that the Supreme Court decision on the *Amistad* mutineers was based less upon the references by Adams to the Declaration of Independence and more upon the laws of property. The Africans were not products of the slave system but rather free people who were illegally seized from their homes in Africa in violation of international agreements outlawing the trans-Atlantic slave trade. In addition, abolitionists such as Lewis Tappan are presented as hypocrites, and the film's conclusion provides a positive ending, suggesting the triumph of American democracy. Yet, twenty years after the events depicted in the film, it would take a bloody Civil War to rid the nation of slavery. Questioning the use of *Amistad* in the classroom, the historian Patrick Rael argues, "The *Amistad* incident lends itself easily to a portrayal in which slavery becomes a figure associated with the silly, moribund, reactionary, monarchical, and anti-republican despots of the Old World rather than as a fundamental economic, social, and ideological component of American society." Rael concludes that Spielberg's film "winds up presenting us with yet another glorified image of American history in which the Nation triumphs without ever coming to grips with its own moral failings."[31] Rather than leave *Amistad* out of the curriculum, students would benefit from instructors who teach both the film and the controversy over how Spielberg addresses the historical record.

Similar controversy surrounds Spielberg's acclaimed *Lincoln* (2012), which will certainly find its way into many history classrooms. It is difficult to criticize Daniel Day-Lewis's Academy Award–winning performance as the sixteenth president, but the question of agency has certainly arisen regarding the film. *Lincoln* is essentially an examination of how the president pragmatically and skillfully maneuvered Congress to approve the Thirteenth Amendment abolishing slavery. The movie is important for its depiction of slavery because enslaved people are entirely absent from the film. As the historian Eric Foner pointed out in the *New York Times*, "Emancipation—like all far-reaching political change—results from events at all levels of society, including the efforts of social movements to change public sentiment and of slaves themselves to acquire freedom."[32] The film, therefore, could generate useful classroom discussion about what it means to exclude the actions of enslaved people in this narrative of emancipation. Additional information on the impact of enslaved people on emancipation can be found in Bethany Jay's essay in this volume. To gain some insight into the diverse historical opinions regarding Spielberg's *Lincoln*, teachers also should examine the articles collected by the History News Network under the heading "Is *Lincoln* the Movie Historically Accurate?"[33]

This overview of slavery on the screen is hardly exhaustive, but it should provide an introduction to the ample opportunities available for bringing the study of slavery into the history classroom through the medium of film, both documentaries and features. As the discussion suggests, slavery on the screen is not without considerable controversy. But history teachers must not be afraid to tackle a subject such as slavery, which continues to cast such a large shadow over American democratic aspirations, and in an increasingly visual age we must work to equip our students with critical viewing and thinking skills to analyze the impact of film upon American history and culture. In addition, a cinematic approach to teaching slavery should also provide an opportunity for team teaching, in partnership with English teachers, the novel *Beloved* (1987) by Toni Morrison and the corresponding 1998 film directed by Jonathan Demme and starring Oprah Winfrey. Natalie Zemon Davis suggests that teaching *Beloved* allows for the examination of the all too often ignored impact of slavery upon African American women.[34] Also, history teachers might collaborate with filmmaking classes, where such programs exist, to encourage students to try their hand at making documentaries on American slavery and its legacy. Cinema and the visual image offer both students and history teachers a rich opportunity to enhance the study and teaching of American slavery through the medium of film, which merits an important role in the history curriculum.

NOTES

1. The negative stereotypes of teachers who employ film is addressed by John E. O'Connor, one of the founding fathers of film history. O'Conner recollects, "Friday afternoon was film time when I was in school, and the teacher who planned carefully could have the reel spin off the projector just as the dismissal bell sounded. This avoided the need for a sometimes strained class discussion." John E. O'Conner, "Reading, Writing, and Critical Viewing: Coordinating Skill Development in History Learning," *The History Teacher* 34, no. 2 (February 2001): 183.

2. *"Middle Passage* Shown to Nine-Year Olds: Educational or Too Graphic," *Huffington Post*, February 23, 2011, www.huffingtonpost.com/2011/02/23 /middle-passage-film-graphic_n_827124.html.

3. For a discussion of scholars who employ film in the classroom, teachers should consult Natalie Zemon Davis, *Slaves on the Screen: Films and Historical Vision* (Cambridge, MA: Harvard University Press, 2000); Robert Brent Toplin, *Reel History: In Defense of Hollywood* (Lawrence: University Press of Kansas, 2002); Robert Brent Toplin, *History by Hollywood: The Use and Abuse of the American Past* (Urbana: University of Illinois Press, 1996); and Robert A. Rosenstone, *History on Film/Film on History* (New York: Pearson, 2006).

4. Mark C. Carnes, ed., *Past Imperfect: History According to the Movies* (New York: Henry Holt, 1995), 10.

5. James J. Lorance, *Screening America: United States History through Film since 1900* (New York: Pearson, 2006), 2.

6. "Teaching Film and History," ed. Ron Briley and Robert Brent Toplin, special issue, *OAH Magazine of History* 16, no. 4 (Summer 2002): 3.

7. John E. O'Conner, "Image as Artifact: Historians and the Moving-Image Media," in Briley and Toplin, "Teaching Film and History," 23.

8. The possibilities of a high school film history class elective is explored in Ron Briley, "Reel History: U.S. History, 1932–1972 as Viewed through the Lens of Hollywood," *The History Teacher* 23, no. 3 (May 1990): 215–36.

9. For overviews of Ken Burns's *The Civil War* see Gary R. Edgerton, "Chalk, Talk, and Videotape: Utilizing Ken Burns's Television History in the Classroom," in Briley and Toplin, "Teaching Film and History," 16–22; and Robert Brent Toplin, ed., *Ken Burns's The Civil War: Historians Respond* (New York: Oxford University Press, 1997). Teachers using *The Civil War* might also consult the companion volume: Geoffrey Ward, Ken Burns, and Ric Burns, *The Civil War: An Illustrated History* (New York: Knopf, 1992), and lesson plans available on the PBS website http://www.pbs.org/civilwar/.

10. In a piece for the *OAH Magazine of History*, James W. Loewen observes that four out of five Americans, including many teachers, maintain the "basic misconception" that the war was about the rather abstract concept of "states' rights." Drawing upon Confederate secession documents, Loewen develops an

interesting lesson plan that restores the issue of slavery as a core reason for the South's secession and the Civil War. James W. Loewen, "Using Confederate Documents to Teach about Secession, Slavery, and the Origins of the Civil War," *OAH Magazine of History* 25, no. 2 (April 2011): 35–44.

11. James M. Lundberg, "Thanks a Lot, Ken Burns," *Slate*, June 7, 2011, http://www.slate.com/articles/arts/culturebox/2011/06/thanks_a_lot_ken_burns.html.

12. Bruce Chadwick, *The Reel Civil War: Mythmaking in American Film* (New York: Knopf, 2001), 292–93.

13. Kevin M. Levin, "Using Ken Burns's *The Civil War* in the Classroom," *The History Teacher* 44, no. 1 (November 2010): 9–17.

14. Dante Josef James, "PBS *Slavery and the Making of America* Producer Responds to Critique," *The Black Commentator*, March 17, 2005, www.blackcommentator.com/130/130_pbs_response.html.

15. Public Broadcasting System, *Slavery and the Making of America*, 2004, www.pbs.org/wnet/slavery/about/index.html; James Oliver Horton and Lois E. Horton, *Slavery in the Making of America* (New York: Oxford University Press, 2004); David W. Blight, "America Made and Unmade by Slavery," The Gilder Lehrman Center for the Study of Slavery, Resistance and Abolition, http://www.yale.edu/glc/events/moareview.htm.

16. Ron Briley, "Hollywood's Reconstruction and the Persistence of Historical Mythmaking," *The History Teacher* 41, no. 4 (August 2008): 453–68; Everett Carter, "Culture History Written with Lightening: The Significance of *The Birth of a Nation* (1915)," in Peter C. Rollins, ed., *Hollywood as Historian: American Film in a Cultural Context* (Lexington: University Press of Kentucky, 1983), 9–19; Mark E. Benbow, "Birth of a Quotation: Woodrow Wilson and 'Like Writing History with Lightning,'" *Journal of the Gilded Age and Progressive Era* 9 (2010): 509–33; and Fred Silva, ed., *Focus on The Birth of a Nation* (Englewood Cliffs, NJ: Prentice Hall, 1971).

17. William A. Dunning, *Reconstruction: Political and Economic, 1865–1877* (New York: Harper & Row, 1907), 1.

18. Martha Hode, *White Women, Black Men: Illicit Sex in the Nineteenth-Century South* (New Haven: Yale University Press, 1997).

19. Leon F. Litwack, "*The Birth of a Nation*," in Carnes, *Past Imperfect*, 140–41.

20. Darden Asbury Pyron, ed., *Recasting Gone with the Wind in American Culture* (Gainesville: University Presses of Florida, 1983); Richard Harwell, ed., *Gone with the Wind as Book and Film* (Columbia: University of South Carolina Press, 1983); and Trisha Curran, "*Gone with the Wind*: An American Tragedy," in Warren French, ed., *The South and Film* (Jackson: University Press of Mississippi, 1981), 47–57. While classic Hollywood cinema of the 1930s and 1940s often perpetuated the stereotype of loyal slaves such as those found in *Gone with the Wind*, abolitionists were often featured as crazed individuals who sought to disrupt the southern way of life and American unity. In *Tennessee*

Johnson (1942), Van Heflin portrays President Andrew Johnson as valiantly resisting the Reconstruction plans of vindictive Radical Republicans such as Thaddeus Stevens. In the amazingly historically inaccurate *Santa Fe Trail* (1940), J.E.B. Stuart (Errol Flynn) and George Armstrong Custer (Ronald Reagan) seek to foil the plans of the abolitionist John Brown (Raymond Massey) at Harper's Ferry. See Chadwick, *Reel Civil War*, 244–46.

21. Alex Haley, *Roots: The Saga of an American Family* (New York: Doubleday, 1976).

22. Harriet Jacobs, *Incidents in the Life of a Slave Girl* (1861; reprint, New York: Dover Thrift Edition, 2001); and Jane Fagan Yellin, *Harriet Jacobs: A Life* (Cambridge, MA: Harvard University Press, 2004).

23. Bill Gorman, "Top 100 Rated TV Shows of All Time," May 21, 2009, tvbythenumbers.com; and Chadwick, *Reel Civil War*, 269–70.

24. William L. Van Deburg, "Slavery as TV: A True Picture?," in "Teaching about Slavery," ed. Kathy Rogers, special issue, *OAH Magazine of History* 1, no. 2 (Fall 1985): 13–16.

25. Robert Brent Toplin, "Making a Slavery Docudrama," in Rogers, "Teaching about Slavery," 17–19; and Robert Brent Toplin, "*12 Years a Slave* Examines the Old South's Heart of Darkness," *Perspectives on History* 52, no. 1 (January 2014): 39–40.

26. James McPherson, "*Glory,*" in Carnes, *Past Imperfect*, 130–31.

27. Daniel Nathan, "The Massachusetts 54th on Film: Teaching *Glory*," in Briley and Toplin, "Teaching Film and History," 38–41.

28. Robert Burgoyne, *Film Nation: Hollywood Looks at U.S. History* (Minneapolis: University of Minnesota Press, 1997), 16–17.

29. Howard Jones, *Mutiny on the Amistad: The Saga of a Slave Revolt and Its Impact on American Diplomacy* (New York: Oxford University Press, 1987); and Howard Jones, "*Amistad*: Movie, History, and the Academy Awards," *The History Teacher* 31, no. 3 (May 1998): 380–82.

30. Davis, *Slaves on the Screen*, 81.

31. Jesse Lemisch, "The Question of Agency," *The History Teacher* 41, no. 3 (May 1998): 386; and Patrick Rael, "Why This Film about Slavery," *The History Teacher* 41, no. 3 (May 1998): 387.

32. Eric Foner, "*Lincoln*'s Use of Politics for Noble Ends," *New York Times*, November 26, 2012.

33. "Is *Lincoln* the Movie Historically Accurate?," History News Network, http://historynewsnetwork.org/article/149560; Mark E. Neely Jr., "The Young Lincoln," in Carnes, *Past Imperfect*, 124–27; and Phillip M. Guerty, "Lincoln, Race, and Slavery," *OAH Magazine of History* 21, no. 4 (October 2007).

34. Toni Morrison, *Beloved* (New York: Knopf, 1987); and for a discussion of *Beloved* on the screen see Davis, *Slaves on the Screen*, 93–119.

Art and Slavery

RAY WILLIAMS

This chapter is meant to encourage history teachers and other non-art specialists to make use of works of art in teaching about slavery. I will introduce two pedagogical frameworks used in the field of visual art education to support nonspecialists in facilitating classroom conversations about works of art. Although these frameworks will prepare you to work with any image—selected from a textbook, newspaper, or popular culture—I have selected four works of art that raise provocative issues important to the study of American slavery to get you started.

Our key images include a modernist depiction from 1967 of Harriet Tubman leading slaves to freedom; an illustration from the influential abolitionist novel *Uncle Tom's Cabin* from 1852; a complex portrait of a former slave, painted by the sitter's grandson in 1924; and a print from a 1993 series that appropriates nineteenth-century imagery and combines it with text that describes the artist himself as a runaway slave. All three of the twentieth-century works are by African American artists; they demonstrate the ongoing impact and significance of the history of slavery on American culture. These images and related contextual information, along with research-based protocols for facilitating interpretive conversations with students, will support you in experimenting with the power of art to stimulate thinking, feeling, and learning. The chapter concludes with references to additional sources and individual artists that will, I have no doubt, inspire you to develop your own image-based lesson plans.

Although many non-art specialists are hesitant to introduce works of art in their history or literature classes, art can act as a catalyst for important and wide-ranging conversations. These conversations, rooted in close looking at a primary source, foster analytical skills and ways of thinking that historians need. Lessons featuring works of art will motivate the visual learners among your students; you may see increased participation from individuals who typically hold back in class discussions based on reading assignments. Images make historical events more memorable to students, and they activate the empathetic imagination. Works of art ask that we operate in both analytical and emotional domains—again, providing entry points for diverse learning styles.

What can works of art contribute to the history classroom?

- Provide primary source material for analysis.
- Make historical events seem more "real" and memorable.
- Cultivate empathy; cause students to care about historical issues and the individuals affected.
- Focus a class conversation on a specific set of visual "facts."
- Encourage ways of thinking that historians value, especially the intellectual habit of grounding interpretive theories in evidence.
- Raise important issues of voice, perspective, and bias.
- Pique curiosity and raise questions that lead to further research.

Visual Thinking Strategies

The Visual Thinking Strategies (VTS) approach is rooted in research on aesthetic development by Abigail Housen and has been developed for application by the museum educator Philip Yenawine.[1] VTS has been widely adopted in both school and museum settings, and the method is particularly well suited to the developmental needs of inexperienced viewers. Students are asked to look closely at works of art, generate theories of meaning grounded in visual evidence, and listen to alternative points of view. Research has shown that students who use VTS in schools improve their critical thinking skills and increase the amount of time they are motivated to spend with (still) images.

VTS is designed to address the common interest among beginner viewers (who, incidentally, make up the majority of museum visitors) in discerning a narrative when considering a work of art. It was developed especially for use by non-art specialists—museum volunteers and classroom teachers—and has the advantage of providing three core questions that, when skillfully used, motivate and sustain close looking and evidential reasoning.

After inviting students to *look closely* at an image for a couple of minutes, teachers use the following three questions to facilitate a wide-ranging discussion:

- What's *going on* in this picture?
- What do you *see* that makes you say that?
- What *more* can we find?

The teacher's role is to facilitate a lively conversation among the students without providing additional information or encouraging any particular line of discussion. The facilitator must listen carefully, paraphrase student comments, and, using question 2, ask that students ground their ideas in visible evidence that can be considered by all. They must also try not to praise or discourage particular student comments; this is a challenge, but praising any one specific student's response can have an inhibiting effect on other potential participants. Student contributions are affirmed by the facilitator's close listening and careful paraphrasing, which includes pointing to the relevant visual evidence and providing a more sophisticated vocabulary to express the students' ideas.

Teachers should also help the group keep track of the conversation by pointing out when one student builds on another's idea, when a comment leads to a reconsideration of an earlier bit of evidence, or when competing theories are being considered. Remember, it is often possible for complex works of art to generate more than one meaning. In any case, it is up to the students to consider alternative theories of meaning with reference to the visual evidence. VTS conversations do not need to end with consensus; after about twenty minutes, at a logical moment, the teacher will thank the students for their close looking and active participation, drawing the conversation to a close.

Now comes the challenging part for many history teachers: resisting the urge to provide information about the artist, the image, or the historical context they have been considering. Doing so will teach students to wait for you to tell them the right answer, instead of engaging in the close looking, evidential reasoning, and vigorous debate that are the great strengths of VTS. Consideration of the work of art might well, however, lead to real curiosity—and new research questions that students can pursue.

Try the Visual Thinking Strategies with Jacob Lawrence's 1967 painting, *Forward*. Remember to ask: "What's going on in this picture? What do you see that makes you say that? What more can we find?" You might follow up on the conversation with a reading assignment about Harriet Tubman—or a look at Jacob Lawrence's other images related to slavery. The artist did a narrative series of paintings based on Harriet Tubman's life and work to rescue enslaved people, as well as one on the uprising led by Toussaint L'Ouverture that ended slavery in Haiti and resulted in its independence from France.

Jacob Lawrence (1917–2000) grew up in Harlem and began painting as a teenager, studying with Charles Alston, Augusta Savage, and other important figures associated with the Harlem Renaissance.[2] Lawrence was very interested in history and achieved international recognition for narrative series of paintings based on the lives of Harriet Tubman, Frederick Douglass, and Toussaint L'Ouverture, as well as a powerful series about the Great Migration of African Americans from the South during the mid-twentieth century. Lawrence once said, "When the subjects are strong, I believe simplicity is the best way of treating them."[3] Lawrence's powerful, modernist style and socially concerned subjects earned widespread public recognition, and his work is well represented in public collections. *Forward* is an excellent example of Lawrence's style; the strong colors and simplified forms work to emphasize the tension and drama of the scene.

Harriet Tubman was certainly an example of the sort of "strong subject" that inspired Jacob Lawrence.[4] Students will likely be familiar with stories about this famous "conductor" on the Underground Railroad. Tubman led more than three hundred slaves to freedom through nineteen visits to southern plantations between 1849 and 1860. During one such rescue mission, recounted in her autobiography, Tubman used her revolver to motivate one in her group who had lost heart and

Jacob Lawrence, *Forward*, 1967. North Carolina Museum of Art, Raleigh, purchased with funds from the State of North Carolina, © 1967 Jacob Lawrence / Artists Rights Society (ARS), New York.

wanted to turn back; this scene inspired the Lawrence painting we have been considering.

Paideia

Paideia is an approach to school reform that promotes a pedagogy combining lecture, coaching, and Socratic "seminar" discussion. The philosopher Mortimer Adler developed his Paideia Proposal in the early 1980s as an alternative to academic tracking and to assert that all students need to practice higher-order thinking to prepare for engaged citizenship in a democracy.

Like VTS discussions, Paideia seminars are wide-ranging conversations in which students examine a primary text or image and explore its meaning(s).[5] Again, the teacher acts as a facilitator, posing a series of open-ended questions and encouraging all students to engage respectfully with one another and with the central "text." Unlike the scripted questions central to VTS, which were developed especially to promote aesthetic development, Paideia seminar questions may be rooted in a particular discipline. They may be sequenced so as to ensure that big questions in the curriculum are addressed. The teacher's preparation is to consider the central image or text and related background information carefully; identify key connections to the curriculum; and write five to eight questions with reference to the Paideia framework. Depending on how the conversation develops, some of these questions will not be used.

After reminding students of the agreed-upon behavioral guidelines for a seminar, the teacher poses an *opening question* designed to encourage a focus on the central image and participation by all students. For example, she may ask for a "round robin" response in which each member of the seminar offers a one-word response or ask students to "vote" on a question. Such opening questions generate energy and provide a sense of the range of first reactions.

Core questions ask students to look more closely at the work in question, moving beyond initial responses and accounting for the available information. Paideia protocols for working with images are less developed than those for working with texts. After a period of close looking at the visual information in a work of art—and identifying areas of interest—I often find that there is a moment in which providing additional contextual information is helpful in deepening the discussion (see example later in this chapter).

Closing questions ask students to move beyond the historical situation and to consider what lessons or connections might be relevant to their own lives or contemporary society.

Try a Paideia seminar with your students featuring Hammatt Billings's illustration to *Uncle Tom's Cabin*, Archibald Motley's portrait of his grandmother, or Glenn Ligon's print from his "Runaway Slaves" series. I have provided images, background information, and some sample questions to get you started.

Background Information for the Teacher

First published in March 1852, less than two years after the passage of the Fugitive Slave Act, Harriet Beecher Stowe's abolitionist novel *Uncle Tom's Cabin* dramatically depicts the injustice and horrors of slavery. It quickly became an international sensation and a touchstone in the charged public discussion of American slavery. Stowe's family tradition

Hammatt Billings, illustration for *Uncle Tom's Cabin*, 1852. Clifton Waller Barrett Library of American Literature, Special Collections, University of Virginia.

has it that when President Lincoln received the novelist in the White House in 1862, he said, "So this is the little lady who made this big war!"[6]

Hammatt Billings, a talented illustrator based in Boston, was widely recognized by his contemporaries for his ability to capture the essence of a range of literary texts. He illustrated works by Shakespeare, Dickens, Keats, Hawthorne, and Alcott, among others. Billings produced seven illustrations for the first edition of *Uncle Tom's Cabin*. When the so-called Splendid Edition was published in time for Christmas sales, he had created well over one hundred images. Like the text that inspired them, Billings's illustrations were radical for their time in their sympathetic, nonstereotypical portrayals of black people.

Later illustrations and theatrical performances of Stowe's story departed from the original emphasis on Tom's integrity and courage; sadly, "Uncle Tom" eventually became used in common parlance to describe a weak and embarrassingly subservient figure. (This uninformed misunderstanding of Stowe's character may need to be addressed in the classroom discussion.)

In her preface, Stowe wrote that her objective was "to awaken sympathy and feeling for the African race, as they exist among us; to show their wrongs and sorrows, under a system so necessarily cruel and unjust as to defeat and do away the good effects of all that can be attempted for them, by their best friends, under it."

Seminar Questions

For this seminar we will be looking at an illustration by Hammatt Billings for Harriet Beecher Stowe's novel, *Uncle Tom's Cabin*, first published in 1852.

Opening: Look closely at the image and try this round-robin question (quick response from each participant): Try to come up with *one word that describes your own reaction* to the scene.

Core: Consider this book illustration as if it were a scene enacted onstage. What can you tell from examining the setting? Costumes and props? Gestures and facial expressions? What's going on in this picture?

Core: What would it feel like to be in this situation? Can you imagine yourself in the position of one or more of the characters shown here?

Information: The novelist Harriet Beecher Stowe was an ardent abolitionist. She wanted *Uncle Tom's Cabin* to engage public sympathies on behalf of individuals held in slavery and to influence public policy.

Read aloud an excerpt from *Uncle Tom's Cabin*, a conversation among slave traders, that relates to the image being considered:

> Last summer, down on Red River, I got a gal traded off on me, with a likely-lookin' child enough, and his eyes looked as bright as yourn; but, come to look, I found him stone blind. Fact—he was stone blind. Wal, yer see, I thought there warn't no harm in my jest passing him along, and not sayin' nothin'; and I'd got him nicely swapped off for a keg o' whiskey; but come to get him away from the gal, she was jest like a tiger. So it was before we started, and I hadn't got my gang chained up; so what should she do but ups on a cotton bale, like a cat, catches a knife from one of the deck hands, and, I tell ye, she made all fly for a minit, till she saw 'twan't no use; and she jest turns round, and pitches

head first, young un and all, into the river,—went down plump, and never ris.[7]

Core: How does the image work with this text to engage our empathetic imagination? Which do you find more powerful—the image or the words?

Closing: What does this scene have to say about the human experience of slavery? How do these fictional sources compare to information we have from other types of sources?

Why might fiction or pictures be effective in shaping public opinion and policy? Can we identify any current artists, writers, or filmmakers who seek to influence our opinions or behaviors?

Background Information for the Teacher

Archibald Motley (1891–1981) was born in New Orleans but spent most of his life in Chicago.[8] He studied painting at the School of the Art Institute of Chicago, graduating in 1918. Motley achieved early success, winning awards from the Harmon Foundation and a Guggenheim Fellowship for study in Paris, where he was greatly inspired by the art of European masters such as Rembrandt, Hals, Velasquez, and Delacroix. *Mending Socks* won the award for most popular painting in a large group exhibition at the Newark Museum in 1927, and in the following year Motley became the first African American artist to have a one-person exhibition in New York City. In addition to his portraits, Motley painted vibrant scenes of daily life—and nightlife—among African American communities.

Despite his recognition as an important figure in the New Negro movement of the 1930s and his work for the Works Progress Administration (WPA), Motley fell into obscurity after World War II. Since being featured in a retrospective exhibition at the Chicago Historical Society in 1991, Motley's work has attracted new interest and may now be seen in major museums, such as the Museum of Fine Arts in Boston. Duke University's Nasher Museum of Art presented an important Motley exhibition in 2014.

Motley once said, "It is my earnest desire and ambition to express the American Negro honestly and sincerely, neither to add nor detract, and to bring about a more sincere and brotherly feeling, a better

Archibald J. Motley Jr., *Mending Socks*, 1924. Ackland Art Museum, University of North Carolina at Chapel Hill. Burton Emmett Collection.

understanding, between him and his white brethren. I sincerely believe Negro art is someday going to contribute to our culture, our civilization."[9]

Seminar Questions

For this seminar, we are going to be looking at a painting from 1924 by Archibald Motley, called *Mending Socks*. It is a portrait of the artist's grandmother.

Opening: Round robin: What one word might you use to describe Mrs. Emily Motley?

Core: List all of the objects you can recognize in the scene. Consider whether any of the items Motley included in the scene might have symbolic meaning.

Information: Motley painted this portrait of his paternal grandmother in 1924. He wanted the portrait to show important aspects of his grandmother's life and to provide insight into her character. The setting of the portrait is the sitter's own home; she is doing useful work, mending socks for her family, surrounded by familiar household items. The brooch that pins her shawl together has a portrait of her daughter; the patterned tablecloth may represent her first husband, who was of Native American heritage.

Emily Motley was born into slavery in New Orleans and put to work in the plantation house. She was taught to read and, in later years, described those early days as happy ones in which she was treated well by the plantation owners and slaveholders. When the slaves were freed, her "Mistress" gave Emily a portrait of herself as a gift. Archibald knew that his grandmother had kept the portrait and asked if he could bring it out of a closet and incorporate it into the composition of the portrait as a reminder of her past.

Core: How does this new information influence your understanding of the portrait? What new questions come up for you at this point? How might you pursue these questions?

Closing: What might cause a person to present a positive or even sanitized version of a difficult past? Can you think of current examples in which a carefully constructed "portrait" is presented to the public? What issues arise for the historian or journalist who seeks to work with interviews, photographs, and other sources provided by the subject?

Background Information for the Teacher

Glenn Ligon (1960–) is a New York–based artist known for work that explores issues of race, sexuality, and identity. Ligon works in various media—painting, photography, sculpture, print making, neon—drawing inspiration from both historical and contemporary sources. His work has been shown internationally and collected by major museums, such as the Museum of Modern Art, the Philadelphia Museum of Art, the Walker Art Center, and the National Gallery of Art in Washington, DC.

R AN AWAY, Glenn. Medium height, 5'8", male. Closely-cut hair, almost shaved. Mild looking, with oval shaped, black-rimmed glasses that are somewhat conservative. Thinly-striped black-and-white short-sleeved T-shirt, blue jeans. Silver watch and African-looking bracelet on arm. His face is somewhat wider on bottom near the jaw. Full-lipped. He's black. Very warm and sincere, mild-mannered and laughs often.

Glenn Ligon, *Runaways*, 1993. Harvard Art Museums/Fogg Museum, Margaret Fisher Fund, 2008.95.

Ligon made *Runaway Slaves*, a series of ten lithographs, in 1993. The images, typefaces, and format come directly from nineteenth-century advertisements used by slaveholders or bounty hunters to track down individuals who had escaped from slavery. The texts, however, are contemporary. They provide a physical description of Ligon himself, including references to his hairstyle, clothing, mannerisms, and voice.

Ligon discussed his work with images of slavery in a 2011 interview:

> We always imagine that slavery is something in the past and that we as a society have gotten over it—it's sort of gone. But if you think about slavery as there when our laws and institutions are being created, when our Declaration of Independence is being written, when our courts are being formed—that it is this sort of moral dilemma at the core of American democracy, and we still feel its effects.
>
> And so that's why there is an autobiographical element. It looks like a slave narrative, but if you read it, the information is about me. But also it's not about me, because it's pieced together from dozens and dozens of slave narratives as a way to think about the past in the present.[10]

Seminar Questions

Opening: After inviting students to look closely, ask for a vote: When was this work of art made? Between 1820 and 1860; 1860 and 1900; 1900 and 1960; 1960 and 2000?

How did you try to situate the image on the timeline? What clues were most useful?

Core: How does reading the text aloud affect our thinking and feelings about the work of art? Knowing that the work was made in 1993, why might a living artist choose to appropriate and change nineteenth-century advertisements for runaway slaves?

Closing: How might America's painful history of slavery continue to affect our society today?

Conclusion

I believe that you and your students will find the featured images powerful, provocative, and relevant to your study of American history. In addition to the affecting and influential nineteenth-century illustration, I chose works of art made at various historical moments of the twentieth century, in part because they show the ongoing impact of slavery on American life. There are many more contemporary artists whose work you might investigate for classroom use: Fred Wilson's installations for the Maryland Historical Society that juxtaposed slave shackles with fine silver and Kara Walker's disturbing silhouettes of antebellum violence come immediately to mind. Looking back to nineteenth-century images, you might develop seminar questions for the diagrams of slave ships that often appear in history textbooks; other images from among Hammatt Billings's persuasive and moving illustrations for Harriet Beecher Stowe's *Uncle Tom's Cabin*; or the political cartoons illustrating Henry "Box" Brown's arrival via express shipping at the Anti-Slavery Society of Philadelphia. There is a wealth of visual material to consider!

Visual Thinking Strategies and Paideia seminars are proven tools for stimulating the kind of thinking that historians value. Works of art can act as important primary sources for historical understanding. Interpretive conversations develop evidential reasoning, empathy, tolerance for ambiguity and diverse perspectives, and creative problem solving. Using art in the history classroom will provide a welcome change of pace and cultivate the skills of visual literacy essential to an informed citizenry.

NOTES

1. You can find out more about VTS and its application across classroom disciplines by reading Philip Yenawine's *Visual Thinking Strategies: Using Art to Deepen Learning Across School Disciplines* (Cambridge, MA: Harvard Education Press, 2013) and by visiting the website http://www.vtshome.org/.

2. This background information is not recommended for VTS discussions, but may be useful should you want to develop Paideia seminar questions for *Forward*.

3. Elizabeth McCausland, "Jacob Lawrence," *Magazine of Art*, November 1945, 254.

4. For more information about Harriet Tubman, consider Catherine Clinton's excellent biography, *Harriet Tubman: The Road to Freedom* (Boston: Little, Brown, 2004).

5. Seminars typically last about forty-five minutes and may be augmented by didactic instruction. You can learn more about using Paideia seminars in the history classroom by visiting the website of the National Paideia Center at the

University of North Carolina at Chapel Hill (www.paideia.org) and by reading Mortimer Adler's *The Paideia Program: An Educational Syllabus* (New York: Touchstone, 1984).

6. David Herbert Donald, *Lincoln* (New York: Simon & Schuster, 1995), 542.

7. Harriet Beecher Stowe, *Uncle Tom's Cabin* (Boston: Jewett, 1852; reprint, Oxford: Oxford University Press, 2011), 93.

8. You may find additional useful background information in an oral history interview with Archibald Motley. "Interview with Archibald Motley, 1978 January 23–1979 March 1," Archives of American Art, Smithsonian Institution, www.aaa.si.edu/collections/interviews/oral-history-interview-archibald-motley-11466.

9. Frank James, "The Colorist," *Chicago Tribune*, October 9, 1991.

10. Glenn Ligon interviewed about work in his 2011–12 exhibition at the Los Angeles County Museum of Art, available on YouTube, https://www.youtube.com/watch?v=IrVHo5Z8oHc.

In the Footsteps
of Others

Understanding History
through Process Drama

LINDSAY ANNE RANDALL

You never really understand a person until you consider
things from his point of view—until you climb into his skin
and walk around in it.

ATTICUS FINCH in To Kill a Mockingbird

It is 1775, and under the cover of night a small group of
slaves huddles in secret among the shadows of their
crudely constructed wooden cabins. They assemble in the one place
that is hidden from view of the main house. On the slope where the
kitchen trash is thrown each day, they discuss startling new information.
They have heard of Lord Dunmore's promise of freedom to any male
slave who escapes and takes up arms for the British.

Those who choose to run face great obstacles and brutal consequences. They will be hunted and tracked and separated from their
families and, if caught, will face severe punishments. Even if they are
successful and reach the British forces, they must still survive armed
conflict. There is no guarantee that the British government will even

uphold Lord Dunmore's pledge. Only if the slaves are successful and the British are victorious and honorable will the slaves be freed.

Each person must decide the course that he or she will follow. Are the slaves willing to risk everything for a chance of freedom? Or is the risk too great? The choice that each must make has consequences that cannot be foreseen.

What would you do? If you were faced with the same uncertain future, would you take a chance at freedom? Would you be willing to leave family members, even children, behind? Would you be willing to risk the possibility of death? Or would you stay on your plantation, knowing that you may have missed your only chance at freedom? How would you weigh these excruciating choices?

These are not simple questions with clear answers. They are complex and painful and have no easy resolution. By forcing students to struggle with and answer these types of questions, teachers allow them to more fully realize the complexities of history and to employ skills that are critical to the study of the past. This is the strength of process drama.

Process Drama as a Method to Teach Slavery

Process drama teaching, using unscripted dramatic activities, is one method that teachers can use to instruct students about various aspects of slavery.[1] Although drama is an essential part of process dramas, the focus of the method is *not* about creating a performance for the benefit of an audience. Students receive a factually based historical problem or scenario and together must use prior knowledge and improvisational techniques to problem-solve their way to a conclusion. This form of instruction allows students to relate to historical agents and material while exploring topics at their own pace, which makes their discoveries and understanding more meaningful.[2]

The history classroom is well suited to utilize the flexible nature of process drama, because any aspect of the past can be turned into a process drama scenario and the technique can be used to meet many topical objectives. Process drama has the ability to teach historical inquiry skills such as logical and critical thinking, the relationship between cause and effect, the importance of historical context, and the analytical skills that are necessary to understand the past. In addition, the approach process drama uses—engaging students through interactive activities—encourages their ability to use inquiry and dialogue. This nurturing of historical analytical skills fosters a deeper knowledge of a subject than the simple memorization of facts.[3] In short, these dramatic activities foster an awareness and a knowledge of the history of slavery that prepare students to take on the role of historian in a unique manner.

Importantly, process drama helps students "to select, assemble, and analyze" events in a manner similar to historical writing and inquiry.[4] The topics that students focus on during the activity are the ones that they find to be the most crucial to their role. This activity parallels the method of identifying central points or issues while researching a paper. Students make arguments throughout the activity, which are constantly summarized and expanded throughout the lesson. This is analogous to the amassing of a variety of historical sources and facts in traditional research. During the concluding discussion, students then analyze the various opinions, facts, and issues that were raised in order to create their own interpretation and understanding of the subject. This step mimics the final step of historical writing, where all information is synthesized into a coherent narrative. These skills are ones that today's students need in order to be proficient and successful in the field of history. Additionally, using these dramatic methods may help educators reach students who might otherwise struggle with more traditional teaching methods.[5]

Unscripted historical exploration creates a flexible narrative that can change depending on student questions and thoughts, allowing students to interact with historical characters and situations in a manner that enables them to connect more fully to the topic. Through this learning style, students are able to understand better that individuals in the past had thoughts and feelings and reacted to external pressures in various ways. Engaging with material in this manner allows students to develop historical empathy, or the ability to navigate "a complex balance between considering the perspectives of and connecting with people in the past."[6] Through process drama activities, students react to the pain, celebration, and conflicting emotions that surround the history of slavery. By their own experience in the classroom, students are given a different perspective on events of the past and begin to see the connections between history and what is occurring in the world today.[7]

In order for a process drama activity to be successful, students need to have a basic knowledge of slavery in a specific time and place so that they do not make ahistorical assumptions. While students do often realize the ways in which circumstances surrounding an historical event are different from the way things are today, they react to those facts with a mindset that imposes their contemporary views on the past. Students might not fully comprehend why slaves made specific choices until they confront the same range of options that was open to slaves at any given moment. In the scenario that opened this chapter, for example, slaves in tidewater Virginia had a very narrow time frame in which to decide whether to run to the British. Slaves had to time their flight to coincide with a nearby and often temporary British military presence (naval or ground). A male slave capable of taking up arms, furthermore, might have made the decision to flee, but if he had a pregnant wife and an elderly ailing mother who could not travel safely with him, then he might have decided to stay. As much as possible, process drama helps students to understand how to examine the actions of individuals and groups through the values and norms that belong to a particular period in time.[8]

Creating and Running a Process Drama Lesson

Constructing a process drama lesson about slavery, or about any other topic, is not an insurmountable task that can be done only by an extraordinary educator. With some guidelines, anyone can create a dramatic activity that is based on a period in history and achieves any identified educational goals.

To create a process drama lesson, teachers first need to select the topic. In this example the topic focuses on the experiences and choices that slaves faced in the British colonies during the American Revolution. After selecting a topic, teachers should identify a goal to anchor the lesson and subsequent teaching technique. The goal of the example lesson is to have students understand that the British Army and American colonists were not the only groups participating in the American Revolution and that enslaved people were engaged with the conflict in various ways.

After a teacher has identified the topic and the goal of the lesson and completed any necessary research regarding the topic, it is time to decide upon the dramatic method that will be used as a window into a larger historical context.[9] There are several dramatic learning methods, such as Forum Theater and Tableau, that teachers can employ in a process drama activity.[10] The following explanation of how to create such a lesson focuses on the Whole Class Role Play method. The Whole Class Role Play technique forces the entire class, including the teacher, to participate in an unscripted role play in which each participant spontaneously interacts with and responds to other participants. In this way, this particular method suits the needs of both secondary and post-secondary classrooms. Teachers also can easily modify it to fit the specific needs of their classrooms.

When constructing a process drama activity, instructors need to be aware of and sensitive to the historical context in which students will be navigating. When dealing with sensitive topics such as slavery, teachers need to construct the scenarios carefully and thoughtfully so that no power imbalances occur between students, such as those that existed between masters and slaves. Students should interact within the constraints of the scenario only as equals. In this scenario, for example, all students take on the role of an enslaved person who has decided whether to run away or stay on the plantation. Other scenarios, such as participating in a rebellion, could also be included in the activity.

To begin the lesson, teachers need to clearly explain the scenario and thereby frame the world of the activity. Reading a fabricated situation and a factual historical account are both good ways to accomplish this task. During the setup for the lesson, teachers should also note that everyone in the class will participate in the activity. An example of a scenario that might be used is this:

> The year is 1775 and you are a slave on a plantation in Virginia. Lord Dunmore, the British royal governor of the Colony of Virginia, has issued a proclamation. The proclamation states that *"all indentured Servants, Negros, or others, (appertaining to Rebels,) free that are able and willing to bear Arms, they joining His Majesty's Troops as soon as may be . . ."* This means that any slaves of American patriots who fight for the British will be given their freedom upon British victory in the conflict. You have heard stories about the British, especially their Ethiopian Regiment, which is comprised of runaway slaves. It is said that slaves who join are given plenty of food and nice clothes, in addition to their freedom. Many colonists, however, have begun patrolling for runaway slaves and those who are caught trying to make it to the British are severely punished, even hung. A group of you have come together in secret to discuss the choice that Lord Dunmore's proclamation has given you.[11]

In the example, students are asked to take on various identities and to interact with the scenario and one another as their characters might. Since few students at any level have been asked to engage in such an improvisational lesson, they may experience worry and stress. To help alleviate some of their tension, it can be helpful to give each student a short write-up, or Character Card, about what role or scene he or she is being asked to engage in, along with a name tag. By providing information for students to refer to throughout the activity, teachers allow them to focus on the interaction instead of trying to remember information. Any information that is meant to help students understand their role should be given before the formal activity begins. It should be clear and succinct so that it does not inhibit the creativity and spontaneity of the students or take more than a few minutes to read. An example of a write-up that might be given to students is:

Name: Elizabeth
Age: 25
Background: You were born on this plantation along with your sister, Celia, who still lives here and is married to another slave, Abraham. Everyone here calls you Bett. You have a three-year-old daughter named Abigail. Your husband was sold away from the plantation two years ago, and you have not seen him since. Your primary job on the plantation is to serve as a cook and laundress for your owner and his family.

Since the information found in a write-up can help inform students about their characters, it should be varied. The Character Card might tell students whether they are single or married, have children or are childless, or are male or female, among many other possibilities.[12] Creating these different characteristics helps to make the lesson more engaging by allowing for an infinite number of outcomes and forcing students to confront difficult decisions on multiple levels.

To produce a more complex and dynamic lesson, teachers should integrate a situation with a potentially unexpected outcome. Instructors might, for example, reveal an important yet concealed role to a student in a Character Card. To add more depth to the learning, the student may decide if she will accept this covert role. This exercise will foster a discussion not only with the student but with the entire class regarding the ramifications of a single choice and why it was made. A write-up that allows a student to have a direct yet unforeseeable effect on the outcome of the lesson might look like this:

Name: Caesar

Age: 40

Background: You were born in Africa, where you were captured and from where you were brought to the West Indies. You labored in the sugar cane fields for a year before you were sold again, to a ship's captain. While working on the sugar plantation you saw many slaves die from sickness and disease. The captain brought you up to Virginia, where your current owner bought you at auction. You have lived here now for fifteen years. You have a wife, Josephine, who lives here at the plantation also.

Optional Personal Decision: If you choose to inform your owner about the plans of another slave to run away to the British, he will not sell Josephine to another plantation nearby. There is no guarantee, however, that your owner will keep his word since in the past he has repeatedly failed to fulfill promises he has made.

If you decide to inform on another student, you must wait for directions from the teacher before informing the student of your choice. Do not let other students know that you are an informant.

Throughout the lesson, educators must steer the direction of the learning process and ensure that all participants can interact with the group. Still, educators should not be afraid to give some control of the classroom to students. Student-led learning is a valuable teaching method and a central component of process drama education. Students might choose to break into smaller groups, team up in support of their views, move about the room, act out emotions, and so forth. Students also may interject and talk over each other in a manner that still allows for each participant to hear and listen to others.

Asking students to be responsible for their own learning does not mean that the teacher has no control and that the classroom is operating in complete anarchy. In fact, the role of the teacher is very important in a process drama activity, even though it should not inhibit student autonomy throughout the lesson. On a basic level, the facilitator should pause the lesson if it seems that students are no longer engaging with the activity in a constructive manner. To help the class focus on the lesson, the teacher might pose a simple question to a student, such as "What are you thinking of doing?" Such redirection allows students to calm down and re-engage positively with the activity.

While improvisation is an integral part of process drama, sometimes classes need help and encouragement initially to engage with the lesson. Facilitators may do this by giving a student who dominates the class in a positive manner a central role. A wish to engage and earn the trust of this particular student will positively influence the other students to participate. When assigning roles to students or creating scenarios, however, educators need to be aware of the social dynamics of the class. The lesson should never exacerbate any negative social dynamics that may already exist between students.

Facilitators also can use gentle hints or suggestions, such as "Remember, you have a daughter but he does not" to encourage students to participate. These prompts help students feel more confident that what they say or do is correct because the teacher has validated an important point. Typically this direct form of support needs to occur only once, as students will begin reacting to their classmates' actions and statements without more prompts. Educators should offer suggestions or other encouragements to students sparingly and only after sufficient time has elapsed to allow students to engage in the activity on their own—it is essential not to hamper their spontaneity.

While it is important to ensure that more reserved students have the courage to participate in the activity, teachers should also ensure that a few students are not permitted a monopoly on the control of the lesson. The teacher must create a balance by both encouraging strongly engaged students to continue participating and establishing opportunities for other students to contribute. Through the use of encouragement and prompting for more reserved students, the educator can ensure that all students come to see their involvement and thoughts as valuable and important to the activity.

The facilitator also can encourage student participation by getting involved with the activity. The teacher should not act simply as a spectator but should serve as a contributor. Students often get nervous when they believe that they are being observed and critiqued, which is the classic dynamic between students and educators. When educators place themselves within the activity, they effectively remove the perception that this type of judgmental interaction is taking place, which allows students to more readily participate in the lesson. This does not mean that the teacher is not informally evaluating student learning throughout the lesson; instead, the process is not so overt that it makes students feel self-conscious.

One way in which the facilitator can have a central role that still enables students to be spontaneous is by assuming a "devil's advocate" position. While students interact with one another as their characters, the teacher could periodically offer verbal pros and cons regarding statements that students make. Interacting with students in this manner not only allows the teacher to subtly ensure the lesson moves toward a conclusion within the allotted time frame but also allows the instructor to interject additional information into the lesson. It also forces students to look at information in a manner they may not have before, while also making them defend their stated positions. Engaging students in this manner expands their ability to think critically.[13] Some pros and cons a teacher might offer are:

Run Away

Pro: The more slaves run away, the better their chances of not being caught, since the resources available for catching runaways will be stretched.

Con: If caught, they will face very harsh punishment, such as physical beating or lashing, or they may be sent to a sugar plantation in the West Indies, which will mean certain death.

Stay on Plantation

Pro: They will not face severe punishment for running away, and their families, at least for the present, might remain intact.

Con: If many slaves choose to run away, then those who remain could get into serious trouble because the owner will think that they knew and did not inform him, and so they will be punished harshly. Also, if others in a family run away, then the family will be broken up and those who remain will never see their loved ones again.

In order to be effective in such a central role, teachers need to think on their feet, as it is impossible to know what students will bring up and what particular issues will be the focus of the activity. To overcome any hesitation regarding this aspect of process drama, it can help to think about some typical stances and perspectives that students might have. For example, a student might say that he would be happy to run away from his family. The teacher, being aware that the character has a pregnant wife, could then play devil's advocate and point out possible issues regarding that initial decision, such as the fact that he would never see his child and questions about what would happen to his family if he were not around. The teacher can formulate some pros and cons prior to the start of the activity and help to redirect, in a positive manner, any comments that could become inappropriate.

When the facilitator has determined that students have engaged with others for enough time, he should give the class a moment to think about what choice it will ultimately make: to run away to the British army or to stay on the plantation. Once all the students have come to a conclusion, they should each state the reasons for their decisions. To enhance student understanding, there should be a full class discussion regarding why students were or were not surprised by a decision made by a peer. For example, if two characters are married but the two students portraying them decide on opposite actions, this might be an area for exploration. A conversation about what factors and considerations went into making these decisions and why others might have made different ones can help students grapple with how historical individuals made difficult choices, which in hindsight may or may not have been the best one for them.

After students have discussed and explained their decisions, teachers should hand them envelopes with the outcome for their character. The outcomes can be predetermined excerpts of historical accounts, or the teacher can create them on the basis of historical facts. Students should share their varied outcomes, and the whole class can discuss any unfamiliar information contained within the outcome. This activity will benefit all of the students. Multiple endings should be given to students in order to reflect the fact that individuals who made similar choices still faced radically different outcomes. The following are examples of three different outcomes that students might face, despite having chosen the same action.

Outcome: Run away to the British (Alternative 1)

You successfully made it to the British Army! You served in Colonel Tye's elite Black Brigade in New Jersey. Despite all of your efforts, the British ultimately conceded victory to the American colonists. For those who were near New York, the British created a list called the Book of Negros.[14] You were able to convince a British official that you were a runaway slave and had fought for the British, and so your name was added to the list. The British brought you to Nova Scotia, where they promised to give you land and freedom. Although they did keep their promise, the land that you were given was rocky and could not support crops. You also faced discrimination and physical threats from your white neighbors.

Outcome: Run away to the British (Alternative 2)

You successfully made it to the British Army! You served in the Ethiopian Regiment with about three hundred other runaway slaves and free blacks. Despite all of your efforts, the British ultimately conceded victory to the American colonists. For those near New York, the British created a list called the Book of Negros. If you could have convinced a British official that you are a runaway slave and have fought for the British, your name might have been added to the list. Then you would have been given your freedom and relocated. Unfortunately, like the majority of slaves and free blacks who fought for the British, you were not near New York and thus did not even know that the list existed. Since the British would not help

258

anyone whose name was not in the Book of Negros, the American colonists confiscated you as property and sold you back into slavery.

Outcome: Run away to the British (Alternative 3)

You successfully made it to the British Army! You served in British Army and were working under General Cornwallis. You traveled with the army and helped fight as well as gather supplies as you marched across Virginia. During your march through Virginia there was a breakout of smallpox, but you were lucky and did not succumb to the sickness. This meant that you were able to join Cornwallis and the rest of the army at Yorktown. While under siege, even more soldiers, both white and black, died of smallpox. Since large numbers of the army were sick, the American and French forces were able to successfully take Yorktown, effectively winning the war. When the American troops entered Yorktown, they began to confiscate British property. The Americans took you and sold you back into slavery.

If there was a secret aspect to a character or scenario, such as a character being given the opportunity to be an informant, the student will reveal it at this point. If a student accepts the opportunity to change the outcome for another student—by informing on his or her plans, for example—the class should discuss the impact of this decision for the individuals involved and the group as a whole. If a student declines the opportunity to change the outcome of the activity, the class should discuss the reasoning behind the decision.

Educators should extend discussion of this activity beyond a single class period. Incorporating an extension of the lesson through a writing assignment or another formal assessment can help students to internalize what they did during the activity and to make connections between the activity and other historical and contemporary topics. An extension might consist of having students write about how their knowledge and perception of the American Revolution changed because of the process drama lesson. Such an assignment helps teachers evaluate how well students grasped the central goal of the lesson and determine what they learned by engaging with the topic in this unique manner.[15]

Conclusion

Process drama offers educators an interactive method to teach students about any historical situation in a manner that not only meets specific standards and skills but also moves beyond them. Through process drama, students use improvisation, their imagination, and historical facts to construct and interact with a narrative of the past. This process provides students with a perspective on how events of the past affected individuals and groups in diverse ways.

To engage with historical thought, students need to become aware that history is complex and multifaceted. When students learn that history encompasses many views and perspectives, they are able to think critically about topics such as slavery. Educators can use the experience of a process drama lesson to provide students with a concrete and tangible example of how multiple viewpoints come together to inform any historical topic. This knowledge can, in turn, help students with other historical skills, such as analyzing primary and secondary sources.[16]

NOTES

1. Some process drama practitioners argue that, when employing dramatic activities to teach about the past, teachers should not use historical facts to teach about specific events. Others assert that a predetermined ending cannot be part of process drama because the outcomes should be created organically through action. The author, however, believes that the two goals are not mutually exclusive and that one can utilize process drama to teach students concrete historical information and skills. In the context of this work, the term "process drama" is a combination of improvisational techniques developed by Dorothy Heathcote and Cecily O'Neill and the structural and factual constraints of story drama. Dorothy Heathcote and Gavin M. Bolton, *Drama for Learning: Dorothy Heathcote's Mantle of the Expert Approach to Education* (Portsmouth, NH: Heinemann, 1995); Cecily O'Neill, *Drama Worlds: A Framework for Process Drama* (Portsmouth, NH: Heinemann, 1995); Cecily O'Neill and Alan Lambert, *Drama*

Structures: A Practical Handbook for Teachers (London: Hutchinson, 1982); Philip Taylor, *Redcoats and Patriots: Reflective Practice in Drama and Social Studies* (Portsmouth, NH: Heinemann, 1998), 152; Philip Taylor and Christine D. Warner, *Structure and Spontaneity: The Process Drama of Cecily O'Neill* (Stoke on Trent, UK: Trentham, 2006), 38.

2. Taylor, *Redcoats and Patriots*, 15–16.

3. Ibid., 30–33.

4. Ibid., 154.

5. Ibid., 153–54.

6. Jada Kohlmeier, "'Couldn't She Just Leave?': The Relationship between Consistently Using Class Discussions and the Development of Historical Empathy in a 9th Grade World History Course," *Theory and Research in Social Education* 34, no. 1 (Winter 2006): 37.

7. Jason L. Endacott, "Reconsidering Affective Engagement in Historical Empathy," *Theory and Research in Social Education* 38, no. 1 (2010): 6–8; Jada Kohlmeier, "The Impact of Having 9th Graders 'Do History,'" *The History Teacher* 38, no. 4 (2005): 500; Kohlmeier, "'Couldn't She Just Leave?,'" 34–35; Taylor, *Redcoats and Patriots*, 60–62.

8. Terrie Epstein, "Preparing History Teachers to Develop Young People's Historical Thinking," *Perspectives on History* 50, no. 5 (May 2012): 36–39; Kohlmeier, "'Couldn't She Just Leave?,'" 34–35.

9. For more information about the role of free blacks and slaves in the American Revolution see Woody Holton, *Black Americans in the Revolutionary Era: A Brief History with Documents* (New York: Bedford/St. Martin's, 2009); Alan Gilbert, *Black Patriots and Loyalists: Fighting for Emancipation in the War for Independence* (Chicago: University of Chicago Press, 2012); Gary B. Nash, *The Forgotten Fifth: African Americans in the Age of Revolution* (Cambridge, MA: Harvard University Press, 2006).

10. O'Neill, *Drama Worlds*.

11. *Africans in America*, http://www.pbs.org/wgbh/aia/home.html.

12. The majority of these options were largely available only to men. While women might have been allowed to join the British Army as cooks or nurses, children and the elderly were often excluded from these options. This exercise has been adapted to allow teachers and students to think more broadly about the complexities surrounding individual decisions about running away from a plantation. The issues surrounding gender and even age could be examined during the wrap-up discussion as a means to add layers of historical knowledge and to illustrate the very different realities faced by men and women.

13. Sylvia A. Walton Jackson, "Everybody's History," in Anita Manley and Cecily O'Neill, eds., *Dreamseekers: Creative Approaches to the African American Heritage* (Portsmouth, NH: Heinemann, 1997), 24.

14. The Book of Negros was specific to New York. There are other examples of black loyalists who were granted freedom, such as the ones who gained Certificates of Freedom from Brigadier General Samuel Birch.

15. Kohlmeier, "'Couldn't She Just Leave?,'" 54–55.

16. Ibid., 37.

"A Likely Negro"

Using Runaway-Slave Advertisements to Teach Slavery

ANTONIO T. BLY

A Runaway's Heroic Tale

On January 3, 1770, "a likely Negro man, named Adam," ran away from his master, John Fox of Gloucester County, Virginia. Days after he left, Fox had an advertisement printed in William Rind's *Virginia Gazette* for the "23 years of age" absconded slave who stood six feet tall and had a "yellowish complexion" and a downward countenance.[1] By his account, the supposedly diffident Adam, "by trade a cooper and sawyer," planned to hire himself out, preferably to someone in South Carolina. In his endeavor to pass for free, the slave carpenter took with him an assorted bundle of clothing, "among them one suit of grey cloth, a pair white yarn stockings," and steel-buckled shoes. And so began Adam's story, printed amid notices for a choice stallion, eight lots, and a runaway indentured servant named Charles Richardson.

RUN away from *Greenwich*, in *Gloucester* county, on the 3d of January last, a likely Negro man, named *Adam*, about 23 years of age, 6 feet high, of a yellowish complexion, and has a down look; he is by trade a cooper and sawyer, and can read and write. Before he went off, he was heard to say that he intended for *South-Carolina*. He carried with him sundry cloaths, among them one suit of grey cloth, and a pair of white yarn stockings, and generally wore steel buckles in his shoes.

Whoever apprehends the said slave, and conveys him to me, shall, if taken in *Virginia*, have FIVE POUNDS reward, if in *North-Carolina* TEN POUNDS, and if in *South-Carolina* TWENTY POUNDS, besides what the law allows; or if confined in any gaol, and notice is given, half the above rewards will be allowed.[2]

Sometime before the end of the month, the fugitive was taken up only to run away again. Not long after his January flight, an advertisement printed in the *Gazette* on February 22, 1770, revealed that Adam had left his master's Gloucester County plantation, Greenwich, a week before Fox returned to the printer. When he went away that time, the country-born man carried with him not only additional articles of clothes but also "some books; as he can read." Although he wrote in an "indifferent hand," Fox continued, he forged "himself a pass to go to Carolina." As had been the case when he first ran away, Adam seemed determined to make his way to the Carolinas to "pass as a freeman." He succeeded for two months before being recaptured.

GREENWICH, *Feb.* 15, 1770. RUN away from the subscriber, in *Gloucester* county, the 5th instant, a very likely *Virginia* born Negro fellow named ADAM, of a yellow complexion, about 25 years old, near 6 feet high, by trade a sawyer and cooper; he had on when he went away a white plains waistcoat and breeches, knit yarn stockings, *Virginia* shoes, steel buckles, an oznabrigs shirt, and a felt hat. He carried with him a light coloured suit of cloth cloaths, and other things unknown, and some books; as he can read and write an indifferent hand, he purposed, when he went off, to forge himself a pass to go to *Carolina*, to pass as a freeman. I will give FORTY SHILLINGS reward, besides the allowance by law, to any person that delivers the said slave to me, or either of my overseers, in this county; and if taken in *Carolina* FIVE POUNDS.[3]

Almost a year passed before Adam would reappear in the newspaper. On July 11, 1771, the "slow of Speech" man ran way again. Printed this time in Alexander Purdie and John Dixon's *Virginia Gazette*, the notice disclosed new information. Besides his customary remarks about Adam's "yellow Complexion" and "down Look," Fox noted that his slave "Cooper" had grown a beard and that some of his hair had turned gray. Gone were his steel-buckled shoes. Absent were the "waistcoat" and "yarn stockings" he had worn before. Moreover, perhaps because he absconded more times than Fox had committed to print or possibly because he had used force to make Adam stay put, the Gloucester County grandee also noted that the slave's "Shins" were "Hurt."

GLOUCESTER, July 11, 1771. RUN away from the Subscriber, in *February* 1770, a likely Negro Fellow named ADAM, by Trade a Cooper and Sawer, near six Feet high, of a yellow Complexion, down Look, rather slow of Speech, his Beard grows much under his Chin, has some gray Hairs on his Head, though but twenty five Years old, and one of his Shins has been Hurt.—He was some Months advertised in the *Virginia Gazette*, and in the Night of the 25th Instant made his Escape from Mr. *Spilsby Coleman*, at an Ordinary in *Henrico* County, who was bringing him from *Orange* County, *North Carolina* (where he had indented himself, by the Name of *Thomas Jackson*, to one *Hugh Dobbins*) but has since been seen at the Plantation of Colonel *William Macon*, in *New Kent*. He had on, when he made his Escape, a Pair of coarse patched Rolls Trousers, a Cotton or white Plains Waistcoat much worn about the Sleeves, a pretty good brown Linen Shirt, but very dirty, a small new Felt Hat, and a Pair of old Shoes. He took Nothing with him but what he had on, which perhaps he may change the first Opportunity. He Pretends to be a Newlight, can read and write a little, and had when taken up a forged Pass. Whoever brings the said Negro to me in *Gloucester* County, or to Colonel *William Macon* of *New Kent* County, shall have FIFE [*sic*] POUNDS Reward if taken in this Colony and TWENTY FIVE POUNDS if out thereof.[4]

In spite of his "Shins," Adam made it to the Carolinas. With "a Pair of old Shoes," the indomitable man walked more than two hundred miles to freedom. For several days, he eluded slavecatchers. During his sojourn, the runaway probably found refuge, a meal, and a friendly face or two among slaves he might have encountered along the way. But not everyone Adam came across helped him in his journey. Some may have threatened to tell the authorities where he was. Considering the reward Fox was offering, they had good reason to reveal his whereabouts. Still, as he planned, after making his way to the Carolinas, Adam hired himself out to "one Hugh Dobbins" of Orange County. He also assumed a new name: Thomas Jackson. Finally, or so it seemed, Adam passed for free.

Not long afterwards, slavecatchers discovered his artfully crafted ruse and took him up as a fugitive. His detention, however, did not last long. At an "Ordinary in Henrico County," Adam escaped from Mr. Spilsby Coleman, carrying with him simply the clothes he wore that day: "a Pair of Coarse patched Rolls Trousers, a Cotton or white Plains Waistcoat much worn about the Sleeves, [and] a pretty good brown Linen Shirt, but very dirty." The antagonist in his slave's heroic tale, John Fox proved ever determined to reclaim his property. He offered a reward of £5 to slavecatchers if they seized Adam in Virginia, £25 (5 more than originally offered) if they caught him outside the colony.

We can deduce from Fox's advertisements in the *Virginia Gazette* that Adam was artful. Despite his supposedly slow demeanor, he disproved his master's assessment of him. Successfully, Adam convinced others that he owned himself. Successfully, he found work. Successfully, he wrote himself a pass; he moved about freely.

Apparently, when not working, Adam attended church, where he found comfort and sanctuary. Caught up in the evangelical fervor of the day, he witnessed firsthand the First Great Awakening, or, as Fox put it, albeit in passing, "He Pretends to be a Newlight."[5] In any case, months passed without any new news about Adam. In April 1772, it looked as though the "Negro fellow" had successfully passed for free. Late that month, Adam remained at large.

GREEENWICH, *Gloucester* county, *Feb.* 22, 1772. RUN away from the subscriber, in *February*, 1770, a likely Negro fellow named ADAM, by trade a cooper and sawyer, near 6 feet high, of a yellow complexion, down look, rather slow of speech, his beard grows much under his chin, and has some grey hairs in his head, though but 26 years old; he was some months advertised in the *Virginia* Gazette, and was taken up in *Orange* county, *North Carolina*, but on his way home made his escape (where he had indented himself by the name of *Thomas Jackson*, to one *Hugh Dobbins*) he was seen some time ago in *Gloucester*, when his dress was a cotton or plains waistcoat, though I imagine he has found means of changing it before this. He pretends to be a Newlight, and reads and writes a little (generally a very small hand), and forges himself passes, by examining which he may be easily discovered. Whoever takes up the said slave and conveys him to me, shall receive, if taken in *Virginia*,

TEN POUNDS reward; if in *North Carolina*, TWENTY FIVE POUNDS; or, if further, in proportion to their trouble.[6]

A year later, on April 23, 1773, John Fox placed another advertisement in the *Gazette*. Although Adam's name is not mentioned directly in the 1773 notice, several references in the ad suggest that it probably referred to him. Considering the fact that Adam had run away many times before, Fox's omission of his name is not unusual. By way of the print and oral culture that bound Virginians together, the grandee's neighbors far and wide were probably intimately aware of Fox's troubles with regard to his unruly slave. Throughout the eighteenth century, Virginians relied on printed news but also on news transmitted orally. At church, courthouses, taverns, and other places of assembly, manuscript advertisements were read aloud and were the subject of conversation. With the emergence of the printing press in Virginia, these old practices continued anew. Consequently, Fox's omission represented a silence in his text, a silence his neighbors understood all too well.[7]

THERE is now at my house at Capahosick ferry a Negro man about 26 years of age, by trade a carpenter and sawyer, and is of a yellowish complexion. This fellow nearly answers the description of one that I advertised some time ago as run away from me, and was brought to me as such, having confessed, when taken up, that he was my property. However, as he has had the smallpox during the time he was absent from me, which makes a considerable alteration in him, and as he now says he does not belong to me, I am unwilling to claim him, and therefore desire any person, who may think himself entitled to him, will appear in a reasonable time after this notice, for which purpose I have advertised him. He says he passed at Baltimore, in Maryland, as a free man, by the name of George Green, and at Annapolis, in said province, by that of Charles Chevier, and that he lived in North Carolina upwards of three years. He has prevaricated much with respect to the person whom he belongs to, having first said that he was the property of Thomas Nelson, Esquire, of York, then that he belonged to one White on the Eastern Shore, and, afterwards, to Samuel Sowerbutt's, a butcher in Fredericksburg. He has been much whipped by constables, since run away, for his irregular behaviour.[8]

Background: Fugitive Slaves in Slavery Studies

Like the WPA slave narratives compiled during the Great Depression, notices for eighteenth- and nineteenth-century runaways provide scholars and students with a wealth of information about slavery. Advertisements challenged the erroneous notion that bondage in the North was mild. A "Negro Man named Cato" surely did not think so when he ran away from his master in July 1741. As his owner told it, the "tall well-set Fellow," a known truant, "lost all of his Toes by Frost." This passing admission clearly underscores the abusive nature of many master-slave relationships. Indeed, Cato's missing digits suggest either that he did not receive adequate clothing or that his clothes were extremely worn or of poor quality. Like those of runaways in the South, Cato's story demonstrates that neither time nor space mattered. Far from it: runaway advertisements in the North challenge our traditional understanding of slavery. Notices like Cato's showing Puritan New Englanders in hot pursuit challenge the benevolent image of northern slavery as a type of "adoptive kinship" in which slaves were considered a part of the family. Additionally, they reverse the popularly held, overstated image of fugitive slaves using the North Star as their guide to freedom.[9]

An artist of African descent, Tunde Afolayan Famous infuses his painting *The Refuge* with his knowledge of African American slavery and with the rich and vivid color symbolism of the Yoruba people of modern Nigeria. In a similar vein, teachers should encourage students to use color and texture to reveal the depth of slavery and of the fugitive's plight.

Instructors can consult a variety of monographs that use runaway slave ads to understand slavery. In Gerald W. Mullin's *Flight and Rebellion* and Lathan Windley's *A Profile of Runaway Slaves*, for example, notices describe slaves who refused to submit. Many slaves considered freedom a most sacred natural right, long before Jefferson wrote the Declaration of Independence. In 1745, for example, after several unsuccessful attempts to keep his domestic from running away, John Custis warned the readers of William Parks's *Virginia Gazette* that his man-servant, who had repeatedly run away, had been taken to court and officially declared an "outlaw." Because he refused to stay put, Custis forced "Peter" to wear "irons" underneath his clothing while he performed his usual tasks about his house. But the slave did not think

Art can be used to unlock a student's understanding of a subject. Using this abstract painting—*The Refuge* by Tunde Afolayan Famous—as a model, teachers can have students create their own painting, sketch, or drawing, inspired by their reading of the assigned fugitive notice. Courtesy of Tunde Afolayan Famous.

much of his master or of his chains. Not long after being brought back, Peter ran away yet again.[10]

Historians have asked a lot of questions about slave ads. Students and teachers who closely examine them may find them similarly revealing. In *The Punished Self*, for example, Arnold Bontemps describes how advertisements expose a complex world wherein masters and slaves engaged one another in a nuanced struggle for power. In anger, many masters noted how slaves pretended to have certain skills or who took for themselves a name different from the one their master had given them. In his study of the multifaceted politics of race in the North, John Sweet demonstrates how runaway notices captured peculiar narratives in which colonial elites constructed a society wherein African Americans were considered valuable chattel and nonslave-owning whites simple but necessary accessories in a hostile environment, full of suspicion, surveillance, and alarm. Woody Holton's work reveals how runaways were active in the American Revolution. In Virginia, these men and women played a pivotal role in the burgeoning conflict, forcing an otherwise reluctant tobacco colony into declaring independence. Not long after John Murray, the royal governor of Virginia, issued a proclamation that freed slaves who were willing to enlist in the British Army, enslaved African Americans ran away and joined the regulars. In W. Jeffrey Bolster's *Black Jacks*, we see how notices gave evidence of a thriving maritime culture in which slaves hired themselves out as sailors, pilots, and ferrymen. In Michael Gomez's *Exchanging Our Country Marks* and in Shane White and Graham White's *Stylin'*, the authors demonstrate how advertisements provide evidence of a unique African American culture, one in which slaves borrowed from both their African past and their American present to forge meaningful lives. Many fugitives, for instance, cut and worked their hair in explicitly African styles. Herbert G. Gutman's *The Black Family in Slavery and Freedom* documents the powerful record of a strong black family. In *Love of Freedom* Catherine Adams and Elizabeth Pleck describe how notices document slave women's determination to achieve dignity in a world that tried to deny them humanity.[11]

In the Classroom: Using Advertisements to Teach Slavery

For all the advertisements reveal, scholarship related to them has yet to make its way into the high school or the university history class. Few scholars have focused on advertisements for absconded slaves. Remarkably, even fewer high school teachers or professors have used them to explore slavery. Instead, these stories of brave and courageous African Americans have been reduced in importance. Because they have been designated as simple acts of resistance or defiance, they have been stripped unintentionally of their true meaning. They have been robbed of their complexity.

But, as Peter Wood once noted, runaway advertisements are the tip of the iceberg.[12] Printed among notices for absentee indentured servants, malingering horses, and truant spouses, they are an interesting window into the past. Unlike court or church records, these proto-slave narratives provide teachers and students with fuller accounts not only of slavery but also of individual slaves. While most probate or church documents supply vital information (e.g., dates of birth, death, and baptism) and illuminate kinship ties and naming practices, advertisements supply other useful information, complementing the firsthand accounts of Olaudah Equiano, Venture Smith, Harriet Jacobs, Frederick Douglass, and others.

Exercise 1: Annotating

You can begin using runaway slave ads to teach about slavery by having students annotate them. This exercise can be done in groups or individually. In its simplest form, annotation requires that students read a notice and write comments in the margins about the document. If annotation is done as a group assignment, the advertisements are read aloud and become the center of class discussions. Annotating is a useful assignment in that it encourages students to think critically. In either case, when annotating, teachers should provide little to no context. Instead, because this exercise is designed to get students to engage with the material, they should be allowed to freely interpret, evaluate, and question the advertisements, exploring the words and the wording of the notices. To choose advertisements to annotate, teachers should consult one if not several collections in print. Lathan Windley's *Runaway Slave Advertisements*, for example, is a magisterial, four-volume collection of eighteenth-century notices for slaves in the South. Billy Smith and Richard Wojtowicz's *Blacks Who Stole Themselves* is an equally useful collection of runaway advertisements for colonial Pennsylvania. Graham R. Hodges and Alan E. Brown's *"Pretends to Be Free"* is a collection of fugitive notices printed in New York and New Jersey. My volume *Escaping*

Bondage documents notices that appeared in newspapers in eighteenth-century New England.[13] For antebellum collections, teachers should consult John Hope Franklin and Loren Schweninger's *Runaway Slaves* and Daniel Meaders's *Advertisements for Runaway Slaves in Virginia.* There are also several useful collections online. The most comprehensive and accessible is Tom Costa's "Geography of Slavery in Virginia."[14]

In their examination of the myriad possibilities encoded in the notices' meaning, teachers and students should be sure to consult the resources link, specifically the teaching materials, on the Virginia runaway website, the glossary sections of Smith and Wojtowicz's *Blacks Who Stole Themselves* or Hodges and Brown's *"Pretends to Be Free,"* and my own *Escaping Bondage.* The *Oxford English Dictionary* will also prove helpful. Ultimately, regardless of the collection used, by annotating notices, students and teachers will begin exploring a series of questions concerning slavery. What, for instance, do the notices tell us about slaves' physical appearance, work skills, linguistic ability, race, gender, character and temperament, and apparel?

Consider Adam's profile. At twenty-three, he stood six feet tall. He had learned the art of carpentry. He had also learned to read; it appears he taught himself to write. The advertisements Fox had printed also indicate that he was a country-born slave; in other words, he was born in America. Furthermore, his "yellowish complexion" suggests that Adam might have been racially mixed. When he left, the slave artisan carried with him additional clothes. Teachers and students should ponder why Adam brought those clothes; they will eventually come to the conclusion that they could have been used for multiple purposes. Superfluous articles, for instance, could have been used as currency. He could have worn them to pass for free. Depending on the weather, he might have used the additional clothing simply to allow him to rough it outside, hidden from the suspicious eyes of slavecatchers or patrols. Whatever the case, annotating encourages students to ask questions, inspiring reflection and critical thinking.

Exercise 2: Analyzing

Students should use the advertisements to examine other questions about slavery. You can start, however, by asking them simply what they see. From there, using the annotating exercise, ask students to describe what they can discern about the subject from the clues the advertisement reveals. Beforehand, teachers should consult essays from this volume or perhaps a textbook that covers the early history of African Americans. The online, searchable database version of William W. Hening, *Statutes at Large: Being a Collection of all the Laws of Virginia*, is also a useful resource.[15] Using the keyword "runaway," teachers could create handouts and discuss with students the legal circumstances runaways and slaves confronted daily. Third, ask students to interpret what the notices reveal about slavery by posing a series of questions. What was the nature of the master/slave relationship? What was the composition of the slave community? In what ways, if any, did slaves manage to retain aspects of their memory of their African past? And what do runaway notices reveal about slave resistance, agency, and culture?

Another look at Adam's story, for example, reveals not only his determination but also his peculiar relationship with his master. Well before he ran, Virginia moved from being a society with slaves to a full-blown slave society, one in which Fox could have had Adam severely punished.[16] To be sure, after leaving the first time, Adam should have been, as a point of law, whipped. After his second flight, the law provided an even harsher remedy: branding. In most instances, the constable would burn the letter "R" on the slave's cheek. Maiming usually followed the third or fourth disappearance, and after that the number of lashes doled out for each offense increased, sometimes leading to death.[17]

Fox, however, chose not to punish Adam in the manner prescribed by the law. Rather, he attempted to solicit, entice, and deputize the public as potential slavecatchers to retrieve his "likely Negro." The prize he offered for Adam's return was considerable. If captured in Virginia, slavecatchers or patrols would receive "FIVE POUNDS reward, if in *North-Carolina* TEN POUNDS, and if in *South-Carolina* TWENTY POUNDS." "Besides what the law allows," these incentives represented no small sum. However they were calculated (in tobacco weight or in precious metal), the awards Fox promised were significant. During the eighteenth century, a decent calf cost approximately £10, a good horse between £7 and £10. Depending on his or her age, a slave could be purchased for £15 to £20. Typically, a skilled slave cost between £50 and £100.[18]

To Fox, the reward for Adam's safe return clearly meant comparably little. Here, students could explore even deeper questions about slavery using runaway advertisements. For example, students should ask why Fox did not punish Adam. What could he hope to gain by employing force? What could he lose? Paternalism, or slave masters' view of themselves as benevolent father figures to their enslaved population, is a complex subject raised by the notices Fox and other masters had printed.[19] Although it is clear that Fox valued the man, his desire to see himself as a paternal figure may explain why he did not use the lash more often or threaten Adam with dismemberment to discourage the slave's unruly behavior. There is also the complicated question of paternity that might explain Fox's magnanimity.

Exercise 3: Synthesizing

With context, the advertisements reveal deeper questions about slavery. What, for example, do they tell us about race, class, gender, resistance, and agency? In examining these questions and others, students should contemplate the stories that lie in between the lines. They can delve into the subtext concealed in plain sight.

One exercise that allows them to explore the complexity of runaway advertisements in this way requires that they engage them creatively. To start, break students into groups consisting of at least five members. Each group should be assigned a specific advertisement. The notice should represent different runaways, either in the same colony or in different ones. Within each group, each student should be assigned one of the tasks described here.

Advertisements illustrated. One student should draw, paint, sketch, or construct a two-dimensional portrait inspired by the assigned advertisement. Instead of seeking a literal interpretation (see illustrations by Eastman Johnson and George Cruikshank), teachers should challenge

---

Top right: In this 1862 painting, *A Ride for Liberty*, Eastman Johnson captures several aspects of a runaway's flight. To be sure, many slaves ran away with other slaves; sometimes, as this painting suggests, they ran away to preserve their families. Others stole away with a horse or a favorite pet. Using Johnson's painting as a literal example, teachers could encourage students to create their own art. The more abstract the work, such as *The Refuge*, the deeper the potential reading of the assigned runaway advertisement. Brooklyn Museum of Art.

Bottom Right: George Cruikshank, "Eliza Crosses the Ohio on the Floating Ice," *Uncle Tom's Cabin* (London: Routledge, 1853). Collection of Jo-Ann Morgan.

ELIZA CROSSES THE OHIO ON THE FLOATING ICE.

students to think abstractly (see painting by Tunde Afolayan Famous). After completing their portraits, students should explain their artwork.

Runaway soundtrack. The second student should compose and perform or, for the musically challenged, select a song inspired by the assigned notice. After students have selected the song, they should explain their choice.

Dramaturgy. Using the assigned advertisement for inspiration, the third and fourth students should develop two short performances, one involving a printer typesetting an advertisement, the other involving a runaway contemplating his or her plight. Titled "Advertisement concerning Advertisements," the first dramatic presentation should focus on the printer, who explains the form and the process of putting an advertisement in the newspaper. This performance should focus on the language of advertisements. The second vignette, titled "The Fugitive Speaks," should imagine a fugitive explaining slavery from his or her perspective. This performance focuses on the varied reasons why slaves protested with their feet. Here some understanding of the punishments runaways suffered if captured would be helpful. Note: teachers should be mindful not to dramatize the pursuit of the runaway or the master-slave relationship, as both of these subjects are nuanced and complex and the discussion has the potential to go wrong, reinforcing racial stereotypes.

Accessorizing. The fifth student should dress the part of the runaway. Drawing on clothes referenced in the notice, students could select an article of clothing or a piece of textile cited and explain their choice. In exploring the language of clothing, Linda Baumgarten's *What Clothes Reveal* will prove invaluable.[20]

After consulting each group, teachers should create a program wherein each group presents, performs, and reenacts its interpretations of its respective advertisements. Before each presentation, the assigned notice should be read aloud. Afterward, each group should respond to questions from the teacher and the class.

Ideally, all of these exercises are designed to encourage critical thinking. Advertisements are important resources for exploring slavery. Each conveys a bold act, a multilayered minidrama. Each conveys a not-so-concealed aspiration for freedom that all students can identify with, regardless of race, class, or gender. By encouraging students to engage the material through these exercises, we can help students to see Adam's story as their own.

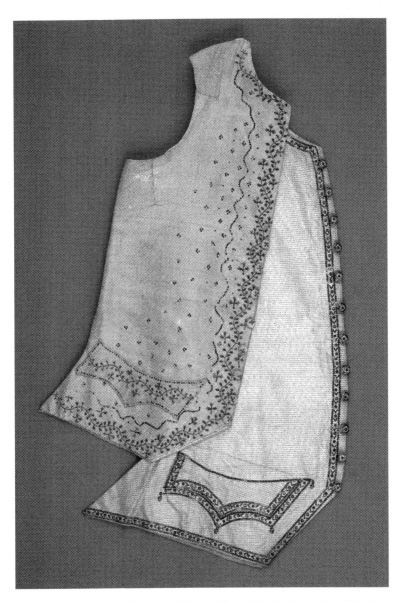

When he went away the third time, Adam took with him "a Cotton or white Plains Waistcoat." During the eighteenth century, cotton, a fabric made from the cotton plant, and heavy wool were increasingly available. For most runaway slaves, clothing served multiple purposes. Besides its obvious importance, for example, clothes communicated status and individuality. Depending on the garment, specifically the materials from which it was made or its texture, clothing also provided slaves with something to barter or a way to pass for free. The Colonial Williamsburg Foundation, Museum Purchase.

Conclusion: A Master's Peculiar Story

Of course, in addition to Adam's story, the advertisements printed in the *Virginia Gazette* reveal John Fox's story as well. Born in 1742, Fox was the son of the Reverend John Fox and his wife, Isabel. Like most gentry, Fox enjoyed a life of privileges. A graduate of William and Mary, he owned well over three thousand acres of land in Gloucester County. In addition to Adam, he owned at least nine other slaves. Like most grandees of his day, Fox thought himself a modern-day patriarch. The master of Greenwich Plantation, he took delight in his fatherly role.[21]

Fox's notice for Adam reveals this sense of paternalism. Unwittingly, near the end of the last two advertisements he had posted in the *Gazette*, he made that much plain when he attempted to mock his slave's newfound sense of faith or, as he put it more concisely, "He Pretends to be a Newlight." Clearly, this reference embodied contempt for his slave's new faith. But it also registers something else, something akin to fatherly pride. The Baptists were, as Rhys Isaac's study of the First Great Awakening in Virginia notes, a bold and impudent lot who challenged the established Anglican Church.[22] Rather than sit in church in accordance with rank, they chose to worship outside without regard for each worshippers' social and economic standing. Instead of deferentially acknowledging the gentry's status, the Baptists elected to call everyone either "brother" or "sister," thus leveling the old Church's views about class and faith. In his effort to deny Adam his humanity, by mocking his faith, Fox inadvertently achieved the opposite goal: acknowledging that he was something more than chattel. In the end, when he placed the advertisements for his slave's safe return in the newspapers, he tried to reclaim not only his valued property but also an orderly cosmos in which "a likely Negro" such as Adam had little choice but to recognize his master's power and likewise his own proper place, a place ironically fading with the burgeoning tide that would be the American Revolution.

NOTES

Antonio Bly would like to thank Bethany Jay and the editorial staff of the Harvey Goldberg Series for Understanding and Teaching History for their helpful comments. He would also like to thank Tom Costa, Elizabeth Rose, Matthew

Mason and Rita G. Koman, and Donald C. Lord, whose work proved invaluable in the development of this article. Tom Costa, "What Can We Learn from a Digital Database of Runaway Slave Advertisements," *International Social Science Review* 76, nos. 1–2 (2001): 36–43; Elizabeth Rose, "Teaching about Slavery with Runaway Slave Advertisements," *Connecticut History* 46, no. 1 (Spring 2007): 117–27; Matthew Mason and Rita G. Koman, "Complicating Slavery: Teaching with Runaway Advertisements," *Organization of American Historians Magazine of History* 17, no. 3 (April 2003): 31–34; and Donald C. Lord, "Slave Ads as Historical Evidence," *The History Teacher* 5, no. 4 (May 1972): 10–16.

1. Notices cost between three and five shillings, a third of the cost for a yearly subscription to the *Virginia Gazette*.

2. William Rind's *Virginia Gazette*, April 26, 1770 (Supplement), 2. Although printed in April 1770, this advertisement notes that Adam ran away in January.

3. William Rind's *Virginia Gazette*, February 22, 1770. This advertisement suggests that Adam had been captured after he ran away on January 3, 1770. Unlike the earlier notice, it also indicates that the slave carpenter repeatedly protested with his feet.

4. Alexander Purdie and John Dixon's *Virginia Gazette*, July 18, 1771. After Adam ran away a third time, John Fox had this advertisement printed in the Williamsburg-based newspaper. This notice reveals that Adam had remained at large for well over a year.

5. A "Newlight" is the name given to converts made by the evangelical movements, known as the Great Awakening, which were passionate religious revivals in American history. The first of these millennial revivals occurred in the eighteenth century, a second in the nineteenth century, and a third in the twentieth. Millennialism is the Christian belief that there will be a Golden Age on Earth after Christ has returned, a thousand years prior to the final judgment. Book of Revelation 20:1–6.

6. William Rind's *Virginia Gazette*, April 23, 1772. This is the fourth advertisement Fox had printed in the paper. Besides marking the fourth occasion that Adam ran away, it shows that the fugitive had passed for free for more than two years.

7. Rhys Isaac, *The Transformation of Virginia* (Chapel Hill: University of North Carolina Press, 1982), 121–25. A close reading of the notice Fox placed in the *Gazette* on April 23, 1773, suggests that the runaway in question was indeed Adam. As he had done before, the fugitive had assumed an alias: "George Green." For three years, he lived in North Carolina and "has been much whipped by constables, since run away, for his irregular behavior." During the time he spent away from Fox, Adam contracted smallpox, which left him disfigured.

8. Printed in April 1773 in William Rind's *Virginia Gazette*, this advertisement concerns an unnamed runaway, more than likely Adam, who managed to

remain at large for more than three years. As he had done before, Fox references the absconded slave's skill, complexion, and previous flights and, most important, his life in North Carolina.

9. Although slavery varied over time and space, most people still hold fast to the simple image of slavery during the antebellum "King Cotton" era, largely due to the influence of popular movies, starting with D. W. Griffith's infamous *Birth of a Nation* through more recent cinematic productions such as Quentin Tarantino's *Django Unchained* and Steve McQueen's *12 Years a Slave*. What's more, because of the impact of the Civil War, most people also hold fast to a benevolent view of slavery in the North. For the quotations concerning Cato, see my *Escaping Bondage: A Documentary History of Runaway Slaves in Eighteenth-Century New England, 1700–1789* (Lanham, MD: Lexington Books, 2012), 79; Lorenzo J. Greene, *The Negro in Colonial New England* (New York: Atheneum, 1968); and William D. Piersen, *Black Yankees: The Development of an Afro-American Subculture in Eighteenth-Century New England* (Amherst: University of Massachusetts Press, 1988).

For useful accounts about New England runaways, see Lorenzo J. Greene, "The New England Negro as Seen in Advertisements for Runaway Slaves," *Journal of Negro History* 29 (1944): 125–46; and my own "A Prince among Pretending Free Men: Runaway Slaves in Colonial New England Revisited," *Massachusetts Historical Review* 13 (2012): 87–117.

10. Gerald W. Mullin, *Flight and Rebellion: Slave Resistance in Eighteenth-Century Virginia* (New York: Oxford University Press, 1972); and Lathan A. Windley, *A Profile of Runaway Slaves in Virginia and South Carolina from 1730 through 1787* (New York: Garland, 1995). For the quotations concerning Peter, see *Virginia Gazette* (Parks), May 2–9, 1745, 4.

Incidentally, by law, parish clerks in Virginia were obliged to read notices for runaways before church services. Besides being thus part of divine service, advertisements were affixed to the doors of county courthouses and were read aloud on court days. William W. Hening, *The Statutes at Large: Being a Collection of all the Laws of Virginia from the First Session of the Legislature* (Richmond, VA: Samuel Pleasants Jr., 1819–23), 4:169. Last, for a fuller account of fictive kinships between masters and slaves, see Orlando Patterson's *Slavery and Social Death: A Comparative Study* (Cambridge, MA: Harvard University Press, 1982), 62–65.

11. Arnold Bontemps, *The Punished Self: Surviving Slavery in the Colonial South* (Ithaca, NY: Cornell University Press, 2001); John Wood Sweet, *Bodies Politic: Negotiating Race in the American North, 1730–1830* (Philadelphia: University of Pennsylvania Press, 2006); Woody Holton, *Forced Founders: Indians, Debtors, Slaves, and the Making of the American Revolution in Virginia* (Chapel Hill: University of North Carolina Press, 1998); Woody Holton, "Rebel against Rebel: Enslaved Virginians and the Coming of the American Revolution," *Virginia Magazine of History and Biography* 105, no. 2 (Spring 1997): 157–92; W. Jeffrey Bolster, *Black Jacks: African American Seamen in the Age of Sail* (Cambridge, MA:

Harvard University Press, 1998); Michael A. Gomez, *Exchanging Our Country Marks: The Transformation of African Identities in the Colonial and Antebellum South* (Chapel Hill: University of North Carolina Press, 1998); Shane White and Graham White, *Stylin': African American Expressive Culture, from Its Beginnings to the Zoot Suit* (Ithaca, NY: Cornell University Press, 1999); Herbert G. Gutman, *The Black Family in Slavery and Freedom, 1750–1925* (New York: Vintage Books, 1976); and Catherine Adams and Elizabeth H. Pleck, *Love of Freedom: Black Women in Colonial and Revolutionary New England* (Oxford: Oxford University Press, 2010).

12. Peter Wood, *Black Majority: Negroes in Colonial South Carolina from 1670 through the Stono Rebellion* (New York: W. W. Norton, 1975), 240.

13. Lathan Windley, *Runaway Slave Advertisements: A Documentary History from the 1730s to 1790* (Westport, CT: Greenwood, 1983); Billy Smith and Richard Wojtowicz, *Blacks Who Stole Themselves: Advertisements for Runaways in the Pennsylvania Gazette, 1728–1790* (Philadelphia: University of Pennsylvania Press, 1989); Graham R. Hodges and Alan E. Brown, *"Pretends to Be Free": Runaway Slave Advertisements from Colonial and Revolutionary New York and New Jersey* (New York: Garland, 1994); Bly, *Escaping Bondage*.

While all of these runaway advertisement collections are useful, teachers might want to start with northern notices, as they promise to challenge students' traditional views of slavery. Because of the abolitionist movement and the Civil War, most students hold fast to the idea of the North as the land of the free and the South as the land of slavery.

14. John Hope Franklin and Loren Schweninger, *Runaway Slaves: Rebels on the Plantation* (New York: Oxford University Press, 2000); Daniel Meaders, *Advertisements for Runaway Slaves in Virginia, 1801–1820* (New York: Garland, 1997); "The Geography of Slavery in Virginia" is available online at http://www2 .vcdh.virginia.edu/gos/.

15. See http://vagenweb.org/hening/.

16. Societies with slaves are those wherein slavery represents a marginal part of that community's economy. In contrast, slave societies are those in which slavery forms the foundation of a community's economy.

17. Hening, *Statutes at Large*, 3:456–57 [whipping]; 1:254–55 [branding]; 4:132 [dismemberment]. For a more detailed account of runaway punishments, see Windley, *Profile of Runaway Slaves*, 3–15.

18. To determine the monetary value of property, I consulted several randomly selected inventories from the Gunston Hall Probate Database (http:// www.gunstonhall.org/), specifically those of Charles Clark, John Fendall Beall, John Fenall, Thomas Clark, and William Hall.

19. Paternalism is an ideology that developed during the 1730s and 1740s among the slave-owning elites who rationalized the institution of slavery and their relationship with slaves as necessary to extend civilization to African Americans. For a fuller discussion, see Anthony S. Parent, *Foul Means: The*

Formation of a Slave Society in Virginia, 1660–1740 (Chapel Hill: University of North Carolina Press, 2003), 197–235.

20. Linda Baumgarten, *What Clothes Reveal: The Language of Clothing in Colonial and Federal America* (New Haven: Yale University Press, 2002).

21. John Fox advertised for Robin and Daniel, Ben, Emanuel, George Green, Jack, Caesar, Peter Brown, Gabriel, and Robin. *Virginia Gazette* (Purdie and Dixon), March 21, 1766, 3; *Virginia Gazette* (Rind), March 3, 1768, 3; *Virginia Gazette* (Rind), April 19, 1770 (Supplement), 2; *Virginia Gazette* (Rind), April 22, 1773 (Supplement), 2; *Virginia Gazette* (Rind), May 20, 1773, 2; *Virginia Gazette* (Rind), September 30, 1773, 3; *Virginia Gazette* (Purdie and Dixon), June 16, 1774, 3; *Virginia Gazette* (Pinkney), December 1, 1774, 3; *Virginia Gazette* (Dixon and Hunter), February 18, 1775, 3. For John Fox's story, see *Genealogies of Virginia Families: From Tyler's Quarterly Historical and Genealogical Magazine* (Baltimore: Genealogical Publishing Company, 2007), 723–24. Incidentally, Adam could have been the property of Fox's father, who also lived in Gloucester County and who was born in 1706. The senior Fox attended the College of William and Mary. After graduating, he traveled to England, where he received his license to preach. In 1736 Fox became rector of the Ware Parish in Gloucester. A year later, he married Isabel (Booth) Richard. From 1729 to 1738 he served as master of the Brafferton School for Native American children in Williamsburg. Like most Anglicans, he advocated the Church's mission to teach Native and African Americans Christianity through reading. If Adam were in fact his slave, this might explain how he learned to read. Between 1761 and 1763 Fox served as a visiting teacher at the college. During his tenure there, Adam could have attended the school sponsored by the associates of Dr. Thomas Bray in Williamsburg. At age 14, the teenage boy could have been the school's oldest known scholar. However, Fox's son appears to be the more likely choice for Adam's owner because his plantation in Greenwich is referenced in the notice for his return. For a fuller account of the Brafferton School, see Karen A. Stuart, "'So Good a Work': The Brafferton School, 1690–1777" (PhD dissertation, College of William and Mary, 1984); Terri Keffert, "The Education of the Native American in Colonial Virginia, with Particular Regard to the Brafferton School," *Colonial Williamsburg Interpreter* 21 (Fall 2000): 20–21. For a useful account of the Bray school, see E. Jennifer Monaghan, *Learning to Read and Write in Colonial America* (Amherst: University of Massachusetts Press, 2007), chapters 5 and 9; and my own "In Pursuit of Letters: A History of the Bray Schools for Enslaved Children in Colonial Virginia," *History of Education Quarterly* 51, no. 4 (November 2011): 429–59. For Fox's father's story, see *Genealogies of Virginia Families*, 722–23.

22. Rhys Isaac, "Evangelical Revolt: The Nature of the Baptists' Challenge to the Traditional Order in Virginia, 1765 to 1775," *William and Mary Quarterly* 31, no. 3 (July 1974): 345–68.

Teaching the History of Slavery and Its Legacy through Historical Archaeology

Project Archaeology

SARAH E. MILLER, JAMES M. DAVIDSON, and
EMILY PALMER

Authors' Note: Archaeologists and educators came together to form a curriculum that would help students better understand the past of enslaved people at Kingsley Plantation. The established supplemental history and science curriculum of *Project Archaeology: Investigating Shelter* provided a template to discuss the geography, history, and archaeology of Kingsley Plantation. These lessons are available for teachers to purchase through the *Project Archaeology* website and are made available at workshops across the country. As the Kingsley shelter unit was developed using Teacher-Ranger-Teachers and staff of the National Park Service, the materials discussed in this essay, including the teacher instructions and the student notebook, are available for free download on the Timucuan Ecological and Historical Preserve's website.

Dreaded questions like "When am I going to use this?" and "Why do I care?" plague teachers. These comments can be especially daunting in history classrooms. How do you ground students in historical material and methods while making them relevant to modern life? Archaeology helps to bridge that gap through its emphasis on the material record of human behavior. Discoveries made in the field not only teach us more about how people lived in the past; they influence how we understand our present. In the study of slavery, archaeology reveals artifacts and structures that allow those silenced by enslavement to speak. Teachers can use studies from active archaeological sites, such as Kingsley Plantation on Florida's northeast coast, to watch as history is revealed with every scrape of the trowel.

Kingsley Plantation offers two unique ways of understanding slavery. First, its location within what was once Spanish colonial Florida provides an opportunity to understand slavery under the Spanish system, which was very different from British colonial rule. Second, ongoing archaeological investigations by the University of Florida provide a different avenue for learning about slavery, that of historical archaeology. This chapter presents a brief history of Kingsley Plantation, an introduction to public archaeology, and an overview of the *Project Archaeology: Investigating Shelter* curriculum, which is available for purchase or download online.[1] By understanding what archaeology has revealed about the lives of enslaved people in Florida, students experience the history of slavery as an active and ever-expanding field of scholarship that touches lives and communities today, including their own.

Slavery under Spanish Rule

Europeans and their immediate descendants in the English (as well as the Spanish and the French) colonies of North America during the early seventeenth century innovated and practiced what arguably became the harshest form of chattel slavery that the world had ever known. It was one part of an emerging global system of colonialism and capitalism that combined economic and military expansion with exploitation. The rationale underlying the practice of slavery grew from an elaboration of what had previously been viewed as a curious difference, the simple physical distinctions between black and white, European and African. Within decades of interaction, this simple mindset of difference evolved into the nascent idea of race, or racial difference, to the point where the notion became real, became naturalized, and finally became viewed as a natural law. This evolution allowed whites to view anyone of African ancestry as regrettably less than human. This

284

view allowed whites to treat them as expendable labor and, later, as simple property, no more or less than cattle.[2]

When these same colonies threw off British rule and became the United States of America, in the late eighteenth century, some states continued the practice of slavery even as it was abandoned piecemeal by the North and increasingly condemned as a moral and economic evil by some. Within the Spanish colony of La Florida, a form of slavery existed that, while cruel, had some protections that were unknown under the British/American system. When Florida became an American territory, in 1821, it adopted the form of chattel slavery practiced in the American South.[3]

Archaeology as a Means to Teach about Slavery

Archaeology, when it is done well, is as much about the present as it is about the past. As the archaeologist Parker Potter noted, the past is gone and irretrievable; we live in the present, and our research must be of use in the here and now, must be a positive good for living people, as much as it is an attempt at giving honor and voice to those who are gone.[4] The field of public archaeology emerged in the 1980s as one means to teach the American public about its collective history. Public archaeology's primary goal is engagement, but engagement with whom? As Carol McDavid discovered in her work at the Levi Jordan Plantation in Brazoria County, Texas, in the 1990s, there is no such thing as a single public but, in fact, many publics with different agendas, perspectives, and backgrounds.[5] Students and schools, however, have emerged as a crucial audience for public archaeologists.

Teachers of all levels grapple with difficult questions when they teach about slavery. If it is not taught properly, students may find the concept too abstract or too traumatic.[6] Additionally, when one is teaching or learning about slavery, there are the psychological barriers of anger, fear, apprehension, and disgust, among myriad emotions. In short, dealing with slavery is hard. As the historian James Oliver Horton noted in his essay on the perils of teaching about slavery and racism to the American populace, "The tendency is to turn away from history that is upsetting, but Americans cannot afford to ignore their past, even the less flattering parts of it. As countless scholars have recently reminded us, 'history matters.' It provides our identity, it structures our relationships, and it defines the terms of our debates."[7]

One means to make the study of slavery more relevant and concrete in a student's life is to focus on how enslaved people met their daily needs, including procurement of food and water as well as construction and organization of their homes.

Archaeology at Kingsley Plantation

Plantation archaeology can trace its origin to 1968 and the efforts of Charles Fairbanks of the University of Florida, who was the first to ask questions pertaining to slave life through archaeological investigations of slave cabins at Kingsley Plantation, Fort George Island, Florida.[8] Beginning in 2006, the University of Florida's Department of Anthropology began a series of eight summer archaeological field schools at Kingsley Plantation that were designed to revisit the original work of Fairbanks and to ask new questions about this time, place, and condition.[9]

Upon their arrival on Fort George Island in the spring of 1814, Zephaniah Kingsley and his enslaved Africans built thirty-two tabby slave cabins, sixteen on either side of Palmetto Road, with the cabin arrangement forming an unusual and highly symmetrical semicircle configuration. Virtually all of the cabins consisted of two rooms, with the front room serving as the living room and kitchen, while the smaller backroom likely was used as a bedroom. Researchers directed their excavations to the interior spaces of four slave cabins built in 1814, three of which were abandoned in 1839, when the plantation owners, the Kingsleys, left Florida for Haiti.[10] These cabins revealed information about the home life of first-generation slaves.

In 2006 a partnership was formed among the University of Florida's Anthropology Department, Timucuan Ecological and Historical Preserve (National Park Service), and the newly formed Florida Public Archaeology Network. The partnership aimed to provide updated, accurate knowledge about the ongoing archaeology at Kingsley Plantation. Interpretive panels for visitors were installed that focused on the archaeological search for physical evidence of African identity at the site. Teachers and archaeologists worked together to draft lesson plans for use in classrooms to bring the Kingsley archaeology experiences beyond the borders of the park. In the summer of 2010, enlisting the help of National Park Service Teacher-Ranger-Teachers, the partners began working toward a Kingsley curriculum that could be used to understand and teach slavery across the United States.

Project Archaeology: Investigating Shelter

One of the best ways to frame learning about archaeology for formal classroom audiences is through the *Project Archaeology: Investigating Shelter* (*PA:IS*) curriculum.[11] Established in the early 1990s, *Project Archaeology*'s National Office has researched, developed, and assessed heritage education materials.[12] Its *PA:IS* curriculum has achieved the highest level of accolades, receiving both official endorsement from the National Council of Social Studies and the Partners in Conservation Award, given by the US Department of the Interior. The lessons can be adapted for use in any secondary or tertiary classroom. In general, this curriculum answers the essential question: How can investigating a tabby cabin help us understand slaves and their culture?

Before students can understand and use archaeology to understand slave culture, instructors will need to build a foundation of knowledge about archaeology as a field. Lessons 1–7 of the *PA:IS* curriculum provide teachers with basic concepts that they need to teach students to help them observe and interpret archaeological data. Once familiar with how archaeologists research, classify artifacts, and search for context within a site, students then become archaeologists and investigate a Kingsley slave cabin.[13]

Investigating a Tabby Slave Cabin

Project Archaeology's inquiry into shelter draws from a Kickapoo saying, "By our houses you will know us."[14] Thus, by understanding a Kingsley tabby cabin, students will begin to know the enslaved people who lived on the plantation.

The Kingsley lesson plan is divided into four parts to guide students through the site using archaeological skills.[15] Part One introduces students to Deborah Bartley-Wallace, a descendant of Easter Bartley, who was born a slave at Kingsley Plantation in the 1820s. Students research flora and fauna of the surrounding estuary to infer potential building materials for the cabins.

Part Two of the Kingsley curriculum focuses on history and includes analysis of select primary resources: historic photographs of slave cabins and two historical documents related to a slave named Jimmy. This section reinforces the idea that research, books, and primary documents are important tools for archaeologists. Two photographs depict the slave cabins as they stood shortly after the Civil War. Students can

Laborers and their children on Fort George Island after the
Civil War. Photograph courtesy of Florida State Archives.

Laborers outside the cabins on Fort George Island. Photograph
courtesy of James Davidson.

Top: A nephew of Zephaniah Kingsley wrote this note giving a slave named Jimmy permission to look for a master. The note also states the minimum price that the writer would accept for Jimmy. Image courtesy of the National Park Service.

Left: Receipt for the sale of two black men, Jimmy Gibbs and Andrew Pow. Image courtesy of the National Park Service.

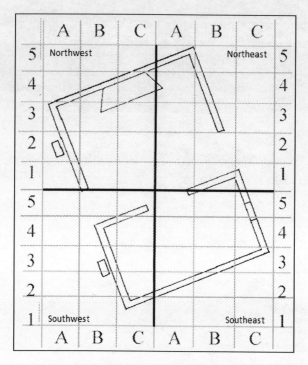

Map of the Kingsley Plantation slave cabin site. Courtesy of the National Park Service.

analyze the photographs and list objects, note materials used to build the cabins, infer activities related to the photos, and posit when the pictures were taken. In addition to asking when, students consider why the photo was taken and guess at the photographer's intentions. They then read two short pieces from the life of an enslaved man named Jimmy: a pass allowing him to search for a new owner and a receipt of sale from his purchase. Examining the photographs and the existing records emphasizes the importance of primary documents in the study of the past but also opens up discussion on how rare these documents can be for a demographic denied access to the written record. The scarcity of historical documents emphasizes the elevated importance of material culture in studying enslaved people.

The third part of the Kingsley curriculum steps away from historical documents and delves into understanding enslaved people at Kingsley through the material culture recovered during excavation of a tabby cabin. Before beginning, it's important for students to understand site formation processes, essentially how buildings on the surface leave a footprint in the soil. At Kingsley, cabins were constructed from the most readily available resource: oyster shells and timbers for framing. Oysters mixed with lime were used to make tabby, a cement-like mixture used to form the walls of the cabins. Stage 1 of the site formation process is the initial construction; stage two occurs years later, when the tabby and timbers start to naturally degrade; and stage 3 is the site in its current condition: some aboveground tabby ruins but intact footprint and soil deposits below the ground.

After students understand how an aboveground structure becomes an archaeological site over time, it's time to expose them to artifacts. Students explore the footprint of a tabby slave cabin at Kingsley by reverse-mapping material culture recovered from the site. Archaeologists collected artifacts, including food remains, personal items, building material, tableware, and ammunition (see table 1). An additional category of ritual/house charms is also present and consists of blue beads, an amber bead, iron objects, Spanish coins, and, most notably, a fully articulated chicken burial. The cabin is broken into quadrants, and students are given the artifact locations to place representations of the artifacts onto the actual location on a tarp that takes up an area measuring ten feet by ten feet, with the footprint laid out.

Teachers can guide students through the categorizing of the artifacts found in each quadrant and ask them to draw a graphic representation of the data. Relying on the authentic material culture collected, students write down observations and draw inferences as to what activities took place at the site. They are asked to combine findings from all quadrants and inevitably adjust their initial interpretations about how people at Kingsley Plantation lived.

Reverse-mapping is a powerful activity from a pedagogical perspective; archaeology is not about the discovery of individual objects but about the analysis and interpretation of material culture to help us understand people of the past. A single artifact in the hand tells you relatively little, whereas multiple objects in concentrations tell a more complex story. For example, iron objects found individually on site might have been used for agriculture or for architecture, but if they are found under the floor in entryways they can be interpreted as house

Table 1. Select artifacts by quadrant for the Kingsley Plantation slave cabin site

Northwest Quadrant

Cow bone (2)	Food remains	B-4, C-4
Pig bone	Food remains	B-4
Fish bones (20)	Food remains	C-4
Lead shot (3)	Ammunition	B-1
Bone button	Clothing	C-3, B-3
Hook and eye	Clothing	C-3

Northeast Quadrant

Iron concretion	Ritual/house charm	A-5
Clay object	Ritual/house charm	B-3
Gunflint (2)	Used in firearms	A-3
Pipe bowl	Personal effects	A-3
Bone button	Clothing	A-4
Lead shot	Ammunition	A-1, A-4
Glass blue bead (3)	Ritual/house charm	B-2

Southwest Quadrant

Iron hoe head	Ritual/house charm	A-5
Hatchet	Ritual/house charm	B-5
Spanish coin (2)	Ritual/house charm	C-4
Artillery button	Ritual/house charm	C-3
Trigger	Used in firearms	C-2
Back plate for padlock	Personal effects	B-4
Pipe stem	Personal effects	C-2
Fishing weights	Personal effects	A-2, C-2, C-3, C-4
Lead shot	Ammunition	C-3, C-5

Southeast Quadrant

French pipe	Personal effects	B-5
Brass nail	Boatbuilding materials	B-5
Glass lens	Sailing equipment	C-4
Chicken burial	Ritual/house charm	C-5
Iron concretion	Ritual/house charm	C-5
Amber glass bead	Ritual/house charm	C-5
Lead bale seal	Melted down to make shot	C-4
Lead shot	Ammunition	A-3, A-5, B-3
Bottle glass	Personal effects	B-5
Fishing weights	Personal effects	A-2, B-3, B-4

charms. Context matters. The location of objects changes our interpretation of how artifacts were used and ultimately helps students understand the cultures of those enslaved at Kingsley.

The chicken burial truly is a spectacular find and grabs the attention of students of any age. Chickens on plantations are commonplace as a food resource. But placement of the chicken burial under the floor in the entrance to a cabin offers other avenues of interpretation. The teacher handbook provides more detail on the academic understanding of animal sacrifice from historians, archaeologists at other sites, and cultural anthropologists conducting contemporary ethnographic research in Africa. For example, chicken sacrifice is described in numerous documents and includes sprinkling the blood over tombs or during divination rituals.[16] Later, during the 1940s, historical ethnographies were collected as part of the Works Projects Administration (WPA) Federal Writer's Project and demonstrate the continued use of chicken sacrifice during mourning and to keep spirits away.[17] Rituals similar to those described historically continue to be reported in the news in the South and are most frequently attributed to Santeria or Haitian Voodoo.

The other notable category of artifacts students discover as they reverse-map the site is ammunition. The discovery of lead shot and gun flint provides an opportunity for students to deliberate over the daily experience of enslaved people apart from the conventional narrative. Kingsley instituted a task system of slavery that allowed the enslaved to hunt and provide food for their families. Additionally, placement of those arms-related artifacts within the cabin and even the half-arc arrangement of all thirty-two cabins emphasize the danger faced by plantations during the Seminole War. It is important to note that archaeologists continue to adjust interpretations over time using what data are available.

After examining the archaeological record, students should consider the preservation of the slave cabins up to the present day. What is the importance of descendants and descendant communities today in understanding slavery? How might the study of Kingsley inform architecture or housing policies today? To assess learning up to this point, have students draw a futuristic shelter based on what they learned about the Kingsley cabin. Ask them to label at least three ideas borrowed from the past, such as layout, materials used in construction, or designation of a sacred area.

The culminating event for the entire *PA:IS* curriculum is the final performance of understanding, a role-playing activity that divides the class into four groups: descendant community, archaeologist, developers of new homes, and new families moving into the area. The students imagine an expanding community where developers are seeking to build on an archaeological site, in this case a slave cabin. As previously mentioned, archaeology takes place as much in the present as it does in the past. The outcome of studying the material culture can help inform today's decision-making processes: this is the ultimate goal of public archaeology.

Conclusion

Teachers who use archaeology to teach an understanding of slavery can take advantage of the many disciplines that intersect when studying objects. In addition to historical resources, the material culture of slave cabins and the plantation environment can directly connect students with the people who formerly held those objects. Archaeology is directly relatable to all cultures as it seeks to understand how people met their basic needs, notably shelter. The past becomes dynamic once it is understood that interpretations are constantly changing on the basis of decisions we make today. And finally, by including how archaeology can help inform the decision-making processes of current civic issues, we answer the question of why it is important for today's students to examine slavery and history in general.

NOTES

1. *Project Archaeology* is a national heritage education program founded by the US Bureau of Land Management (BLM) for educators and their students. Developed in the early 1990s, *Project Archaeology*'s mission is to develop awareness of our nation's diverse and fragile archaeological sites, to instill a sense of personal responsibility for stewardship of these sites, and to enhance science literacy and cultural understanding through the study of archaeology. For more on *Project Archaeology* and the materials developed for state programs across the country, visit www.projectarchaeology.org.

2. David W. Babson, "The Archaeology of Racism and Ethnicity on Southern Plantations," *Historical Archaeology* 24 (1990): 20–28.

3. Daniel W. Stowell, *Timucuan Ecological and Historical Resource Study* (Atlanta: US Department of the Interior, National Park Service, Southeast Field Area, 1996), 43.

4. Parker B. Potter Jr., "What Is the Use of Plantation Archaeology?" *Historical Archaeology* 25 (1991): 94–107.

5. Carol McDavid, "Descendants, Decisions, and Power: The Public Interpretation of the Archaeology of the Levi Jordan Plantation," *Historical Archaeology* 31(1997): 114–31.

6. Edward A. Chappell, "Museums and American Slavery," in Theresa Singleton, ed., *I, Too, Am America: Archaeological Studies of African-American Life* (Charlottesville: University Press of Virginia, 1999), 243.

7. James Oliver Horton, "Presenting Slavery: The Perils of Telling America's Racial Story," *The Public Historian* 21 (1999): 19–38.

8. Charles Fairbanks, "The Plantation Archaeology of the Southeastern Coast," *Historical Archaeology* 18 (1984): 1–14.

9. James M. Davidson, "Interim Report of Investigations of the University of Florida 2007 Historical Archaeological Field School: Kingsley Plantation (8DU108), Timucuan Ecological and Historic Preserve National Park, Duval County, Florida," University of Florida, Gainesville, 2007.

10. James M. Davidson, "Interim Report of Investigations of the University of Florida 2008 Historical Archaeological Field School: Kingsley Plantation (8DU108), Timucuan Ecological and Historic Preserve National Park, Duval County, Florida," University of Florida, Gainesville 2008.

11. Cali A. Letts and Jeanne M. Moe, *Project Archaeology: Investigating Shelter* (Bozeman: Montana State University 2009).

12. Jeanne M. Moe, "Conceptual Understanding of Science through Archaeological Inquiry," PhD dissertation, Montana State University, 2010.

13. Teacher instructions and student notebook for Kingsley Shelter Curriculum are available for free download on the Timucuan Ecological and Historic Preserve website, http://www.nps.gov/foca/learn/education/project-archaeology.htm.

14. Peter Nobokov and Robert Easton, *Native American Architecture* (New York: Oxford University Press, 1989), 11.

15. Pam James, Mary Mott, and Dawn Baker, "Investigating a Tabby Slave Cabin," *Project Archaeology: Investigating Shelter Series #12*, Timucuan Ecological and Historic Preserve, Jacksonville 2013.

16. Yvonne P. Chireau, *Black Magic: Religion and the African American Conjuring Tradition* (Berkeley: University of California Press, 2003).

17. Guy B. Johnson, *Drums and Shadows: Survival Studies among the Georgia Coastal Negroes* (Athens: University of Georgia Press, 1940), 167.

Contributors

LAIRD W. BERGAD is Distinguished Professor of Latin American and Caribbean History in the Department of Latin American, Latino, and Puerto Rican Studies at Lehman College and the Ph.D. Program in History at the Graduate Center of the City University of New York. He is the founding and current director of CUNY's Center for Latin American, Caribbean, and Latino Studies at the Graduate Center. He has written and published extensively on slavery in Cuba and Brazil and comparative slavery in the Americas, as well as on the Latino population of the United States and the New York metropolitan area.

IRA BERLIN, Distinguished University Professor at the University of Maryland, is author of *Slaves Without Masters: The Free Negro in the Antebellum South* (1965), *Many Thousands Gone: The First Two Centuries of Slavery in North America* (1998), and *Generations of Captivity: A History of African-American Slaves* (2004). *The Long Emancipation: The Demise of Slavery in the United States* (Nathan I. Huggins Lectures) was published in 2015.

ANTONIO T. BLY is an associate professor of history and the director of Africana studies at Appalachian State University. His research explores the connections between African American studies and the history of the book in America, an intellectual history of authorship, reading, and publishing.

RON BRILEY has taught American history, film history, and world cinema for almost forty years at Sandia Preparatory School in Albuquerque, New Mexico. His teaching has been recognized by the Golden Apple Foundation of New Mexico, Society for History Education, Organization of American Historians, American Historical Association, and National Council for History Education. He is the author of numerous articles on film and sport history as well as five books. His most recent book is *The Baseball Film in Postwar America: A Critical Study, 1948–1962* (2011), and he is currently at work on biographies of Woody Guthrie and Elia Kazan.

CHRISTY CLARK-PUJARA is an assistant professor of history in the Afro-American Studies Department at the University of Wisconsin–Madison. She is the author of the forthcoming book *Dark Work: The Business of Slavery in Rhode Island*. Her teaching and research interests include African American history before 1865, particularly the emergence and dismantlement of race-based slavery. She is especially interested in the intersections between race, politics, economy, and social hierarchy.

DEIRDRE COOPER OWENS is an assistant professor of history at Queens College, City University of New York, where she teaches courses on US slavery and African American and women's history. She is the author of the forthcoming book *Mothers of Gynecology: Slavery, Immigration, and the Birth of Gynecology*.

JAMES M. DAVIDSON received his doctorate in 2004 from the University of Texas and is currently an historical archaeologist and associate professor in the Department of Anthropology at the University of Florida. His research interests include historic mortuary archaeology and the African diaspora, with a particular focus on two key sites: Freedman's Cemetery in Dallas, Texas, and the Kingsley Plantation on Fort George Island, Florida. Recent publications include documenting an example of an animal sacrifice reflective of early nineteenth-century African religiosity at the Kingsley Plantation (2015), an analysis of artifacts from the slave cabins associated with the historic Couper Plantation site (St. Simon's Island, Georgia) (2012), and a bioarchaeological study comparing a Confederate officer to emancipated African Americans from the 1870s and 1880s (2015).

PAUL FINKELMAN is the Ariel F. Sallows Professor in Human Rights at the University of Saskatchewan School Of Law. He is also a Senior Fellow in Penn Program on Democracy, Citizenship, and Constitutionalism at the University of Pennsylvania, and an affiliated scholar at the National Constitution Center in Philadelphia. He received his B.A from Syracuse University (1971) and his Ph.D. from the University of Chicago (1976). He is a specialist in the history of slavery, American race relations, the civil war era, American constitutional history, civil liberties, and baseball and law. He is the author or coauthor of more than forty books, including *Slavery and the Founders: Race and Liberty in the Age of Jefferson* (2014), *Millard Fillmore* (2011), and *A March of Liberty: A Constitutional History of the United States* (with Mel Urofsky, 2011). The U.S. Supreme Court has cited his scholarship four times in cases on religion and law, firearms regulations, and affirmative action. He is currently writing books on the Supreme Court and slavery, the Oberlin-Wellington fugitive slave case, and a legal history of American Jews.

Contributors

KENNETH S. GREENBERG is Distinguished Professor of History at Suffolk University. He is the author of *Masters and Statesmen: The Political Culture of American Slavery* (1985) and *Honor and Slavery* (1996). He has also edited *The Confessions of Nat Turner and Related Documents* (1996) and *Nat Turner: A Slave Rebellion in History and Memory* (2003). He is coproducer and cowriter of the film *Nat Turner: A Troublesome Property*, nationally broadcast on PBS in 2003.

BETHANY JAY is an associate professor of history at Salem State University. Trained as an American historian, she works in a number of fields including nineteenth-century American history, public history, and history education. She is particularly interested with presentations of slavery in American museums and is currently working on two projects related to that field.

ERIC KIMBALL is an assistant professor of history at the University of Pittsburgh at Greensburg. An Atlantic historian, he is at work on multiple projects that explore the economic relationships between colonial New England and the West Indies.

JAMES W. LOEWEN is the award-winning author of several best-selling books, including *Lies My Teacher Told Me: Everything Your High School History Textbook Got Wrong* and *Lies Across America: What Our Historic Sites Get Wrong*. Loewen holds a Ph.D. in sociology from Harvard University and has taught race relations for twenty years at the University of Vermont. He has written several books specifically on issues of race in American history, including *The Confederate and Neo-Confederate Reader* and *Sundown Towns: A Hidden Dimension of American Racism*.

CYNTHIA LYNN LYERLY is an associate professor of history at Boston College, where she teaches courses in race, slavery, gender, and religion. She is the author of *Methodism and the Southern Mind* (1998) and is currently writing a cultural biography of Thomas Dixon Jr.

JOANNE POPE MELISH is an associate professor of history emerita at the University of Kentucky. She is the author of *Disowning Slavery: Gradual Emancipation and "Race" in New England, 1780–1860* (1998) and several essays on race and slavery in the early republic and slavery in public history. Currently she is working on a book-length project entitled "Gradual Alienation: How a Multiracial Laboring Class Formed, Persisted, and Became Invisible in the Post-Revolutionary North."

SARAH E. MILLER received her master's degree in anthropology in 2001 from East Carolina University, where she developed archaeology education programs at Tryon Palace in New Bern, North Carolina. Upon graduation from ECU, she supervised field and lab projects with public involvement for the Kentucky Archaeological Survey and reviewed compliance projects for the Kentucky Heritage Council. She now serves as director for FPAN's Northeast and East Central Regions, statewide coordinator and leadership team member for Project Archaeology, chair for the Society for Historical Archaeology's public education and interpretation committee, and sits on the historic resource review board for St. Johns County. Her specialties include public archaeology, historical archaeology, municipal archaeology, advocacy, and historical cemeteries.

SOWANDE' MUSTAKEEM is an assistant professor of history and African and African American studies at Washington University in St. Louis. She has authored several scholarly essays and book chapters on the Middle Passage and is anticipating publication of her forthcoming book, *Routes of Terror: Gender, Health and Power in the Seafaring World of Slavery*. She is currently at work on a digital humanities project centering the innovative and active role of history and memory within the millennial generation.

STEVEN THURSTON OLIVER is an assistant professor of secondary and higher education at Salem State University. He is a sociologist of education whose work has focused on the the ways in which race, class, gender, and sexual orientation affect access to educational opportunity. He is currently working on a study that seeks to understand resilience and persistence within the teaching profession.

EMILY PALMER has been with the National Park Service's Timucuan Ecological and Historic Preserve since 2009, and before that she worked as a teacher and at the Historic Sauder Village, Ohio's largest living history museum. A native of Ohio, she received her undergraduate degree in history at Defiance College and her master's at the University of North Florida. At UNF her thesis focused on the preservation of presidential homes.

BERNARD E. POWERS JR. is a professor of history at the College of Charleston. He is the author of *Black Charlestonians: A Social History, 1822–1885* (1994) and has written journal articles and book chapters. His scholarly interests are in nineteenth-century American history, African American history, and the history of the African diaspora. His present work examines the history of African Methodism in South Carolina.

LINDSAY ANNE RANDALL is the curator of education and outreach at the Robert S. Peabody Museum of Archaeology at Phillips Academy, Andover, where she teaches topics in archaeology, anthropology, and Native American history. She holds a B.A. in history from Keene State College and a M.A. in historical archaeology from the University of Massachusetts, Boston. Her research interests include English history, colonial New England, and issues facing minorities, both historical and contemporary.

JAMES BREWER STEWART is the James Wallace Professor of History Emeritus at Macalester College and the author of seven books and more than fifty articles on the American abolitionist movement. He is also the founder of Historians Against Slavery, an international network of academics and activists that opposes today's forms of enslavement.

RAY WILLIAMS is the director of education and academic affairs at the Blanton Museum of Art, University of Texas at Austin. His work as a museum educator has been inspired by the challenge of designing experiences with art that are clearly relevant to issues we face in daily life. His most notable museum projects have focused on supporting interfaith dialogue, preparation for citizenship, empathy and imagination. He makes his home with husband Hao Sheng, daughter Clyde, and an assortment of good dogs, cats, and chickens.

Index

Fairbanks, Charles, 290–94
Famous, Tunde Afolayan, 268
Fassbender, Michael, 226
Faulkner, William, xvii
Federal Housing Administration, 14
Federalist Papers, 74n2
Federal Writer's Project. *See* Works Progress Administration (WPA) slave narratives
Ferdinand (Spain), 47
Festinger, Leon, 20
Fifteenth Amendment, 196, 222
films about slavery and Reconstruction: age-appropriateness of content and, 216–17, 225–26; compression of complex stories and, 217; documentaries versus feature films and, 221–22; evocation of empathy and, 218; fact versus fiction in, 228; interpretive nature of documentaries and, 219; negative stereotypes of film in the classroom and, 216–17, 230n1; preparation of students before viewing, 216–17, 222; as primary sources, 217–18, 222; racist stereotypes and, 226, 231–32n20; subjectivity of documentaries and, 218; team teaching and, 229; value of in the classroom, 216–18, 229; white versus black agency in, 228–29; whole versus partial films in the classroom and, 218. *See also specific films*
Finkelman, Paul, 121
Finley, Robert, 45–46
Florida Public Archaeology Network, 286
Flynn, Errol, 231–32n20
Foner, Eric, 229
Foote, Shelby, 219
foreign relations, 67
Fort George Island, Florida, 286, 288
Forward (painting), 236
Fourteenth Amendment, 196
Fowler, Margaret, 209–10
Fox, Isabel, 278, 282n21
Fox, John, 263–67, 273–74, 278, 279–80nn6–8, 282n21
France, 25–26, 67, 73

Franklin, John Hope, 272
Franklin and Armfield slave trading firm, 24
free blacks: amid gradual emancipation in the North, 125–26; *Dred Scott v. Sandford* and, 64, 74n9, 76n23; employment discrimination against, 126; exclusion of from southern states, 74–75n10; interaction between slaves and, 189; kidnapping of in the North, 26, 67; as noncitizens, 64, 76n23; organizations formed by, 189; Thomas Jefferson's hostility toward, 70–71, 72; Underground Railroad and, 126; in US versus Latin America and Caribbean, 188–89; as without access to federal courts, 64
freedom, xiii–xiv, xv
Freehling, William W., 63–64
Freeman, Morgan, 221
Free the Slaves, 200
French, Austa, 146
French Revolution, 136, 184
fugitive slave laws. *See* escape and fugitive slaves

Gandhi, 17
Garlic, Delia, 209–10
gender: black women as eligible for harsh labor and, 160; caregiving work and, 164; codification of slavery on basis of, 159–60; gender balance among slaves and, 191–92; men versus women in military service, 261n12; skilled slave labor and, 161–62; slave men and women in same labor and, 160–61; slave nurses and midwives and, 162; slave resistance and, 162; task system versus gang labor system and, 163–64; violence against slaves and, 161; women in runaway-slave advertisements and, 270; WPA slave narratives and, 209
General Electric, 28n5
Gerima, Hallie, 86
Gibbs, Jimmy, 289

Iredell, James, 61
Isaac, Benjamin, 56
Isaac, Rhys, 278
Isabella (Spain), 47
Ivy League universities, slaves in building of, 109, 114n42

Jackson, Andrew, 69, 70, 76n23
Jackson, Martin, 214
Jacobs, Harriet A., 141, 220, 224
James, Dante Josef, 220
Jay, John, 67, 70, 76n24, 121
Jay's Treaty (1795), 67
Jefferson, Thomas: contrast of liberty and slavery and, 70, 72, 73; Declaration of Independence and, xiii, 59, 70, 268; election of 1800 and, 69–70; former slaves who fought in the Revolution and, 67, 72–73; Haiti and, 25, 67, 73; Louisiana Purchase and, 68; on manumission, 72; *Notes on the State of Virginia* by, 71–72; number of slaves owned by, 73; racism of, 71–72, 73; Sally Hemings and, xvii, 72, 73; slave-owning presidents and, 69; on slavery in the western territories, 72; slaves of in Washington, DC, 66; slaves sold by, 71, 73; treatment of blacks as governor of Virginia and, 70–71
Jews and Judaism, 47–48, 55–56n8, 56
Johnson, Andrew, 231–32n20
Johnson, Eastman, 274, 275
Johnson, George, 221
Johnson, Richard Mentor, xvii
Johnson, Samuel, 121
Johnson, William, 74–75n10
Jones, Howard, 227
Jordan, Winthrop, 136

Kansas-Nebraska Act (1854), 69
Kennedy, John F., 35
kersey industry, 103–6, 112n22
Kimball, Eric, 21
Kindred (Butler), 86
King, Martin Luther, Jr., xiii, 17, 35

King Philip's War, 116
Kingsley, Zephaniah, 286, 289
Kingsley Plantation (Florida), 283, 284, 286–87, 290–94
Kolchin, Peter, 164
Ku Klux Klan, 222
Kweli, Talib, 88–89

Ladson-Billings, Gloria, 39n1
Las Casas, Bartolomé de, 20
Lawrence, Amos A., 169
Lawrence, Jacob, 236–37
Lee, Robert E., 213
Lehman brothers, 102
Lennon, John, 35
Levin, Kevin M., 220
Levine, Lawrence, 150
Lewis, Bernard, 55–56n8
Library of Congress, 15, 207, 208
Ligon, Glenn, 238, 243–45
Lil Wayne, 89
Lincoln (film), 228–29
Lincoln, Abraham: Emancipation Proclamation and, 173; enlistment of black soldiers and, 173–74, 176; films about, 217; as flawed hero, 35; Second Inaugural Address of, 177; in slave narratives, 213; slavery as cause of Civil War and, 177; southern reaction to election of, 171
Litwack, Leon, 223
Liverpool International Museum of Slavery, 86
Loewen, James W., 29n17, 230–31n10
Lopez, Aaron, 99, 100, 101, 108
Lopez, Moses, 101
Lopez and Rivera company, 100, 106, 109
Lorence, James, 217
Louisiana Purchase, 20, 26, 67, 68
L'Ouverture, Toussaint, 236
Lundberg, James, 219–20
lynching, 29n17, 222

Macy's, 197
Madison, James, 67, 69, 74n2
Mandela, Nelson, 17

Smalley, Laura, 221
Smiley, Tavis, 86–87
Smith, Billy, 271, 272
Smith, John, 57n27
Smith, Kirby, 176
Smith, Venture, 129, 153
Society of Friends. *See* Quakers
Solomon Northup's Odyssey (made-for-TV
    movie), 225, 226
Spanish Florida, 25
Sparks, Elizabeth, 147
Spielberg, Steven, 227–29
Stampp, Kenneth, 134–35
Stephens, Alexander H., 171
Stevens, Thaddeus, 231–32n20
Stewart, Alexander, 102
Stono Rebellion, 153, 220
Story, Joseph, 70
Stowe, Harriet Beecher, xvii. *See also Uncle
    Tom's Cabin* (Stowe)
Stuckey, Sterling, 150
sugar production, 159, 183, 186
Supreme Court, 70, 76n23
Sweet, John, 270

Taney, Roger B., 70, 76n23
Tannenbaum, Frank, xx
Tappan, Lewis, 228
Tarantino, Quentin, 88, 280n9
Target Stores, 197
Taylor, Zachary, 69
teaching about slavery: African American
    voices in readings and, 129, 134, 136,
    139–40, 141–42; analysis of WPA
    slave narratives and, 207–8, 211–13;
    appraisal of sources and, 208–9; ar-
    chaeological artifacts and, 110; au-
    thenticity and, 129; avoidance of, 84–
    85; backward reading of slavery's
    history and, xx; caution about class-
    room dramatizations and, 276; chal-
    lenges in, 4; challenging racism and,
    130; Common Core Standards and,
    27; course titles and descriptions
    and, 85; current events in, 89; difficul-
    ties with primary sources and, 152;

discussions about words and, 44–45;
diverse experiences of slaves and,
158, 165–66, 189–90, 194; documents
about colonial transition to slavery
and, 53–54, 57n27; evaluation of documents and, 139–40; exposure to different historical methods and, 92n8;
fear of, 31–32, 33; feelings evoked by
history of slavery and, 157–58; how
not to teach and, 15–16; learning
communities for teachers and, 33–
34; learning with students from
other schools and, 87; lifelong learning and self-work and, 37–38; meta-
discussions and, 16–18; museum visits
and, 86–87, 94n17; music and, 25, 88–
89, 95n20; northern versus southern
slavery and, 128; "the n word" in, 130;
online databases and, 92n8, 92–93n10,
108–9; Paideia and, 237–38, 240–41,
242–43, 245, 246n2, 246–47n5; poetry
and, 95n20; popular culture and, 85,
88–90; preconceptions about causes
of Civil War and, 167–68; problematic
aspects of WPA slave narratives and,
208–11; problem of selection and, 133;
psychological barriers and, 285; race
of students and, 16; readings by slaves
and free blacks and, 129–30; reenacted
slave auctions and, 158; religious
songs and, 150; resources outside the
textbook and, 34; selection of sources
and, 85–86; sensitivity in, 158; slave
narratives and, 34, 129, 152–53; slave
resistance and, 139; slavery as fraught
subject and, 3; slavery in US versus
Latin America and Caribbean and,
186; slavery's relevance to the present
and, 11–15; sources for, 5–6; starting
point of slavery in American colonies
and, 53–54, 57n27; statistics on comparative slavery and, 180, 193; students' existing contemplations about
race and, 33; students' growth and,
xi–xii; students' opportunities for
action and, 38–39; synecdoches and,

The Harvey Goldberg Series
for Understanding and Teaching History

Understanding and Teaching the Vietnam War
Edited by John Day Tully, Matthew Masur, and Brad Austin

Understanding and Teaching U.S. Lesbian, Gay, Bisexual, and
   Transgender History
Edited by Leila J. Rupp and Susan K. Freeman

Understanding and Teaching American Slavery
Edited by Bethany Jay and Cynthia Lynn Lyerly

Printed in the United States
By Bookmasters